W.J.M.M.   Political Questions

W.J.M.M., 1974

Photo. by courtesy of the BBC

Edited by Brian Chapman
and Allen Potter

W.J.M.M.
Political Questions

Essays in honour of W. J. M. Mackenzie

Manchester University Press

Published by Manchester University Press
Oxford Road, Manchester M13 9PL

ISBN 0 7190 0594 9

Printed in Great Britain by
Western Printing Services Ltd, Bristol

Contents

To William James Millar Mackenzie

Born 8 April 1909, son of Laurence Millar Mackenzie, W.S., Edinburgh, and Anna Marion McClymont. Educated Edinburgh Academy; Balliol College, Oxford, B.A. (1931) and M.A., Edinburgh University, LL.B. (1934).

Married Pamela Muriel Malyon, 1943; one son (James Laurence) and four daughters (Frances Jean, Leslie Margaret, Alison Ann, Catherine).

Fellow of Magdalen College, Oxford, 1933–48, War Historian, SOE (part-time), 1945–48, Faculty Fellow of Nuffield College, Oxford, 1948, Lecturer in Politics, Oxford, 1948. Professor of Government and Administration, University of Manchester, 1949–55. Professor of Government, University of Manchester, 1955–66. James Bryce Professor of Government, University of Glasgow, 1966–70. Edward Caird Professor of Politics, University of Glasgow, 1970–74.

CBE, 1963, FBA, 1968, Dundee University, LL.D., 1968, Lancaster University, LL.D., 1970, Warwick University, D.Litt., 1972.

Special Commissioner for Constitutional Development, Tanganyika, 1952; co-opted member, Manchester City Education Committee, 1953–64; appointed member, British Wool Marketing Board, 1954–66; Royal Commission on Local Government in Greater London, 1957; constitutional adviser to Kenya, 1959; vice-chairman, Bridges Committee on Training in Public Administration for Overseas Countries, 1962; member, Committee on Remuneration of Ministers and Members of Parliament, 1963–64; member, Maud Committee on Management in Local Government, 1964–1966; Parry Committtee on University Libraries, 1964–67; member, North West Regional Economic Training Council, 1965–66; Council member, SSRC, 1965–69; chairman, Political Science Committee, SSRC, 1965–1969; Glasgow University representative on Public Administration Committee of JUC, 1966–74; member, Advisory Committee for Scientific and Technical Information, 1966–71; member, British Council Committee for Foreign University Interchange, 1967–74; chairman, Joseph Rowntree Memorial Trust working party on Social Work (Scotland) Act, 1968, 1968–69; member, Children's Panel Advisory Committee, City of Glasgow, 1969–72; member, Training Resources Committee of CPAC, 1970– ; member, Police Advisory Board for Scotland, 1970– ; member, Academic Executive Committee of Scottish Business School,1970–74; chairman, Children's Panel Advisory Committee, City of Glasgow 1972– ; member, Publications Committee, Advisory Council on Public Records, 1972; member, Joint Working Party on a Diploma in Public Administration, Scottish Council for Commercial, Administrative and Professional Education (now renamed SCOTBEC), 1972–73.

The contributors

MALCOLM ANDERSON
Professor of Politics, University of Warwick. Manchester: *L*, 1960–65.

A. H. BIRCH
Professor of Political Science, University of Exeter. Manchester: *L*, to 1961.

PETER CAMPBELL
Professor of Politics, University of Reading. Manchester: *L*, 1949–60.

BRIAN CHAPMAN
Professor of Government, University of Manchester. Manchester: *R*, *L*, *P*, from 1949.

DAVID DONNISON
Director, Centre for Environmental Studies. Manchester: *L*, 1950–55.

DOROTHY EMMET
Professor Emeritus of Philosophy, University of Manchester. Manchester: *P*, throughout.

JOHN ERICKSON
Professor of Politics, University of Edinburgh. Manchester: *L*, from 1962.

MAX GLUCKMAN
Research Professor in Social Anthropology, University of Manchester. Manchester: *P*, from 1950.

J. W. GROVE
Professor of Political Studies, Queen's University, Kingston, Ontario. Manchester: *R*, *L*, 1949–65.

SHEILA HAMILTON
Secretary, Department of Politics, University of Glasgow. Glasgow: from 1966.

C. C. HOOD
Lecturer in Politics, University of Glasgow. Glasgow: *G*, *R*, *L*, from 1968.

J. M. LEE
Senior Lecturer in Politics, Birkbeck College, London. Manchester: *R*, *L*, from 1958.

JOHN MONEY
Lecturer, Departments of Politics and of Social and Economic Research, University of Glasgow. Glasgow: L, from 1968.

GERAINT PARRY
Edward Caird Professor of Politics, University of Glasgow. Manchester: L, from 1960.

ALLEN POTTER
James Bryce Professor of Politics, University of Glasgow. Manchester: L, 1951–62. Glasgow: P, from 1970.

RICHARD ROSE
Professor of Politics, University of Strathclyde. Manchester: L, from 1961.

JOHN SANDERSON
Lecturer in Politics, University of Strathclyde. Manchester: G, L, 1958–1963.

R. N. SPANN
Professor of Government and Public Administration, University of Sydney. Manchester: L, to 1953.

STEPHEN WHITE
Lecturer in Politics, University of Glasgow. Glasgow: G, L, from 1968.

MAURICE WRIGHT
Reader in Government, University of Manchester. Manchester: R, L, from 1960.

Acknowledgement
The editors are grateful to Sir Charles Wilson, Principal of the University of Glasgow, for contributing some of the biographical information about W. J. M. M. and for taking the chair at the personal presentation of this *Festschrift*.

Preface

This volume is produced on the occasion of W. J. M. Mackenzie's retirement from his Chair of Politics in the University of Glasgow, as an expression of the admiration and affection with which he is regarded by those who have known him and his work. His formal retirement does not presage the end of Bill Mackenzie's contributions to politics. As the *curriculum vitae* on the dedication page indicates, he has for a long time been a member of councils, commissions and other bodies. In recent years he has, if anything, been taking a more continuous initiative in community affairs. He has also been writing more. His retirement from his Chair simply marks a stage in a shift of interests: from academic to community development, from curricula and lectures to more reading (if that is possible!) and writing.

The influence that Mackenzie has had on his academic colleagues is so admirably described in the first of the essays in this volume, 'Mackenzie at Manchester' by Tony Birch and Dick Spann, that we need add nothing on that theme in this preface. We confine ourselves to adding a little to the bare outline of Mackenzie's academic career in the *curriculum vitae*.

It is a tale of four places: Edinburgh, Oxford, Manchester and Glasgow. His father was a Writer to the Signet in Edinburgh. Bill Mackenzie went to Edinburgh Academy, most of whose able pupils moved after Highers to Scottish universities; but a few stayed on, working on Latin and Greek, for Oxford and Cambridge scholarships and entrance. Mackenzie won a scholarship to Balliol (where A. D. Lindsay, previously Professor of Moral Philosophy in the University of Glasgow, had become Master in 1924), arriving there in 1927.

After reading Greats at Oxford, Mackenzie returned to Edinburgh to read law with the intention of practising. In 1933,

however, following the death of his father, he went back to Oxford
as a classics don in Magdalen. In 1936 the increasing interest of students in Modern Greats led the college to appoint a Fellow in politics. Mackenzie asked for and obtained the job.

After serving in the Air Staff secretariat in the war, he returned
to Magdalen: in the immediate post-war years he and two Glasgow
graduates, Charles Wilson at Corpus and Wilfrid Harrison at
Queen's, carried a large part of the burden of the Politics examining
in Modern Greats. In 1948 Mackenzie was appointed the first
Professor of Government and Administration in Manchester: in
1955 he became simply Professor of Government when a Chair of
Social Administration was instituted.

A Chair in Political Economy was established at Owens College,
Manchester, in 1854. When Manchester became an independent
university in 1904 a Faculty of Commerce was created. In 1910
Manchester established the first Chair of Economic History in an
English university, and in 1926 appointed a lecturer in Public
Administration. In 1933 a unit for economic research was created,
several of whose members subsequently rose to eminence in governmental economic and statistical services during and after the war.
Manchester was thus exceptionally well placed to take advantage
of the special 'Clapham' provision made by the University Grants
Committee for the social sciences after 1945: the Faculty of Commerce had been reconstituted as the Faculty of Economic and
Social Studies in 1944. Mackenzie's was one of several appointments
made at Manchester in the immediate post-war years that provided
the basis for pre-eminence in British social studies.

The essay by Birch and Spann deals with Mackenzie's time at
Manchester. It makes manifest why a *Festschrift* for Mackenzie
most appropriately comes mainly from students of politics who
were in his department there, and also why we asked Dorothy
Emmet and Max Gluckman to join us in this commemoration. They
too were 'members' of the Friday seminar, which more than anything else defined the circle of those who participated most intimately with Mackenzie at Manchester in discussing the 'partly
answerable' questions of political science.

In 1966 Mackenzie became the first James Bryce Professor of
Government in the University of Glasgow. He had once tried to
attract Charles Wilson to a Chair in Manchester. Now Sir Charles,
as Principal of Glasgow, succeeded in attracting him.

Many parallels may be drawn between the 'Adam Smith departments' in Glasgow in the mid-'60s and the 'Dover Street departments' in Manchester in the late '40s. Adam Smith had been Professor of Logic and then of Moral Philosophy in Glasgow in the mid-eighteenth century: the Chair of Political Economy was established in 1896. The Department of Social and Economic Research, under a Chair of Applied Economics first filled by Alexander Cairncross in 1950, performed the role that the economic research section had performed in Manchester; its head when Mackenzie moved to Glasgow, Donald Robertson, uncannily resembled Ely Devons of Manchester in his relation to Mackenzie. (Both these economists died tragically young.) In both universities at the time of Mackenzie's appointment the only departmental professorial heads concerned with social studies, apart from Economics and Economic History, were political philosophers. In Glasgow, Mackenzie joined David Raphael, the Edward Caird Professor of Political and Social Theory (later Political and Social Philosophy) since 1960, in heading a department responsible for teaching politics, sociology and social administration.

In association with Robertson and others, Mackenzie helped establish the Glasgow section of the Scottish Business School. He fostered the ties of his department with the Institute of Soviet and East European Studies under Alec Nove and with the Institute of Latin American Studies. There are now separate Chairs of Sociology and of Social Administration. Once again, Mackenzie has been at the centre of a social-science explosion.

In 1970 the Edward Caird and James Bryce Chairs were made co-equal Chairs of Politics. (Edward Caird was Professor of Moral Philosophy in Glasgow from 1866 to 1893, when he became Master of Balliol; James Bryce was a Glasgow graduate—and Professor of Jurisprudence at Owens College, Manchester, in the 1870s on the way to becoming Regius Professor of Civil Law at Oxford.) Mackenzie moved to the Edward Caird Chair, which had been vacated by Raphael's departure to Reading. Mackenzie's retirement from this Chair takes effect on 30 September 1974.

From the moment when his intention to retire became known, those who had been lecturers under him at Manchester assumed that it was their peculiar right and duty to tender this tribute. Some, however, were unable to prepare a contribution in time. It became possible, therefore, to invite essays from the two most recently appointed lecturers in the Department of Politics in Glasgow. This invitation, to which Stephen White and Christopher Hood responded with alacrity, was our recognition that—to allude once more to what Birch and Spann write in 'Mackenzie at Manchester'—in many ways Mackenzie's greatest skills have been with younger members of staff.

We are well aware that many other beneficiaries of Mackenzie's learning and kindness would have liked to contribute: those who have been undergraduate, graduate or research students under him; political scientists in the United Kingdom and elsewhere; other academics; and public servants. Even a cursory listing of the (overlapping) groups shows that it would have been impossible to choose adequately and fairly among them for contributors to a single volume.

In determining the subject-matter the editors were concerned only with the two joint contributions. We wanted a bibliography of Mackenzie's writings. We persuaded John Money to attempt it. A little later Miss Sheila Hamilton, Mackenzie's secretary, was discovered preparing such a listing on her own initiative, to accompany the deposit of Mackenzie's papers in the University of Glasgow archives. We suggested that they combine their efforts, and we thank them very much for the result.

It would be untrue to say that we asked for the piece that Tony Birch and Dick Spann have produced, because in saying so many of the things that ought to be said about Mackenzie they have exceeded any reasonable expectation about anyone finding the words to say them. Each of them proposed writing something on Mackenzie's Manchester years, properly claiming the special competence of having preceded Mackenzie to Manchester. We simply put them in touch with each other. We are sure that the other contributors do not begrudge our giving their essay pride of place in this volume.

The individual contributors chose their own topics. Neither the breadth of Mackenzie's interest nor the time available allowed us to insist on a particular theme. However, while the subjects and approaches (and the extent to which the authors make explicit reference to Mackenzie's work) vary, most, if not all, of the essays seem to us to be in a particular style of political discourse—that of the Friday seminar. ('Style' is a favourite Mackenzie word, which his successor in the Edward Caird Chair uses in his essay.) The authors open up or pursue a subject, clarifying the concepts or issues involved, aware of distinctions between normative and empirical political writing, but not afraid of engaging in both. Above all, they do not pretend to pronounce the last word. They invite further discussion, in the endless task of dealing with the intractable field of politics, in which the important questions are indeed only partly answerable.

Brian Chapman
Allen Potter

A. H. Birch and R. N. Spann

I

Mackenzie at Manchester

By the end of the 1950s the Manchester Department of Government was recognised as one of the three major centres in Britain for the study of political science. It was appreciably smaller than Oxford or the London School of Economics but it was in some ways more adventurous than either, and the work of its members had earned it an international reputation. This achievement was particularly remarkable in view of the fact that the first Chair of government had been created as recently as 1948, and when W. J. M. Mackenzie was appointed to it he had inherited only three members of staff (the authors and the late John Grundy).

When Mackenzie was appointed, in July 1948, he was thirty-nine and still virtually unknown outside Oxford. We had certainly never heard of him, there were no publications to which we could refer, and he arrived in Manchester at the turn of the year[1] with a certain aura of mystery about him.

In fact, as we learned, he was a Balliol Scot, a very good classical scholar who had changed the focus of his interests. He had been Craven scholar in 1928, Ireland scholar in 1929, and was senior scholar of Balliol in 1930. In his final year he attracted the attention of Harold Nicolson, who recorded in his diary that when he was guest of honour at the St Catherine's dinner his health was proposed by Mackenzie 'in an amusing speech with a strong Scotch accent'.[2] He duly got a First, but after graduating he did not fancy a career as a classics don and returned to Edinburgh (where his father was a solicitor) to take a law degree, which he did in two years. However, in 1933 he was back in Oxford as a Fellow of Magdalen College and tutor in classics.

In 1936 he persuaded his college to transfer him to a tutorship in politics and held this post until 1948, with a break for war service. During the war he worked for the Air Ministry and with the joint staff mission in Washington; and then returned to a semi-academic task by writing a history of the activities in France of the Special Operations Executive, the branch responsible for aiding resistance movements in occupied territories. On this he produced a lengthy report, though unfortunately a report too secret to be published.

In appearance Bill Mackenzie was and is tall, ruddy, blue-eyed, solidly constructed, tweedy and vaguely untidy. He has the slow speech and deliberate manner of many Scotsmen, but by the time he came to Manchester he had lost the greater part of his Scots accent. His many years at Oxford had had a more obvious effect on him than his Scottish upbringing, and when he spoke of the English Establishment one had not much doubt that he belonged to it, if in a slightly eccentric way. Yet it turned out that he was a loyal Scot, who took most of his holidays at Kinloch Rannoch and who moved to Glasgow in 1966 to spend the last years of his career in his native country.

In all the obvious characteristics of education and background Mackenzie differed appreciably from his new colleagues in the Economics Faculty at Manchester, and one might have expected him to be a fish out of water there. In fact Manchester suited him well and proved to be very receptive to the special contribution he was to make. To explain this we must say a little about the situation there before he arrived.

The teaching of politics at Manchester started well before the war. A combined honours course in economics and political science had been established in the 1920s, and by the late '30s the senior of the two lecturers teaching the subject was D. N. Chester, a Manchester graduate who went on to become Warden of Nuffield College. Political theory was taught in the Philosophy Department and was for many years in the hands of A. E. Teale, a teacher in the tradition of A. D. Lindsay, who later become Professor of Moral and Political Philosophy at Keele. By 1948 the Arts Faculty had an honours degree in politics and modern history and the Economics Faculty had an honours degree in economics and politics together with the pass degree of B.A. (Admin.). All these degrees were inter-departmental in character. The politics and modern history degree was controlled by a board of studies which contained representatives of the departments of Government, History, Philosophy, Economic History and (later) American Studies; the two degrees in the Economics Faculty were controlled by the faculty board.

This was the structure that Mackenzie inherited and which he modified but did not fundamentally disturb. According to the handbook, the only changes made in the first years were to add a new course on 'government and industry' and a special subject on 'parties and elections'. He taught the latter himself, with a reading list in which Duverger and Lazarsfeld were listed alongside Hume and Burke. In later years more courses were added, but the basic character of the degrees was left unchanged. He never even discussed the possibility of establishing a special honours degree in politics, such as now exists in many British universities, and it is clear that the interdepartmental arrangements at Manchester suited both his own broad intellectual interests and his view of the character of political science as an academic subject.

Departmental frontiers were bridged not only in degree syllabuses but also in staff seminars. In the 1930s there had been the brilliantly orchestrated seminars of Adolf Lowe (later of the New School for Social Research), which had drawn in philosophers and historians as well as social scientists. After the war the seminars in economics, in government and in social anthropology all attracted members from several departments, while Dorothy Emmet, as Professor of Philosophy, formed close intellectual ties with the social scientists.

When Mackenzie went to Manchester, then, he joined a lively faculty with a distinguished group of professors. Ely Devons and Arthur Lewis held Chairs of economics, Michael Polanyi had recently moved from a Chair of physical chemistry to one of social studies, and Max Gluckman was shortly to be appointed to a new Chair of social anthropology. Mackenzie appreciated these colleagues and they appreciated him. They were, indeed, a formidable group of scholars, of powerful mind, strong personality and occasionally sharp tongue, who could stimulate but also sometimes intimidate. More than one visiting academic who addressed a Manchester seminar found it a traumatic experience. Harry Johnson has written of the economics seminar in this period that it was 'the most devastatingly critical forum in the country into which a careless economist could blunder'.[3] Bill himself did not bark or bite on such occasions, but his grunts (Of approbation? Incipient dissent? Simple noting of a point? Who can say?) could be disconcerting.

Approach to political science

We soon became aware that the new professor was a man of very special qualities. His first publication was a chapter on 'The structure of central administration' in a book of essays on British government.[4] This was written before he came to Manchester and one of us proof-read it soon after his arrival. Here was an ostensibly unexciting subject which was for once discussed with a sense of history, of broad theoretical bearings, and also of significance for current problems; and in a stylish prose that gave the whole enterprise a certain dash. These are all qualities characteristic of the best of Mackenzie's later writing; another is the quality of sparking off more extended work by others, as this chapter did.

At the same time, Mackenzie's attitude to the subject of which he had been appointed professor had its paradoxical elements. He once told a group of us that his own first love, namely classical philology, was a model academic discipline for undergraduates, for it had a very limited literature, all of which was worth reading, and a clear internal logic which could be mastered within three years. The study of politics clearly exhibits none of these characteristics, and in the 1950s Mackenzie doubted, as did his contemporary, Michael Oakeshott, whether political science could properly be regarded as an academic discipline at all.

He expressed his thoughts on this matter in an essay discussing Oakeshott's inaugural lecture.[5] In this he wrote in somewhat Oakeshottian terms (though in a very different style) of the queerness of being a political scientist, a 'very odd by-product of our educational system'. He shared Oakeshott's scepticism both about social scientism and about political theology of the Laski or Lindsay kind. 'My own reaction against sermons came very early in life, as both my grandfathers were ministers of the Church of Scotland who "came out in '43".'[6] All the same, he could find no satisfaction in Oakeshott's answer, which was to use political writings as a way of inducting his students into an understanding of historical explanation. Political science was, for better or worse, in the academic curriculum and 'my own inclination is to face the problem rather than to evade it'.[7] At its lowest, there were people who 'want to be taught not traditions, but facts', who need a great deal of information about government to do their work properly. There was a demand for political cookery books, so 'let us apply our minds in order to make sure that they are good ones'.[8] More profoundly, the very political tradition to which Oakeshott appealed included the illusions that he rejected, such as the search for principles, the belief in 'a detectable strand of progress', and so on.

The strongest academic traditions in political education in this country have been, first, to teach principles at the stiffest level of intellectual debate which the pupil can stand: second, to teach empirical method and the use of evidence, with due precautions to ensure that the limits of the method are understood.

With all its defects, this is what we were stuck with. So we were impelled not merely to compile cookery books but to argue about them; and political argument was more than Oakeshottian conversation, it was 'in the last resort an argument about what to do', so one could not 'talk about politics without incurring a share in responsibility for action'.[9] All this now sounds very *avant-garde* in a period when many faces have turned away from 'apolitical politics'.

So for Mackenzie, if the study of politics lives up to few predetermined canons of an academic discipline, it is nevertheless an important academic enterprise to be attempted, with its distinctive problems and brand of scholarship. It would be misleading to say that for Mackenzie in the 1950s political science as a subject had yet to be created, but he certainly saw it as a struggling infant which he had a special duty to nurture, and this included giving its teachers a sense of confidence and a feeling of professional identity. He even liked the term 'political science' itself, at a time when most of his British colleagues, including those who had christened his own Chair, fought shy of it.

Appointments and staff

These attitudes were reflected in many of Mackenzie's activities, including his appointments. At the time he went to Manchester the London School of Economics and Political Science was the main source of junior lecturers in politics. But while London graduates were appointed to jobs up and down the country in the 1950s, very few of them went to Manchester. Mackenzie was rather sceptical about the London degree, and his object was not so much to appoint people who already thought themselves political scientists as to choose able, well-educated graduates who could develop into political scientists in the Manchester environment. He thought first-hand knowledge of other countries was at least as important as a degree in politics, and as head of a relatively small department he was exceptionally generous in arranging leave of absence for his junior colleagues. In the early '50s R. N. Spann, A. H. Birch, J. W. Grove and Peter Campbell took turns to have a year's leave to study abroad, while Brian Chapman was helped to spend a period of each year in France. All this far-sighted, and then unusual, career planning was going on while the department grew from five to eight in its total strength.

A fair number of Mackenzie's appointments brought new kinds of expertise and new perspectives into the department. Thus at a time when there were no Russian-speaking political scientists available to teach Soviet government, and other universities settled for politics graduates interested in Marxism, it was typical of Mackenzie to appoint an historian who spoke Serbo-Croat, on the grounds that, first, he was an educated man; second, if he had learned one language he could presumably learn another; and third (in a characteristic phrase), 'it will be useful to find out what the Jugs are up to'. When D. J. R. Scott left, after learning Russian and producing a textbook on Soviet government, his place was taken by Vladimir Dedijer, a former member of the central committee of the Yugoslav communist party and a friend of Tito's. He enlivened the department not only by his lectures on Soviet government but by his marvellous tales and his unexpected contributions to conversations on a variety of topics. There was, for instance, a seminar discussion on the career of Chandra Bose, initiated by an earnest young Indian scholar, which was transformed when Dedijer revealed that he had been a secret Comintern adviser to Bose before the war.

Later, when the department acquired its first lectureship in African politics, two candidates were interviewed who were both eminently appointable: sound scholars with excellent references who had both had longish periods in west Africa, which in terms of the literature then available was by far the most suitable part of the continent on which to concentrate in an undergraduate course. However, Mackenzie decided to pass both of them over in favour of a Sudanese candidate, Mudathir Abdul-Rahim. He was not available for interview and it was clear from his references that he was more interested in Arab nationalism than in the politics of black Africa. But he was himself from Africa, he had political interests and commitments, and his appointment extended the range of knowledge within the department to include an area with which we were previously unfamiliar.

This tendency to add a new dimension to the department's strength wherever possible extended even to such a mundane subject as British government. In the 1950s the first-year course on this topic at Manchester was a rather heavy one, with an enormous audience of day students and a sizable group of evening students. The man appointed to help A. H. Birch teach this course was a young historian from New Zealand called Harry Hanham, who subsequently became Professor of History at Harvard. The only snag about this appointment was that it came at a time when Birch (perhaps foolishly) was in process of eliminating most of the history from the syllabus, so that Hanham's arrival inaugurated what Harold Wilson would call a period of creative tension about how the course should be taught. But the atmosphere at Manchester was such that personal relations were unaffected by intellectual differences.

We stress all this because it has always seemed to us (who were at Manchester before he arrived) that one of Mackenzie's great qualities is a gift for spotting talent. He did not build his department by appointing people with congenial personalities and similar backgrounds, in the hope that they would weld together into a cooperative team. He built it instead by appointing the most talented young men he could find, with a wide variety of backgrounds and interests, in the hope that they would strike sparks off one another and create an atmosphere of intellectual excitement. In this he succeeded triumphantly. We discussed our research over coffee in the morning, over beer in the College Arms at lunchtime, and over tea in the afternoon; we took part in a staff seminar every Friday afternoon and sometimes arranged special evening seminars as well; and members of the department produced a constant flow of articles and books.

In consequence the Manchester Department of Government became the most productive nursery in Britain for professors of politics: the great majority of those who were lecturers at Manchester in the '50s got Chairs in the '60s, in most cases before they were forty, and the tradition has been continued by their successors. In approximate order of appointment, R. N. Spann went to Sydney, Peter Campbell to Reading, A. H. Birch to Hull (later to

Exeter), Brian Chapman was promoted to a Chair at Manchester, Allen Potter went to Strathclyde (then to Essex and Glasgow), H. J. Hanham to Edinburgh (then to Harvard and MIT), Mudathir Abdul-Rahim to Khartoum. Richard Rose succeeded Potter's successor at Strathclyde, J. W. Grove went to Queen's University, Ontario, Martin Harrison to Keele, John Erickson to Edinburgh, Clement Dodd succeeded Birch at Hull, William Tordoff was appointed to a further Chair at Manchester. Coral Bell (after appointments at Sydney and London) became Professor of International Relations at Sussex, Lewis Gunn now has a Chair at Strathclyde, and Malcolm Anderson at Warwick. Mackenzie's own Chair at Glasgow is being filled by Geraint Parry, who has been teaching political theory at Manchester since 1959.

Mackenzie's eye for talent extended itself to research assistants as well as to lecturers. Holders of that modest post at Manchester included such future stars as F. F. Ridley, now professor at Liverpool and editor of *Political Studies*, Jean Blondel, professor at Essex and first chairman of the Department of Government there, and W. H. Greenleaf, professor at Swansea. We should also mention David Donnison, a former student of Mackenzie's at Magdalen who was appointed to a lectureship in social administration when that subject came under Mackenzie's control,[10] subsequently became Professor of Social Administration at the London School of Economics and is now director of the Centre for Environmental Studies.

Running the Department

Mackenzie ruled the Manchester department with an informal but unchallenged authority. Staff meetings were infrequent and casual. On minor points one sometimes did not know what had been decided until the minutes appeared. Departmental memoranda were in appearance even more casual, thoughts and jottings deliberately not put into full-flowing English sentences and usually open-ended in their message. He ran the department in an apparently loose and indirect way which was nevertheless extremely effective. There were few or no awkward points of confusion, no fierce arguments about admissions or about graduate students, no moments of panic during the examination season. Moreover, there was a singular lack of jealousy. While many university departments keep a careful tally of the number of hours' teaching each individual does and the number of examination papers marked, in Manchester we continued happily for years with a programme under which some lecturers did much more teaching than others.

The secret of this atmosphere lay partly in the personal ascendancy which Mackenzie enjoyed in his department, together with the amount of work he did behind the scenes to see that everything ran smoothly. But what was probably more important was the commitment to research which members of staff developed under his guidance. There was in the cavernous building in Dover Street a sense of intellectual discovery that transcended all else and relegated administrative matters to their proper place. What had to be done was done with the minimum of fuss. There were occasional controversies about teaching methods or the syllabus. But none of the lecturers in the department worried about administrative detail or got engaged in faculty politics, let alone cared about what was happening in Senate, in the many committees of the university, or in the then quiescent Students' Union. It was characteristic of Manchester in this period that the most important event of the week was the Friday afternoon seminar for members of staff and graduate students.

In retrospect, these seminars—arranged almost single-handed by Mackenzie—seem quite remarkable. As we have mentioned, Manchester had a tradition of good staff seminars. In particular, the Economics Department had a long-established and very lively Wednesday seminar in which the present writers had participated regularly before Mackenzie's arrival. He quickly established a government seminar with an ambitious programme of its own. Staff and graduate students took turns to read papers on their own research, but each session we also had a series of discussions devoted to a particular theme. Thus we had a longish series of meetings on the role of pressure groups in British politics, before S. E. Finer's *Anonymous Empire* put this topic on the agenda in most other universities. The series was opened by Mackenzie himself.[11] There followed a paper on methodology by a staff member, a paper by Finer, and a series of meetings addressed by pressure group organisers willing to be cross-examined by academics. It was all highly educative.

A similar mixture of contributions by academics and by practitioners characterised other series. So when we discussed decision-making, an introductory session by Mackenzie was followed by

G. L. S. Shackle on mathematical approaches and a number of papers by people who spent their lives taking decisions. The most memorable were Alastair Hetherington on decision-making in the editor's chair of the *Manchester Guardian* and a scintillating talk by Sir Basil de Ferranti on the problems of running a large engineering firm.

One remarkable feature of the Friday seminar was that it was based on a small department of eight or nine staff members and the tiniest handful of graduate students. Many far larger departments have found difficulty in sustaining a regular staff seminar, let alone one as frequent and successful as this. One reason for its success was undoubtedly the willingness of members of the department to regard regular participation as taking precedence over commitments that might have carried them away from Dover Street on a Friday afternoon. We were helped too by the presence of one or more senior faculty Research Fellows who mostly owed their appointments to the generosity of Lord Simon of Wythenshawe (for many years chairman of the university council). Among these we particularly remember Bertrand de Jouvenel from Paris, George Homans from Harvard, Eveline Burns and Walter Gellhorn from Columbia, Edward Shils from Chicago, C. H. Sisson, who was granted a year's leave of absence from the Ministry of Labour to write his book on *The Spirit of the Civil Service*, Robert Osgood, the strategic theorist from Harvard, and Alexander Werth, the international journalist who was for many years Paris correspondent of the *Manchester Guardian* and later Moscow correspondent of *The Times*.

Mackenzie could also count on the attendance of colleagues from other departments. Nobody ever talked about 'interdisciplinary cooperation' at Manchester, but conversations and arguments across departmental boundaries went on all the time. According to the subject under discussion, the government seminar was attended by colleagues from the Department of Social Administration; by Max Gluckman and other social anthropologists, who attended regularly through a long series on African politics; by Dorothy Emmet and one or two other philosophers; and especially by Ely Devons, the Professor of Applied Economics.

Devons needs a special word. He died, tragically early, in 1967. He was a man of rare quality, of whom Sir Alec Cairncross has truly said that he had 'the elements of greatness in him to a degree not reflected in his career or in his writings'.[12] In the Economics Faculty he was the most dominant of several powerful personalities in the 1950s. He was dean for several years and guided the faculty board while others were dean. He loved the cut and thrust of controversy, and took part not only in the economics seminar each Wednesday but in many social anthropology seminars on Tuesdays and many government seminars on Fridays.

In these Friday meetings—to which he contributed at least three papers—he was a perfect foil to Mackenzie. Where the latter was ruminative and oblique, Devons was incisive and direct. Visiting speakers were conventionally interrupted after twenty minutes, a far longer period of grace than that given to members of the Department. Anyone who spoke in a superficial or boring way was apt to find the discussion taken out of his hands, so that he never reached the end of his paper. The seminar was more argumentative than any we have encountered elsewhere, though Mackenzie's chairmanship stopped it ever becoming ill-mannered or unpleasant. And in the evening visitors were commonly entertained by Bill and Pam at a party to which lecturers and their wives were invited.

Personal influence

Though Mackenzie's writings are important, and his best articles and chapters pass the test of repeated re-reading (they should be collected together in one place) there can be no doubt that his greatest impact on British political science has been made through his personal influence on colleagues and students.

This has not been primarily through any direct expository teaching, though as a formal teacher he was very successful with the bright honours student, or indeed any student who was stimulated by a lecturer more than slightly above his head and clearly anxious to lead him along new and unexpected paths. (Bill did not really approve of the teacher who was too readily comprehensible; he thought that such a person did not leave the student with enough work to do, or with any sense of personal challenge.)

In many ways his greatest skills were with younger members of staff, especially in the 1950s when the department was fairly small. He was in those first years very much available, an early arrival each day in the department, and a ready intruder into the rooms of others with a sheaf of paper in his hands, raising some point or making some suggestion. He gave an impression of age, wisdom and learning that belied the calendar. By about 1953, when still in his early forties (and still having published very little), he had already become a kind of academic father-figure to colleagues who were in their late twenties or even their early thirties. Though never in the least pompous, he was treated by his juniors with a degree of deference that was unusual even in the 1950s and is virtually unknown in the 1970s.

He was always generous with advice about his colleagues' work, and always constructive. While the brisk and cheerful manner of Ely Devons went along with a basic scepticism about the value of most academic research, Mackenzie's cautious Scottish demeanour concealed a fundamental optimism and permissiveness. For him 'All things work together for good to them that love God' or, at its lowest, who do their research thoroughly and present it stylishly. And even if it isn't really so, Mackenzie has believed it best to behave as though it were. When manuscripts were sent to him (as they were, as a matter of course, by his younger colleagues) they were returned promptly with many pencilled comments. These ranged from corrections of fact and detailed suggestions for the improvement of style to remarks which indicated the need for a different approach to the whole problem. Occasionally the comments would end with some small compliment which brought joy to the heart of the author, such as 'If you were to make a few changes I think you could probably publish this without doing your reputation any harm.' Once he is remembered to have said, 'I wish I had written that.' He took pride in the published work of his staff and maintained a special shelf for it in his room. He liked to intrude into all their (academic) affairs, and by and large sensible people let him do so—it was nearly always to their advantage.

He has a number of favourite words that everyone who knows him will recognise, such as the set formed by 'odd', 'puzzling', 'curious' and 'muddle'. It is possible that his fondness for these terms reflects something of his attitude to the respective roles of reason and tradition in politics. He has always taken pleasure in revealing confusions and ambiguities and in sorting out logical or historical puzzles, but at the same time he has never believed that tidiness is an important political virtue. As he once said, 'Human affairs are always in a state of muddle; muddled politics are not the worst sort of politics; and muddles often have a curious stability of their own.'[13]

He wrote a great deal by hand, even most letters in the early days. The administrative assistant to the faculty, Helen Hall, trying to allocate the time of the two and a half faculty secretaries of the late 1940s, was told by the new professor, 'You don't need to bother about me. I write my own letters. I don't need a secretary.' (His opinion changed later.)

We benefited not only from his letters and written comments, but even more from the ideas that he threw off in seminar discussion or in casual conversation. It must be said that one had to work—or at least to think—in order to benefit in this way, His oral manner, reflected in some of his shorter publications, was highly allusive and oblique. He had—doubtless still has—a habit of putting problems in a broader frame of reference than anyone else taking part in the discussion. It could be said of him what Wordsworth said of Coleridge: 'There was always a train, a stream in Coleridge's discourse, always a connection between its parts in his own mind, though one not always perceptible to the minds of others.'[14] The piece of writing which probably comes nearest to capturing his verbal style in his article on Oakeshott's inaugural lecture;[15] readers who have never met Mackenzie could do worse than read this article, and in particular try to work out how it was influenced by the books of T. S. Eliot, Harold Nicolson and E. R. Dodds that he lists on the first page as having helped to shape his thinking.

The allusive character of Mackenzie's conversation gives it a very special charm and stimulation for connoisseurs, as many of us became. The bikini is a revealing garment, but one not to be compared with a skirt ruffled by a summer breeze. Mackenzie's manner of discourse set the minds and imagination of his listeners to work. It shimmered with half-formulated ideas and suggestions which his colleagues were able to develop, and could use with less diffidence because, having mixed their labour with them, they felt they had become their own property.

Mackenzie's erudition is immense. His learning ranges from classical philology and Scottish law to broad fields of literature, history and philosophy. He knows an algorithm from a logarithm, and his head contains a mass of other such lore, available on summons when needed. He bore this learning lightly, but could not wholly conceal his feeling that railway journeys, holidays and illnesses were opportunities to reduce one's ignorance a little.

One of us (A.H.B.) will always remember a heart-warming encounter that took place in 1955. Birch was in a Cheshire hospital recovering from meningitis, unable to read and generally at a rather low ebb. The Sunday afternoon visiting hour in this institution was always singularly depressing, with the patients under instruction not to disturb their tidy bedclothes and the dark-suited visitors speaking in hushed tones as if preparing for a funeral. One Sunday the whole atmosphere was changed by the arrival of the large, untidy and somewhat incongruous figure of Bill Mackenzie, with muddy boots and a vast rucksack, conveying greetings in his deep and booming voice. The boots were muddy because he had hiked several miles across fields instead of driving or taking a bus. The rucksack was full of Victorian novels, to be deposited in a great heap on the bed. There followed a charming disquisition on their political and social significance, on a character in one intended to portray Sir Charles Dilke, in another Benjamin Jowett. Though the novels were not read for a very long time, for the sick man the visit was the greatest possible psychological boost—not only a gesture of friendship and a breath of fresh air, but positive proof that, outside those walls, there was a world of civilisation to which he would one day return. As always with Mackenzie, the message was conveyed indirectly, and with incomparably greater impact than by assuring the patient that he would recover.

Intellectual concerns

Mackenzie has never sought to become a specialist, and in political science his interests have included (*inter alia*) public administration and local government, political and administrative history, electoral studies, African politics, and the methodology of the social sciences. But this gives an impression of scatter that may be misleading. Though Bill undoubtedly has inclinations towards omniscience, one often finds that particular fields of study have been for him points of take-off for a few persistent theoretical concerns; or else matters on which he has written in a 'textbook' frame of mind, to set down clearly some body of information whose dissemination seemed at the time socially desirable: as we have already quoted him as saying, political argument and cookery books. A good example of the latter is that very successful book, *Free Elections*.[16]

An illustration of the first point is his Sidney Ball lecture,[17] ostensibly dealing with 'The export of electoral systems', which promptly states that it will in fact be 'concerned primarily with some rather dry questions about the tactics of research in politics'. This, part of what he later called the political science of political science,[18] has been an abiding interest.

One could track back important elements in his approach to politics to his own education. For example, his early classical and philological interests have influenced his later work in several ways, the most superficial of which are a kind of lifemanship about the use of words and a supply of quotations which he deploys with marvellous skill, as in the chapter headings of *Central Administration in Britain*. A more important reflection of his scholarly training is his interest in precision and craftsmanship, and his desire and capacity to draw fine distinctions. However, Bill would surely have written well, whatever the precise character of his education. He needed no philological training to make that brilliantly apt and amusing 'translation' of the Plowden report.[19]

At a more profound level, his linguistic and historical interests have influenced his whole conception of method in political science. In one discussion of research techniques he refers to 'arts techniques' and describes them in the following way:

... remnants of a rather old tradition in education; the capacity to use our own language with awareness of its limits and its ambiguities; to use two or three other languages more crudely, and to grasp in general the sort of problems which arise in translation from one language to another; to handle printed or written sources in a comprehensive and orderly way; to assess the value of these and other scraps of evidence about doubtful matters; above all, to present conclusions in such a way that the reader trusts the author's judgement but is not bound by it.[20]

Later in the same lecture, in discussing various accounts of the process of scientific discovery, he specifically refers to classical philology, 'the rather archaic science or disipline in which I was brought up', where one can have an effective grammar for a single language without first developing a general theory of linguistics, and learn 'to understand and translate' without explicitly setting out the structure of proof. Again, in *Politics and Social Science* he reminds us that 'even to master one foreign system adequately is a big job, because one can scarcely become an adequate instrument of political analysis without a full knowledge of the spoken language and the *nuances* of personal and political relationships which it conveys'.[21] Elsewhere he has spoken of his related training in the tradition of history as an understanding of unique events in context and sequence.

Then there is his legal training (and the law, as well as the manse, is part of his family background). It is harder to point with certainty to ways in which this has influenced him, but it probably shows up in his interest in procedures, in the formalities of organisation, and in order and continuity. He has often called attention to the unfortunate consequences of the total separation of the study of political science from that of law.

His practical work in government is also important. His war-time experience was supplemented while he was at Manchester in very varied ways. He went as adviser on constitutional development to Kenya and Tanganyika, was a member of various committees and commissions on local government reform, was a co-opted member of the Manchester City Education Committees, and so on. This had a number of consequences. It affected the work of others, from a small train of Africanist successors to fruitful research topics pursued by colleagues and students in local government and public administration. It also fed back into his own work, perhaps not as fully as he would have liked it to do, given the pressures of a mounting schedule of work (including administrative work) in the 1960s. In *Central Administration in Britain*, the book he wrote with Jack Grove, much judicious comment and vividly concrete details display the hand of the knowledgeable insider, as do his articles on local government and his more overtly analytical pieces on administrative theory. Mackenzie knows many things, and has greatly wanted to use what he knows, to rescue his experience and make it available and intelligible to others.[22]

Finally, there were the intellectual associations in Manchester of which we have already spoken, including those with anthropologists, economists, philosophers and others, themselves more than normally ready to explore points of contact with subjects other than their own. In particular, Mackenzie has liked, in the university context, to see his own subject as helping to keep academic communications open between the philosophers, historians and lawyers on the one hand, and the economists, anthropologists and sociologists on the other. Some of what he learned from anthropology is summarised in part IV of *Politics and Social Science*; he also speaks there of the way in which British social anthropologists and political scientists alike have favoured 'structure' over 'culture'. The faculty certainly became the centre for a series of small-town and community studies, starting in the 1950s with A. H. Birch's *Small-town Politics* and including Barbara Rodgers' and Julia Dixon's *Portrait of Social Work* and Michael Lee's *Social Leaders and Public Persons*. Not all such studies owed their first inspiration to Mackenzie, but he usually played an important role at some stage. (As we have hinted, he is adept at seeing ways of overcoming research problems, or guiding a manuscript into publishable form; the unpublishable Ph.D. thesis has always seemed to him a great waste of effort.)

Mackenzie did not take to everything at Manchester, and was less ready to accept its economics, especially some sizable remnants of anti-planning doctrine that survived John Jewkes's departure to Oxford. An early typescript of his laid into Michael Polanyi for seeming to claim that spontaneous co-operation and bureaucratic order were contradictories, whereas Bill found hope for the world only in their possible reconciliation. However, he saw the point of more empirical scepticism of the Devons kind, if still suspicious of its effects on the morale of the troops.

General stance

Perhaps this is the point at which we should say a little more about Mackenzie's general stance in face of his subject. A useful beginning is the sentence he quotes approvingly from Yarmolinsky: 'Social scientists particularly have to deal in situations in which any sensible person would throw up his hands and go home.'[23] For Mackenzie they 'have to' in several distinct, but connected, senses; at its lowest, because that is the way things have turned out. Our societies have evolved social science as they have evolved other forms of self-conscious reflection, and 'there is really no point in grumbling about mistakes or wrong turnings which happened at some time or other in the past'.[24] At its highest, social scientists are morally obliged to fill gaps that others have left empty, to venture forth to deal with the problems that no one else will tackle, doing the most craftsman-like job they can with very imperfect materials and techniques. For political scientists the dilemma is greatest, as they are the residuary legatees of the social sciences, from which others have carved off those areas most amenable to the rigorous use of scientific method.

'Political science . . . must either abdicate or attempt the impossible . . . The job is to talk in an orderly manner, paying regard to consistency and verifiability, about a unique situation, which is extremely complex and changes rapidly.'[25] The data of political science are harder to grasp and interpret, the conclusions more liable to error and distortion, the rationality of the subject in general precarious.

At the same time the findings, if they are important, will 'feed back into politics with the force of recommendations'.[26] Here again Mackenzie seems both to be saying what must inevitably be the case—that non-trivial political science can't help being practically influential—and what ought to be the case—that political science must in the final analysis be useful if it is not to be pointless. Not that he has preached any narrow-minded pragmatism, nor is it reflected in much of his own work. Still, he has had a bent to the kind of political science that 'is to be justified by practical benefits, at all levels from that of world politics to that of efficiency and humanity in public offices'.[27] He knows of the radical attacks on political science as statecraft, and is himself radical enough to see the force of these. But in the end it is for statecraft that he opts. He is conscious of the great, and often succumbed to, temptation of political scientists to be diverted from the great issues, and slide into some more readily navigable backwater of their subject.

The metaphor from seamanship reminds us here to mention the name of Joseph Conrad, a favourite novelist of the young Mackenzie, and who seems to have greatly influenced him in some not easily analysable way—not only his belief in professional competence, and devotion to the task, but some more general attitude to the constraints and promise of life. We have at least this indication, at the end of 'Political theory and political education':

I have no doubt that the search for principles in politics is a romantic illusion. But my taste is for the romantic rather than for the rococo, and there is after all a well known remedy for romance

and Mackenzie quotes the familiar words of Stein in *Lord Jim*:

with the exertions of your hands and feet in the water make the deep, deep sea keep you up . . . In the destructive element immerse . . . To follow the dream, and again to follow the dream—and so—*ewig—usque ad finem* . . .[28]

This at least should make it clear that Mackenzie is far from wishing to confine political science to the wholly answerable questions. Indeed, the questions he likes to ask of society are the 'partly answerable' kind, ones which we can approach and throw light on from several angles and by a variety of techniques, and so make progress, though finality or a single scheme eludes us. Of the three kinds of approach to politics that he refers to in *Politics and Social Science*—roughly, pluralist, generalist and the 'particularistic interdependence of disjointed incrementalism'—the last seems to attract him most, though as 'a matter of temperament and tactics, not of dogma'. Pure pluralism, one may guess, attracts him least, whether in political science or political life itself. He has always wanted to rescue the public interest and the common effort, though never quite sure how. He also asks political science to be venturesome, and (given good training and common sense) he is inclined to scorn caution. In a characteristic sentence he has praised the work of Raymond Aron, whose 'combination of perspective and precision may . . . prove to be a greater contribution to the making of foreign policy than the cautious use of scientific method'.[29]

One should perhaps also mention here a quirky anti-Americanism, evident in his Manchester days, and ranging from remarks about the almighty dollar scribbled in the margins of books extolling (as they then still did) the pluralistic politics of the United States, to the rather curt comment about the behavioural movement in *Politics and Social Science*. Neither did Bill seem keen to visit that country in his Manchester days (he had known war-time Washington), though he has never withheld due praise for individual American scholars. On the value of modern scientific and sociological approaches to politics, he has perhaps shown some ambiguity. His own education hardly prepared him to appreciate them, and in the 1950s he wrote feelingly of 'the nauseating jargon used by . . . American sociologists to conceal banality of thought'.[30] On the other hand, he has always felt it important that political science be hospitable to novelty and above all things eclectic in method, drawing on many approaches and indeed making this almost the defining characteristic of the discipline.

This ambiguity is reflected in *Politics and Social Science*, which represents a massive investment of time and thought in an attempt to summarise and criticise the more important of the scientific approaches to the study of politics. It is the most ambitious of

Mackenzie's cookery books. As Brian Barry has said, it is 'a master-piece of compression' which 'covers an enormous range of recent work, introducing each author with a pat on the back, dismissing him with a dig in the ribs, and usually succeeding in making some pertinent remarks in between'.[31] It is arguable that an equivalent effort in a field of scholarship more congenial to Mackenzie would have produced a book of more lasting value, but it is a remarkable testimony to his dedication to advancing his subject, and full of incidental brilliance and insight.

Mackenzie has desired venturesomeness in politics itself, as well as in political science, its handmaiden. Indeed, he seemed to feel more keenly, as the Manchester years went by, the failure of nerve and well directed intelligence at the root of British troubles, and especially the shortcomings of English elites and establishments. True, he has had a Burkean respect and affection for the wisdom embodied in existing institutions, from tribal village to tribal White-hall. But for him it has been something to be learned from, and built on, not rested in; and often the more enticing the myth, the more (he thinks) it needs a sharp knock. A stern and impatient man has surfaced from time to time in conversation and writings.

... for better or for worse (something of both) our rulers are more clearly aware of the complexity of Britain than African rulers are of the com-plexities of Africa. Perhaps this is one reason why African governments use the political bulldozer too much, British governments too little.[32]

Are we to train the Civil Servants of the future to be good tax-gatherers or good rulers? ... Personally, I should vote for the second alternative; find men who are ruthless, enterprising, well-read, well-travelled, ready to talk to any man in his own language: that keeps the options open ... Representation of the Establishment? Yes, for such men constitute part of the national stock of leaders; no, not *this* Establishment: except in so far as that changes, the Civil Service can neither be abolished nor renewed.[33]

He has admired the vitality of the great Victorian builders of Man-chester and Glasgow, and for that matter of Whitehall. It is no paradox to say both that Mackenzie is many ways a Victorian figure and that his mind is questing, restless and radical in cast. Many of the great Victorians had just those characteristics.

In his attitudes to practical questions of policy Mackenzie has nearly always had a good nose for the future, whether it be in local government reform, or in relation to the 'environment', or foreign policy, or the development of new universities. When petrol rationing ended in 1951, and most academics were enthusiastically buying their first car, Mackenzie was already worried about the effects of the motor car on city and countryside and stressing the importance of maintaining the railway system. He spotted the evasion of major problems of British higher education going on in the Sussex-Essex phase. Well before Suez he astonished some of us by announcing that Britain should remove her forces from the Mediterranean and leave it to the Americans and Russians. He never fitted neatly into a modern political category, lived in large old houses and even looked rather old-fashioned. It took time for his colleagues to detect the temperament of a Victorian radical—a political stance in any case much less common in the 1950s than it has turned out to be in the 1960s and 1970s. In this too he was before his time.

He seemed even more idiosyncratic when he discoursed on the virtues of Manchester architecture, especially those warehouses in the city centre—gaunt, blackened buildings that appeared fit only for the bulldozer. He, almost alone, admired their staircases and galleries, their door panelling, their Ruskinite decorations. Now that the city has finally enough money to demolish those that remain, Mackenzie's attitude has become fashionable, and in February 1973 the *Observer* devoted most of a colour supplement to extolling their virtues. To read this, in cities far from Manchester, was like hearing a voice from the past. No wonder we worry at rumours from Glasgow that Bill now favours self-government for Scotland.

In conclusion

Mackenzie's appointment to Manchester was an outstanding example of the right man going to the right place at the right time. It was either exceptional foresight or great good luck that led the appointments committee to think that this slow-speaking Oxford Scot would fit into the aggressive, even abrasive atmosphere of the Faculty of Economics in Dover Street. That he fitted so well is a tribute not only to him but to the senior people in the faculty when he arrived. It was a very lively faculty, with an alchemy that fused the talents of a disparate group of scholars. Soon Mackenzie had used his own alchemy to create a lively young Department of Government, one that was to establish an international reputation in less than a decade.

This sort of alchemy yields to no simple explanation, and it would be foolish to end this chapter with remarks that purported to summarise a complex story. But it may not be inappropriate to conclude by stressing once more Mackenzie's breadth of mind. Collingwood ended his essay on Ruskin's philosophy as follows:

Ruskin's greatness lay ... in his synthetic power. There were then, and always are, plenty of analytic minds. It is the synthetic mind—the mind that sees the unity of things—that is rare.[34]

Mackenzie too has been a great synthesiser, always peculiarly gifted at seeing the connections between apparently discrete ideas, at understanding the relations between ideas and institutions, at assessing the interplay of human beings in institutional settings. Under his subtle guidance the Manchester Department of Government developed a tradition of scholarship that was lively in approach, eclectic in method, but always humane in character. It is this tradition that those who had the good fortune to work with Bill Mackenzie seek to continue.

Notes

[1] As the university in those days had the gentlemanly habit of paying academic salaries quarterly, he was actually paid from 25 December, and his working habits made this more appropriate than it would have been for most. In a later year a colleague received a long letter on academic matters bearing that very date.

[2] Harold Nicolson, *Diaries and Letters, 1930–39*, Collins, London, 1966, p. 59.

[3] Quoted by Alec Cairncross in 'Ely Devons: a memoir', in E. Devons, *Papers on Planning and Economic Management*, Manchester University Press, 1970, p. 11.

[4] Gilbert Campion *et al.*, *British Government since 1918*, Allen & Unwin, London, 1950.

[5] 'Political theory and political education', *Universities Quarterly*, IX, 4, August 1955.

[6] *Ibid.*, p. 352.

[7] *Ibid.*, p. 360.

[8] *Ibid.*, p. 361.

[9] *Ibid.*, p. 362.

[10] In his first years at Manchester Mackenzie's Chair was one of 'Government and Administration' and he always took a keen interest in the work going on in Social Administration (in which his wife, Pam, took a degree).

[11] This interest was reflected in two articles of the period, 'Pressure groups in British government', *British Journal of Sociology*, VI, 2, June

1955, and 'Pressure groups: the "conceptual framework"', *Political Studies*, III, 3, October 1955.

¹² Cairncross, *op. cit.*, p. 15.

¹³ *Free Elections*, Allen & Unwin, London, 1958, p. 170.

¹⁴ Quoted in D. A. Stauffer (ed.), *The Selected Poetry and Prose of Samuel Taylor Coleridge*, Random House, New York, 1951, p. x.

¹⁵ 'Political theory and political education', *Universities Quarterly*, IX, 4, August 1955.

¹⁶ Allen & Unwin, London, 1958.

¹⁷ Delivered in the University of Oxford in February 1957, and reprinted in *Political Studies*, V, 3, October 1957.

¹⁸ See, for example, 'The political science of political science', *Government and Opposition*, VI, 3, summer 1971.

¹⁹ It appeared first in the *Guardian*, but is also to be found in *Public Administration* (Sydney), XXII, 2, June 1963.

²⁰ 'The export of electoral systems', *Political Studies*, V, October 1957, pp. 243–4.

²¹ *Politics and Social Science*, Penguin Books, Harmondsworth, 1967, p. 312. See also the chapter in that book on 'Law and Language', with its interesting discussion of what future work on political language might be like.

²² 'No one has *known*—for intellectual use—the things you know...' (James to Conrad, 1 November 1906. See *Selected Letters of Henry James*, ed. Leon Edel, Hart-Davis, London, 1956, p. 189).

²³ *Politics and Social Science*, p. 306.

²⁴ *Ibid.*, p. 57.

²⁵ *Ibid.*, p. 383.

²⁶ The political science of political science', p. 278.

²⁷ *Ibid.*, p. 290.

²⁸ 'Political theory and political education', p. 363.

²⁹ W. J. M. Mackenzie, *The Study of Political Science Today*, Macmillan, London, 1970, p. 46.

³⁰ 'Political theory and political education', p. 356.

³¹ Brian M. Barry, *Sociologists, Economists and Democracy*, Collier-Macmillan, London, 1970, p. 185.

³² *Politics and Social Science*, p. 356.

³³ 'The civil service, the State and the Establishment', in Bernard Crick (ed.), *Essays on Reform, 1967: a Centenary Tribute*, Oxford University Press, London, 1967, pp. 201–2.

³⁴ R. G. Collingwood, *Ruskin's Philosophy*, Kendal, 1919, p. 43. We owe the quotation to W. H. Greenleaf.

Malcolm Anderson

2

Frontier regions in Europe

One of Professor Mackenzie's major contributions to the study of politics has been to correct the distortions encouraged by Febvre's striking aphorism 'Peu importe le marge, c'est le coeur qu'il faut avant tout considérer.' Reflections on Bill Mackenzie's redefinition of the frontiers of political science I leave to others. This essay is a tribute to his abiding interest in the politics of peripheral regions. What constitutes a peripheral region, as he knows so well, changes with time. Those provinces once considered on the periphery can be absorbed into metropolitan spheres of influence through improved transport facilities and changed economic circumstances. The drawing of boundaries and questions of definition, which for long periods are the calm preserve of lexicographers, cartographers and pedants can suddenly emerge as the most urgent and intractable problems of public policy and political science.

The preservation or revision of international boundaries has ceased to be an obsessive issue in European politics. In other parts of the world frontier disputes remain an important feature of international relations but in Europe, after centuries of conflict, there is a greater degree of acceptance of existing boundaries than at any other time in recent history.[1] The great question of the first half of the twentieth century, the proper boundaries of the German-speaking peoples, has been all but settled. The minor adjustments to the western frontier after the second world war have not been subject to significant challenge since the Saar plebiscite of 1955. The extraordinarily complex relationship between Germans and Slavs in Bohemia, Silesia, Pomorze, Poznania, East Prussia and the Memel territory—to mention only the most important areas of confrontation—was transformed by the massive *coup de force* of 1944-45. The flight and expulsion of German populations created *de facto* situations which, in the long run, and if no new factor emerged in the international environment, were bound to result in *de jure* recognitions. From the late 1960s the Brandt government's *Ostpolitik* has effectively created a situation which would be difficult for future German governments to challenge.[2] Even that unquiet zone between the Alps and the Adriatic where Teuton, Slav and Latin meet is relatively stable. The Italo-Yugoslav border, the scene of D'Annunzio's theatricals after the first world war, was delimited by the Trieste plebiscite of 1954, although there are still some minor questions outstanding. The Austro-Italian boundary remains on the Brenner after years of equivocation by the Austrian government over the South Tyrol's right to self-determination. In general, the disputes between the successor States of the Austro-Hungarian empire have been held in check by the Russian presence in eastern and central Europe and, west of the Iron Curtain, by the conditions created by the cold war. In a very different part of Europe, the constitution of the Republic of Ireland does not recognise the border of the six counties of Ulster, although the present policies of the Dublin government tend towards such recognition. Existing boundaries are still challenged by minorities but social, economic and military developments have effectively removed these challenges from the realm of practical possibilities.

There is, however, an immense sediment of history remaining to cloud perceptions of boundary or frontier questions.[3] This sediment is composed of several elements—a body of literature, popular stereotypes of peoples who live in frontier provinces, lingering or latent minority problems and apprehensions of national governments about security and sovereignty. The literature on frontiers is of many kinds. Some has been written by soldiers and statesmen, and those who proffered their advice to them, concerned with the problem of delimiting strategically and politically desirable frontiers. Men such as MacMahon and Curzon during the high tide of the British empire, writers during the first world war such as Lyde and Fawcett, to name only the best known British examples,[4] who were succeeded by Americans such as Peattie during the second world war,[5] belong to this tradition. It is a tradition of 'improvement', of attempting to reduce levels of conflict and to make the world safer. If boundaries were correctly drawn, according to this tradition, the risk of war would be minimised. International lawyers have also written much on boundary questions, particularly on the procedures of demarcation and, above all, on boundary disputes. The commentaries of international lawyers are necessarily anchored in the past because they are concerned with those disputes which have arisen and the methods by which they have been settled. Remarkable and now unfashionable views about frontiers can be found in the work of Ratzel and the German school of 'geopolitics'. Crudely summarised, the principal thesis of the geopolitical school is that 'nature abhors fixed frontiers'[6] and that boundaries represent the transitory expression of the power of adjacent States. Most English and American political geographers have, for one reason or another, rejected this view. Their work has been of very varied character. Some of their attention has been turned to placing notions of boundaries in their context of space and time.[7] They have also been concerned with the establishment of classifications or typologies of boundaries. The old distinction between artificial and natural boundaries has been abandoned, and in recent years the focus has been concentrated on the functions which boundaries perform.[8] These functions are seen less in terms of the nature of the boundary line and more in terms of the characteristics of the communities which the boundaries separate.[9]

Commonly held views of the nature of the peoples who live close to frontiers have been compounded of folk memories, historical experiences, literary images and the prejudices of those who live in the heartlands of the old nation States. Frequently these have little direct relevance to contemporary problems but have an important influence on how those problems are assessed. Popular images of frontiersmen are of considerable richness and complexity and can be only briefly sketched here. Four main themes frequently recur. The first is the picture of the frontiersman as the tough, resourceful guardian of the *imperium*, keenly aware of the dangers to security from across the border. This is the image of the frontier officer given by Curzon of Kedleston,[10] and the picture presented by Maurice Barrès of the men of Lorraine, with their eyes fixed on the thin blue line of the Vosges. The second is the lawless brigand, cattle thief or smuggler whose code of honour, although rigidly adhered to, is at odds with that of the rest of the community. This is a picture often drawn of men on remote frontiers—the Scottish border, the Pyrenees, the Carpathians. They are often heavily sentimental and historically inaccurate. As with Pierre Loti's novel about the Basques, *Ramuntcho*,[11] they can strike the people concerned as ridiculous and slightly offensive. The third theme, that of the half-breed or cultural hybrid with no clear identity, is an image with more evidence to support it. The Masurians of East Prussia, speaking an archaic Polish, writing in a Gothic script and Lutheran by religion, whom the Poles wished to retain in Poland in 1945 but who preferred to follow Germans into exile, closely correspond to the stereotype.[12] It is a type which excites anti- pathy—'Cultures turn rotten when they part.'[13] The picture of the frontiersman as a marginal man, also because of his geographical situation, is the fourth theme. One of Kipling's Roman legionaries guarding Hadrian's wall, in *Puck of Pooks Hill*, says, 'We're the last sweepings of the Empire—the men without hope.'[14] The forgotten man of the periphery is, however, not only a literary stereotype but a deeply felt attitude found in frontier populations who have suffered an economic or political decline.

Feelings of separateness, social distance and neglect have en- couraged autonomist movements on the periphery of European nation States. In recent years those national minorities which form an island in an ocean of a much larger national group, like the Sorbs of Lusatia in East Germany,[15] either by lack of opportunity or by calculation, have not sought autonomous political expression. National or quasi-national minorities on the periphery in Brittany, Estonia, Catalonia, Frisia, Scotland and Wales have all conceived of themselves as having a social and frequently a political identity. The Baltic nationalities were, of course, subjected to violent re- pression when they were absorbed by the Soviet Union after the second world war. But European governments in the last quarter of a century have generally regarded the aspirations of these nationalities as of minor importance, considering that they can be dealt with by small material concessions, or by minor constitutional adjustments, or by interminable procrastination. The setting up of the Commission on the Constitution (the Crowther–Kilbrandon commission) in the United Kingdom, after Welsh and Scottish nationalists had caused local electoral difficulties, was a typical reaction. There are two circumstances in which governments have recently taken minority questions very seriously. The first is when the minority is very large, such as the Flemish in Belgium and the Croats in Yugoslavia. These groups pose a very real threat to the unity of the State. The second is when the minority is adjacent to an international frontier. In this circumstance old sensitivities about irredentism, however unrealistic, can be easily aroused. In the former case the problem is usually complicated by the international context. The whole of Belgium is within very easy reach of international boundaries, and only one administrative region, Brabant, has no boundary contiguous with another country: both 'national' groups, the Flemish and the Walloons, speak languages which are very similar to those spoken in neighbouring countries. The Croatian problem is aggravated by the location of the Croats in the western part of Yugoslavia and the economic attraction exercised by countries over the western boundary. But the frontier does not loom large in these situations. For the Tyrolese, the Alsatians, the Northern Irish and, to a much lesser extent, the Basques, attitudes towards the frontier have been a basic element in their political consciousness. When governments have been compelled to take notice of agitation in these provinces, their actions have been influenced by apprehensions and sensitivities about the frontier.

The South Tyrol question presents some of the typical features of conflict in frontier provinces. The Alto Adige, the region in which most German-speaking South Tyrolese live, lies on a frontier which has long been the subject of dispute.[16] The peace conference of 1919 accepted the Italian claim to the crestline of the Alps, traversed by the Brenner pass, as Italy's strategically necessary frontier. This presented Italy with a minority problem, a German-speaking population of over 200,000. The Italian government gave certain undertakings about the cultural, educational and linguistic rights of the South Tyrolese. Mussolini's fascist regime ignored these undertakings and embarked on an aggressive policy of Italianisation which included the establishment of the industrial zone of Bolzano to encourage Italian immigration into the Alto Adige. The revival of German military strength, after Hitler came to power, caused Italian fears that demands for frontier revision would be made. Hitler, however, by the pact he made with Mussolini in 1938, renounced the intention of including the South Tyrol in the greater Reich, and the South Tyrolese were compelled to make the choice, by December, 1939, between emigration and complete integration into Italy. A majority of two to one chose emigration. The war intervened and, although many urban South Tyrolese crossed the Alps to settle in the Reich, virtually all the rural dwellers remained in their homes. In the last two years of the second world war there was a *de facto* annexation of the South Tyrol by the Germans, but the German military defeat restored the *status quo ante*.

The post-war constitution of the Italian republic allowed for considerable regional autonomy. This was readily granted to the small French-speaking community of the Val d'Aoste, but the German-speaking inhabitants of the Alto Adige were grouped with the predominantly Italian region of Trento to form the administrative region of Trentino–Alto Adige. The reason for this arrangement was to reintegrate the South Tyrolese without submerging them, but the motives of the Rome government were suspect to the South Tyrolese. Although cultural and linguistic rights were returned to them and a fairly generous measure of local autonomy was granted, intense mutual suspicion grew up between them and the Rome government. For two decades the problem dragged on, with impatient young South Tyrolese militants conducting a bombing campaign in the early 1960s.

The complexity of the problem was well stated by the moderate South Tyrolese leader, Dr Nicolussi-Leck, in 1961 :

The present social and economic conditions do not give the 240,000 South Tyrolese sufficient chance of surviving for long the competition against the 51 million-strong national population. The same rights for all would mean in this case unequal rights for the weaker minority. From this derives our moral as well as constitutional and treaty-consecrated right to far-reaching self-administration.[17]

The region suffered from an unfavourable economic environment similar to that of many peripheral regions in Europe. The majority of the inhabitants felt (and expressed this feeling by voting for the Südtiroler Volkspartei) that their ethnic identity was threatened both by economic circumstances and by the political system. The South Tyrolese considered that they had been deeply wronged in the past by the Italian State and were not being properly protected by it in the present. The Austrian government supported the South Tyrolese, although there was little it could do, apart from making diplomatic representations. But by refusing to deny the right of the South Tyrolese to self-determination it kept alive deep-rooted Italian apprehensions.

For the Italian government the Alpine crest was a 'natural' frontier in the old sense, a watershed, an obvious topographical feature which was still considered to have military usefulness. For many Italians the South Tyrolese were citizens of doubtful loyalty (in the recent past the great majority had opted for emigration to the Nazi greater Reich and they now voted for an ethnic

Volkspartei); they engaged in direct contacts with a foreign government, the Austrian government, appealed to international opinion on a very doubtful interpretation of the right of self-determination; they showed scanty sympathy for the Italian minority in their own region, and young Tyrolese activists engaged in extremely distasteful terrorist activities. The conflict was difficult to resolve because neither side had much understanding of, let alone sympathy for, the other's point of view.

The struggle of the South Tyrolese was an anachronism—an ethnic struggle based on national hostilities in a context in which there was little or no possibility that the old solution of boundary revision could be effected. The economic links which bound the Alto Adige to the Italian State made that solution progressively less attractive to the South Tyrolese. Further, 'the South Tyrolese realised from bitter experience that they were too weak politically, and possessed no institutions capable of bringing pressure to bear on the Italian government'.[18] The only way forward for them was to adopt a more co-operative attitude towards the Italian State. Eventually, in the summer of 1969, an agreement was reached between the Italian government and representatives of the South Tyrolese. The detail and complexity of this agreement (it contained 137 points, covering administrative, educational, cultural and linguistic matters)[19] is an indication of the depth of the mistrust, but since 1969 tension between the main parties has much diminished.

The South Tyrol is an extreme case of a disaffected frontier province, but some of the same factors are present in other European frontier provinces. It is very difficult to predict when these factors will cause serious political conflict.[20] The failure of the IRA bombing campaign of the 1950s gave little hint that events after 1969 would reveal that the Catholics in Ulster were perhaps the only genuinely irredentist population in contemporary Europe. There are, of course, hints of irredentism elsewhere. The Basque autonomist movement envisages the uniting of the four Spanish with the three French Basque provinces in the context of a united Europe.[21] Factors exist which promote feelings of distinctiveness and perhaps latent irredentism. The inhabitants of Alsace and Moselle remain faithful to the Germanic dialects of their ancestors. They expressed their distinctiveness by voting for regional parties in the inter-war period, but in recent years they have tended to over-compensate by voting Gaullist more heavily than any other region of France.[21] This is an example of the typical extremism of frontier provinces born of two different kinds of insecurity: a sense of military and physical insecurity arising from the proximity of a foreign sovereignty and a psychological insecurity related to uncertainties about cultural and national identity.

'Le voisinage', as Lapradelle called it, can have very different effects.[23] All frontier provinces are special cases in the sense that they are in unique geographical and social situations. They have special problems, different economies and different demographic patterns. Some international boundaries, such as the German–Dutch, do not separate markedly different regions.[24] Other boundaries, such as the Franco-Spanish, mark dramatic breaks in the cultural landscape. The causes of this are not only differences in linguistic patterns and architectural tastes but the layout of communications networks, agricultural patterns, industrial developments, all influenced by government regulation and by the market forces of different economies. The historical experiences of frontier regions have been different, and some have experienced radical changes of fortune.[25] Trieste had a brilliant period from the eighteenth to the twentieth century, when it became a great port and commercial centre in the Austro-Hungarian empire.[26] After its cession to Italy in 1919 its position was reduced to twelfth among Italian ports. It was a prize contested by Yugoslavia and Italy after the second world war.[27] These troubles and relative decline created a nostalgia among the inhabitants of Trieste which has strongly influenced their political attitudes.

Boundary changes have generally had a depressing effect on frontier provinces. The damage to property in some cases has been great because wars have been fought not only over frontiers but on frontiers. The flight of elites from Alsace in 1871 and whole populations from east of the Oder–Neisse line in 1944–46 caused damage of a much more important kind than the damage to property resulting from military operations. Changes in sovereignty have often had depressing effects because of the introduction of new and strange administrative arrangements, the ill-adaptation of previous political habits to the new circumstances and changes in the competitive situation of the industries in the provinces. For rather different reasons, frontiers which have been stable for centuries have tended also to have backward regions adjacent to them. The stability has usually been associated with the ease with which the frontier can be defended: these are not usually in locations favourable to the development of trade and industry. Frontier provinces have therefore often been relatively depressed: they have all, until the development of European co-operation in the recent past, been compelled to face one way—towards the metropolitan centres of their own countries.

When an economic imbalance arises between neighbouring provinces separated by an international boundary,[28] the result can be very disturbing for the population of the ill-favoured regions, and the political consequences are unpredictable. In north Moselle a scattering of medium and small towns, such as Sarreguimines, Saint-Avoid, Merlebach and Forbach, lie within thirty kilometres of the burgeoning industrial contribution of Saarbrüken. Jobs have proliferated in the Saar, whilst on the French side of the border the creation of new jobs, often as a consequence of German investment, has succeeded only in cushioning the effects of the ineluctable contraction of the coal industry. As a result of changes in recent years, mainly monetary, the wages paid in deutschmarks in 1972 were roughly 60–80 per cent higher than those paid in francs on the French side of the frontier.[29] The German- based firms also often provide free transport for their workers. The young leave to work in Germany, and the workers left in Moselle tend to be ageing. Firms on the French side of the border are caught in a vicious circle, because without increasing productivity they cannot pay wages high enough to retain the young, and without the young workers they cannot raise productivity. The local economic development committee, Comité d'expansion de l'est Lorrain (CELOR), has issued alarmist statements and has enthusiastically backed a proposal for a new industrial zone straddling the frontier. The development committee for the whole Lorraine region, Association pour l'expansion industrielle de la Lorraine (APELOR), the Gaullist deputies of the region and the French government have been very lukewarm about this scheme, and it has little chance of getting off the ground. Faced with a situation of inertia and lack of industrial development on the French side of the boundary, the frontier communes are rapidly becoming dormitory suburbs. A similar situation exists in most of Alsace outside the large towns. In these north-east borderlands of France, in towns such as Bitche, Wissembourg, Haguenau and Saint-Louis, there is much discussion of neglect and abdication

by the French government. The prosperity across the border is compared, with some bitterness, to the French situation. Parallels are
drawn with Auvergne, Corsica and Brittany—the traditionally
backward regions which have served as a pool of labour for the
industrial centres of France.

Some account of the special problems of the frontier regions
has been taken by European authorities. The focus of the European
Communities' developing regional policy has been on depressed
regions, which are usually peripheral regions[30] and sometimes
frontier regions. The only specific programme for frontier provinces
was the commission's recommendation in 1963 for the north of
Lorraine and the Belgian province of Luxembourg, which it addressed to both governments concerned.[31] Nothing came of this.[32] The
Council of Europe has been modestly successful in awakening
official and public opinion to frontier provinces and in helping to
stimulate trans-frontier co-operation. In January 1964 the Consultative Assembly of the Council of Europe instructed its committee on local authorities 'to consider the expediency and, if
appropriate, suitable forms of co-operation . . . between municipalities
of different member States of the Council of Europe, in particular
between neighbouring municipalities on their frontiers'.[33] The
committee also considered a resolution of the European Conference of Local Authorities on regional planning and frontier
areas.[34] The committee duly proposed a draft convention on trans-
frontier co-operation between municipal authorities, which was
approved by the Assembly, but the Committee of Ministers refused
to act on it. Despite the obvious procrastination of the national
governments, the Consultative Assembly re-entered the fray with a
resolution in 1969[35] proposing a European symposium on the problems of frontier provinces. This was a modest success when it met in
Strasbourg in July 1972.[36] In its recommendations to the Council
of Europe it observed that the 'intensity of trans-frontier co-operation is a measure of the *rapprochement* between nations in Europe
and of governments' willingness to promote it'. Its most important
practical proposals were that governments should be invited to
establish frontier region commissions composed of local, regional
and national representatives from both sides of the boundary. These
commissions, to which professional associations and interest groups
would have easy access, would propose measures for trans-frontier
co-operation and examine trans-frontier problems such as pollution

control. The problem of frontier provinces should be put on the agenda for the European Security Conference. The European Conference of Ministers responsible for Regional Planning should be encouraged to propose measures in trans-frontier planning.

This latter conference, held in Bonn in September 1972, throwing aside the usual caution of national government representatives on this question, urged governments to co-ordinate planning policies and measures in frontier regions 'with the participation of those directly concerned, in particular, by *creating regional committees* to hold periodic meetings in order to co-ordinate the preparation and timing of regional plans'. The second conference, in September 1973, discussed the problems involved on the basis of on-the-spot appraisals made by senior officials in Alsace, Baden–Württemburg and along the Franco-Belgian border.

These moves at the European level were not, of course, taking place in a vacuum. Studies, arrangements and agreements have been sponsored at the unofficial, local and national levels. Examples of studies are the 'Régions frontalières à l'heure du Marché commun' by the French Permanent Association of Chambers of Commerce, published in 1966; the 'Regions of Europe' seminar organised by the 'Euregio Rhein–Ems–Ijssel'[37] has contributions from representatives of several European borderlands; occasional studies are pubished by the 'Saint-Gotthard community', which brings together the Swiss cantons of Ticino, Valais and Uri with the Italian region of Novara.

There is practical co-operation across frontiers of many kinds. The oldest kind is concerned with transport problems. The conventions on traffic on the Rhine and Danube are venerable examples. There is co-operation at both the national and the local level between Sweden and Denmark about the construction of an international airport on the island of Saltholm linked by bridge and tunnel with Copenhagen and Malmö. The widening of a canal helped to develop trans-frontier co-operation between Zeeland and East Flanders. There has been some joint planning on the routing of motorways between the French *départements* of Nord and Pas-de-Calais and the Belgian provinces of West Flanders and Hainault. The extension of Basle airport requires the co-operation of Haut-Rhin and the French government. There are, however, other types of trans-frontier co-operation. The planning and pollution problems of Lake Constance have brought together the governments of

Vorarlberg in Austria and Baden–Württemburg in Germany. In October 1967 an agreement was signed setting up a Franco-German Dairy Union—the Mosel–Saar dairy co-operative associated a number of dairies in Alsace, Lorraine and the Saar. There is an ambitious scheme in the Dutch–German permanent commission on regional planning. The 1972 symposium on frontier regions found practical trans-frontier co-operation most highly developed in the Alps–Adriatic triangle—Carinthia and Styria (Austria), Croatia and Slovenia (Yugoslavia) and Friuli–Venezia (Italy).

Of all the States west of the Elbe, France has been the most reluctant to contemplate trans-frontier co-operation. This reluctance has not been entirely consistent, and indeed, France could claim to be a pioneer of special arrangements for frontier zones. After the 1947 peace treaty with Italy, readjusting the boundary so that it followed the crest of the Maritime Alps, a fairly close relationship between the areas adjacent to the boundary developed. With the blessing of both governments, a standing committee of French and Italian chambers of commerce of the frontier zone was established to stimulate exchanges, to revive the economy in the border regions and to encourage improvement in communications. In 1951 a Franco-Italian convention was signed creating a frontier zone about ten kilometres in depth on both sides of the boundary, within which there was to be free circulation of persons, livestock, seeds, tools and fertilisers. The efforts to stimulate the economy of the frontier regions had little effect, and representatives from the regions on both sides of the border made a joint approach to both governments, asking for special attention to be paid to their problems.[38] No obvious obstacles have been placed in the way of co-operation but there is still the feeling that, as the senator mayor of Menton puts it, 'The frontier regions find it difficult to control their fate since they, more than others, are under the domination of their respective governments.'[39] In Senator Palmero's view the main difficulty lies not in direct contacts across the frontier but in relations with the respective central governments and with 'the slowness of the administrative machinery'. The old centralisation of the French administrative system which, despite the movement towards regionalisation in the last two decades, has not yet been fundamentally modified, is seen both by the French and by their neighbours as an important obstacle. The president of the regional government of Val d'Aoste, Cesare Dujany, remarked, 'In our day-to-day relations we have found that it is more difficult to conclude agreements with our neighbour, Savoy, because it belongs to the centralised State of France. With Valais it is easier because as a canton of the Con- federation of Switzerland it enjoys greater autonomy.'[40] President Dujany freely admitted that Italy had rigidities in other ways and did not adapt quickly to new situations. He thus implicitly recog- nised that the basic problem lay not in legal and administrative arrangements but in attitudes.

The attitudes associated with Gaullism, but by no means ex- clusively French or exclusively Gaullist, are generally more hostile to trans-frontier co-operation than attitudes associated with social democratic, Christian democratic and 'liberal' parties in France and other European countries. There are three main themes in the former complex of attitudes: firstly, the nation State is *the* basic factor of political life—the nation State is and ought to be the main focus of political obligation and loyalty; secondly, specific national cultures exist whose parameters are a language and a shared historical experi- ence—dilution of the culture and foreign influences on the language are a grievous loss; thirdly, the national territory is a sacred patrimony, and none of it should be alienated—it ought not, to any appreciable extent, be encroached upon economically, socially or militarily by foreigners. These ideas are important inhibiting factors in trans-frontier co-operation. Affronting them is imprudent because this could encourage more extreme forms of nationalism.

Highly educated and cosmopolitan people in many European countries hold the view that 'frontiers once the scars of history ought to be made the points of contact and communication between nations and their inhabitants'.[41] Studies, declarations of intent and proposals for co-operation create a climate of progress and achieve- ment among some politicians and senior administrators. But there remain many reticences, one example of which is the reluctance of the members of the European Communities to dismantle their border controls. Many factors conspire to make frontier regions areas of particular difficulty and confrontation.[42] Economic, social and political changes inevitably render some boundaries obsolescent. Unpredictable conflicts will arise if there is a *de facto* shift in fron- tiers whilst the same *de jure* boundaries are maintained. The rhetoric of European integration is unlikely to calm these conflicts. Conflict in frontier regions raises tangled historical, political, psy- chological, administrative, legal and economic questions. Perceptions of the nature and causes of conflict are almost always widely divergent. Some harmonisation of administrative arrangements in frontier regions will, through the European institutions, certainly be achieved. Political harmony in those regions is always at risk.

Notes

[1] On a global scale, however, boundary disputes remain an important feature of international relations. For a list of current disputes see E. Luard (ed.), *The International Regulations of Boundary Disputes*, Thames & Hudson, London, 1970, pp. 7–10. An impressive collection of papers on boundaries and frontier provinces was presented to a colloquium in March 1972 at the Institute of International Sociology at Gorizia: see *Confini e regione (Boundaries and Regions)*, Lint, Trieste, 1973.

[2] In particular, it would be difficult to go back on the unequivocal recognition of the Oder–Neisse frontier between Poland and East Germany contained in the Warsaw treaty (1970) between the German Federal Republic and Poland.

[3] The conventional, though rather loose, distinction between a boundary and a frontier is followed in this article: a boundary is a line which demarcates the limits of the jurisdiction of a State, whereas a frontier can be a zone part of which may be within the jurisdiction of a State.

[4] See especially G. P. Tate, *The Frontiers of Baluchistan*, Witherby, London, 1909, introduction by Col. Sir A. Henry MacMahon; G. N. Curzon, Viscount Kedleston, *Frontiers* (Romanes lecture, 1907), Clarendon Press, 1907; C. B. Fawcett, *Frontiers: a Study in Political Geography*, Clarendon Press, Oxford, 1918.

[5] Especially R. Peattie, *Look to the Frontiers: a Geography of the Peace Table*, Harper, New York, 1944; S. B. Jones, *Boundary-making: a Handbook for Statesmen*, Columbia University Press, New York, 1945.

[6] E. C. Semple, *Influences of Geographic Environment*, Holt, New York, 1911, p. 204. For an extreme example of the geographical position see K. Haushofer, *Grenze in ihre geographischen und politischen Bedeutung*, Heidelberg, 1939.

[7] For example, S. B. Jones, 'Boundary concepts in the setting of place and time', *Annals of the Association of American Geographers*, XLIX, 1959, pp. 241–55; and the excellent articles by N. J. Pounds, 'The origin of the idea of natural frontiers in France', *ibid.*, XLI, 1951; 'France and "les limites naturelles" from the seventeenth to the twentieth centuries', *ibid.*, XLIV, 1954, pp. 51–62.

[8] A pioneering work on this subject from one particular perspective is O. E. Lessing, *Minorities and Boundaries*, Nijhoff, The Hague, 1931.

[9] Little progress has been made. See R. V. Prescott, *The Geography of Frontiers and Boundaries*, Hutchinson, London, 1965, pp. 102–3.

[10] Curzon, *op. cit.*, pp. 54–8. It is sometimes argued that these qualities of energy and resourcefulness have been a particularly creative force in history: new States have grown out of the frontier provinces of old empires.

See O. Lattimore, *Studies in Frontier History*, Mouton, Paris and The Hague, 1962.

[11] Calman Levy, Paris, 1896.

[12] E. Wiskemann, *Germany's Eastern Neighbours*, Oxford University Press, London, 1956, pp. 15–16, 96–118. For another example of a hybrid see Institut d'études politiques de Toulouse, *Les Problèms actuelles des vallées d'Andorre*, Pédone, Paris, 1970.

[13] R. Conquest, 'For the 1956 opposition of Mars', in R. Conquest (ed.), *New Lines* II, Macmillan, London, 1963, p. 113.

[14] Macmillan, London, 1906, p. 184.

[15] G. Stone, *The Smallest Slavonic Nation*, Athlone Press, London, 1972. See p. 32 for a not very serious move in 1919 for self-determination for the Sorbs.

[16] A. T. Alcock, *The History of the South Tyrol Question*, Joseph, London, 1970.

[17] *Ibid.*, p. 361.

[18] *Ibid.*, p. 471.

[19] *Ibid.*, pp. 433–52. F. Ermacora, 'Die Südtirolfrage, 1969–1970', *Donaurum*, XV, 1–2, 1970, pp. 1–10.

[20] See, for example, the extraordinarily sanguine assessment of prospects in the South Tyrol in G. G. Weigand, 'Effects of boundary changes in South Tyrol', *Geographical Review*, XL, 1950, p. 37.

[21] Motion of the congress of Itxassou quoted in M. Anderson, 'The political life of the French Basques', working paper No. 1, Department of Politics, University of Warwick.

[22] M. Anderson, 'Regional identity and political change: the case of Alsace from the Third to the Fifth Republic', *Political Studies*, XX, 1, 1972, pp. 17–30.

[23] P. de Lapradelle, *La Frontière: étude de droit international*, Editions internationales, Paris, 1928. For a systematic case study of 'le voisinage', based on survey data, see R. Gubert, *La situazione confinaria*, Lint, Trieste, 1973.

[24] R. S. Platt, 'A geographical study of the Dutch–German border', *Siedlung und Landschaft in Westfälen*, No. 3, Münster, 1958. For an attempt to classify European frontier regions see V. Freiherr von Malchus, 'Méthodes et pratique de la coopération internationale des régions frontalières européens', in *Confini e regione, op. cit. supra*, pp. 179–98.

[25] An excellent study of a frontier region over several centuries in S. Daveau, *Les Régions frontalières de la montagne jurassienne*, Trévoux, 1959.

[26] J. B. Duroselle, *Le Conflit de Trieste, 1943–54*, Institut de Sociologie, Brussels, 1966: A. E. Moodie, *The Italo-Yugoslav Boundary*, Philip, London, 1945.

[27] G. Valussi, *Il confine nordorientale d'Italia*, Lint, Trieste, 1972, pp. 165–268, for the implications of these boundary changes.

[28] R. Gendarme, 'Les problèmes économiques, des régions frontalières européens', *Revue Économique*, November 1970.

[30] The peripheral regions feel a similar sense of identity. See the meet-

ing of representatives of European peripheral regions organised by the Comité d'études et de liaison des intérêts bretons, *Le Monde*, 26 June 1973.

[31] 'Recommendation de la Commission ... concernant un project de co-operation sur le plan régionale entre le nord de la Lorraine et le sud de la province belge du Luxemburg', *Journal Officiel de la CEE*, 97/63, 27 June 1963.

[32] For one account of this see D. Coombes, *Political and Bureaucracy in the European Community*, Allen & Unwin, London, 1969, pp. 217–39.

[33] Council of Europe, Consultative Assembly, order No. 27, 1964.

[34] *Ibid.*, resolution No. 46, 1964.

[35] *Ibid.*, document No. 2529 and reference No. 734, 1969.

[36] *Ibid.*, document No. 3228, 1973. This contains the recommendations of the symposium and a summary of reports presented to it. The full reports can be found in Council of Europe, AS/Coll/Front 1–18.

[37] Council of Europe doc. AS/GT/AT (17) 12.

[38] See J. W. House, 'The Franco-Italian boundary in the Alpes-Maritimes', *Transactions of the Institute of British Geographers*, XXVI, 1959, pp. 107–31; and *id.*, 'A local perspective on a boundary zone: two examples from the European Economic Community', in C. A. Fisher (ed.)., *Essays in Political Geography*, Methuen, London, 1968. A similar arrangement was made for the Italian-Yugoslav boundary—the agreement of Udine, 20 August 1955; see L. Buratti, *La frontiera italiana*, Forni, Bologna, 1971, pp. 190–3.

[39] Senator Francis Palmero, 'Psychological problems of frontier co-operation', Council of Europe, ASS/Col/Front (72) 6.

[40] *The Times*, 21 February 1973. On the French side of this boundary the *conseil général* of Haute-Savoie is very conscious of its frontier situation and, as a consequence, does not wish to be a part of the Rhône–Alpes administrative region. *Le Monde*, 28 June 1973.

[41] Council of Europe, Consultative Assembly, document No. 3228, 1973, p. 26.

[42] See E. Fischer, 'On boundaries', *World Politics*, I, 1949, pp. 196–222.

Peter Campbell

3

Militancy, democracy and the universities: a review with reflections

It is now over ten years since the Robbins report heralded the great expansion of higher education that was the natural consequences of the Butler Education Act of 1944 and that was, indeed, already under way when the report appeared. That decade has ended with the drastic economy measures of December 1973 and January 1974 and with the troubled and rather diffuse reappraisal of the future of higher education initiated by the White Paper of December 1972. These years have seen not only a great increase in the number of students in higher education but also important developments in the range of institutions within that sector, in the relationship between the State and those institutions, and in the attitudes of students towards their education and the institutions in which they are studying. This essay is concerned with those attitudes and their consequences for university government.

The expansion of higher education was accompanied by a transformation of the relationship between students and the institutions in which they are studying: from being one of acceptance it became one of challenge. To say this is not to imply either that before the 1960s all students accepted the values prevailing in those institutions and approved of the ways in which things were done in them or that from the 1960s onwards all students have been repudiating the values and condemning the ways. Nonetheless, a marked change has occurred, which is part of the general change in the attitudes of adolescents and young adults that has resulted from the economic social changes of the middle decades of the century.[1]

The development of a distinctive youth culture and the assertion of what might be called the class-consciousness of youth by behaviour ostentatiously different from the general life-style of the parental generation has had extremely important consequences for the institutions in which the young and their elders find themselves together with roles that are inevitably related to their age groups. In employment (including educational employment) younger and older people are to a very great extent mixed together; young workers and older workers are alike in being under the authority of the foreman or manager, who may be younger than some of them although older than others. The overwhelming majority of students are younger than the academic and administrative staff who are concerned with them.

Moreover, the motives which many of them have for undertaking higher education are very different from those of the academic staff, who are committed to their subjects and who should be committed to their teaching and to their general relations with their students. Many students are committed neither to their subjects nor to studying; they are in the university because of the way the educational band-wagon rolls in a society which regards higher education as the essential (or at least natural) route to the jobs carrying most prestige and/or pay. Current talk about the 'right' to higher education relates more to equality of opportunity for getting on or for having whatever may seem the good things of life than to equality of opportunity for engaging in scholarship. The vocational purposes which higher education has always had have become vaguer and more generalised, the belief that higher education is something that should not be missed has become more widespread, but concern with scholarship is hardly fashionable. The trend towards undertaking higher education with motives that are not strictly vocational and without much appreciation of either its scholarly purposes or its liberalising potential is particularly important amongst students of the arts and social sciences. Their numbers have grown most, their vocational purposefulness is least, their predisposition to critical awareness is greatest, and their readiness to press their challenge and to assert their values is most vigorous.[2] The expansion of higher education has meant that the university is to an increasing extent a mass society or, rather, that the student population is a mass whose members are socialised by each other rather than by the total society—the university as a whole—which they have joined. The self-consciousness of the generation group in general and of students as a 'class' in particular enables the most active sections of the student population to mobilise considerable support for certain causes and in certain contexts. Those sections have tended to be the various forces of two distinct but overlapping movements—the Marxist Left (particularly its Trotskyite factions) and the counter-culture. They have seen universities as potential red bases for attacking the capitalist order or as potential locations for the alternative society. The conduct (as well as the objectives) of a campaign has a political purpose: the development of group feeling and radical attitudes by the statement of demands of a kind and in a way likely to cause repugnance, the failure of negotiations, the extension of the issues to mobilise more students and accentuate the conflict, and the use of mass meetings—preferably in occupied buildings—to enhance group solidarity so that all feel committed to the purposes and methods of the vanguard, who often take action which is held to commit the whole body and is therefore ratified subsequently.

Like American universities, where these developments had started earlier, gone further, and had the special incentives of the campaigns first about civil rights and then about the Vietnam war, British universities began to experience the politics of protest and the assertion of student power. Here this assertion took place in the context of a widespread idealistic disappointment with national 'consensus politics' (of which CND was an early expression) the frustration engendered by the Wilson government, and the disgust (partly indigenous and partly imported) with the Vietnam war and racialism in selected African countries. By 1966 agitation at LSE proved to be the start of a nation-wide movement of student protest both on issues local to universities and on matters of national and international politics: the LSE agitation itself linked the two, for it concerned the appointment of Dr Walter Adams as Director and united two themes—his alleged involvement in the system of white supremacy in Rhodesia and the non-involvement of students in the process for selecting the Director. In the following few years militant activity became a familiar feature of the life of universities and colleges. Some of this militancy directly affected the conduct of university activities: the occasional boycotting and picketing of ordinary lectures and the disruption of lectures by visiting scholars whose views or themes were regarded as particularly obnoxious; the disruption of meetings of governing bodies and disciplinary committees; the occupation of administrative offices (with their tempting filing cabinets), lecture blocks, libraries and residential accommodation reserved for the other sex; and rent strikes by students in university residences. Some of it affected other activities on university property, such as recruitment interviews held by the armed forces, Barclay's Bank, and other bodies; scientific meetings sponsored by NATO and other defence organisations; meetings due to be addressed by members of the Wilson and Heath governments, right-wing Conservative MPs, and representatives from the American and South Vietnamese embassies; and visits from the House of Commons select committee investigating in 1968–69 students and their relations with universities and colleges. The daubing of slogans on walls became commonplace; more serious vandalism—including arson—occurred from time to time.[3]

A comprehensive review of militant action shows, very naturally, that the overwhelming majority of incidents within the unversities are concerned with issues arising within the universities themselves, and it is desirable to consider the kinds of issue in order to see better the implications which student protest has for university government. They can be grouped roughly into ten categories.

1. The contents of courses, methods of teaching, modes of assessment, and the general conduct of academic departments and Faculties. On first consideration it might be thought that issues of this kind would be the most frequent cause of agitation, yet they are not, even although some of the conflicts concerning them were very serious, such as the early troubles in 1968 at the University of Hull and at the Colleges of Art in Hornsey, Guildford, Croyden and Birmingham, the conflicts at Cambridge in 1971–72 and 1972–73 and Manchester in 1972–73, and the most recent ones at York and Kent in 1973–74. Moreover, many of the incidents were caused by academics and administrators committing faults which only a few years earlier would have been endured with exasperation rather than challenged by agitation and litigation; it is significant that although from time to time the NUS has held conferences and organised brief campaigns about examinations and classification it has never attempted a really vigorous and prolonged campaign about them despite the fact that they arouse amongst many teachers a good deal of anxiety, doubt, and hostility, which such a campaign might exploit.[4]

2. The 'private lives' of students: rules of visiting hours (particularly for the opposite sex) and other matters in residential buildings, university cognisance of convictions in the courts (which involves 'double punishment').

3. The procedure and decisions of adjudicating bodies concerned

with students whose academic progress has been unsatisfactory or who are charged with violating disciplinary codes by their individual behaviour or their involvement in collective disruption.

4. The appointment and dismissal of academic staff. Cases such as those in which the Left protested on behalf of Mr A. Arblaster at Manchester, Mr R. Atkinson at Birmingham, Dr B. Dasgupta at SOAS, Dr D. Craig and others at Lancaster, and Mr W. Jenkins at the Polytechnic of North London but against Professor W. Coupe at Southampton raised directly issues concerning scholarly standards and academic freedom.[5]

5. The provision of catering, residential, social and sporting facilities (which caused serious occupations at Kent and at Portsmouth Polytechnic in 1972).

6. The wages and/or conditions of work for university employees (including postgraduate students in respect of teaching and academic demonstrating, as at Swansea and elsewhere in 1974).[6]

7. The university's involvement in student business; the provision of buildings for a students' union (as in Oxford in 1973 and 1974), scrutiny of the union's constitution (the conflicts at LSE in 1971–72 and the Polytechnic of North London in 1972–73 and 1973–74 were particularly severe) and accounts, the raising of the union's subscription, the use of the union's facilities by people who are not students and for whom the university does not receive funds (this last topic being the cause of very prolonged agitation in Bristol in 1968).[7]

8. Student involvement in university business; the initial demand for participation and the subsequent protests against the university for devaluing student representation (by such means as putting students only on 'rubber-stamping' bodies, transferring important business to committees on which students are not represented, shunting business from one committee to another, withholding information, deferring matters until it is essential to reach a decision too swiftly for student representatives to get the views of their constituents).

9. The involvement of the university or individual staff in those sectors of the external world which are regarded by some students as obnoxious: the business world at large (e.g. Warwick[8] and Lancaster), investments in companies with business in South Africa (e.g. Edinburgh and Hull), research contracts and other academic dealings with bodies concerned with British, American, and NATO

defence (e.g. Essex and Reading) recruitment by the armed forces (e.g. East Anglia, Reading, and Salford), files that might include details of students' political activities (e.g. Warwick and many other places); to a considerable extent certain appointments (which happened to be essentially administrative) should be included in this category (thus the appointments of Dr W. Adams and Professor T. G. Miller as Directors of LSE and North London Polytechnic respectively were attacked chiefly because of alleged compliance towards Mr Smith's regime in Rhodesia, and the appointment of Lord Sherfield as Reading's Chancellor was attacked because of his involvement with firms doing business with South Africa); perhaps visits by members of the royal family for ceremonies should be included here, even though the demonstrations are often explained (as at Stirling in 1972) as being in favour of spending on other purposes the funds needed for the visit.

10. The external world's involvement with universities at large: the Labour government's decision that overseas students should be charged fees some three or four times as much as those charged to British students, the Conservative government's proposals about students' unions, the level of government grants to students; these have been the objects of various demonstrations, including occupations and rent strikes aimed at getting the university to support NUS campaigns or even to disregard UGC accounting controls.

This list of issues about which there has been militant action somewhere or other (and the institutions cited are only examples of the most serious turbulence) shows how great a range of topics can arouse amongst a good many students feelings intense enough to cause them to take part in disruptive action. Its effects can be summarised as follows. There have been some dramatic successes, such as the agreement of some universities to placing students on governing bodies, the withdrawal of disciplinary charges against disruptive students, York's decision to revise the structure and contents of its Social Sciences course and Kent's decision not to expel a student whose academic performance had seemed unsatisfactory. There have been some noticeable failures, such as the failure of the sustained campaigns against the Directors of LSE and the North London Polytechnic. In the great majority of incidents, however, the outcome has been less clear-cut. Compromises have been negotiated—or concessions made—in such a way that the university has been able to assert that it has been influenced by argument but not by force and the militants have felt that they owed their gains to force rather than to argument. In a host of situations there has been a fairly effective exercise of student power, defined by 1968 by David Adelstein as 'the ability of the students' bloc to inflict, if necessary, sanctions of sufficient economic, social and political magnitude to force its opinions to be heeded'.[9]

It seems difficult to deny that some of the most effective participation by students in university government has been by agitation rather than by representation: conflict has achieved more than the co-operation which the NUS and the Committee of Vice-Chancellors and Principals announced in October 1968 and which the NUS negotiated with the appropriate bodies in other sectors of higher and further education. During the following few years student representation was widely extended in a favourable climate of opinion (exemplified by the Latey report on the age of majority and the report which the House of Commons Select Committee on Education and Science made on students and their relations with universities and colleges) and with the aid of militant action in many places. By the end of the quinquennium 1967–72 student representatives took part in the meetings of the main governing bodies (senate and the council—outside Scotland—or court—in Scotland) of most universities, were on key general purposes, planning or finance committees in some thirty universities and in most of the London and Welsh colleges, were on Faculty boards in some twenty universities and university colleges, were on some of the committees with decision-making powers in respect of residence, libraries, safety and other common service matters in almost all universities, and were on a host of staff–student committees at various levels.[10] Yet in practice representation seems to have been ineffective and frustrating.[11]

For this outcome there seem to be three reasons. First, universities have naturally repudiated the fundamental argument of the student Left for treating the university as a political system ripe for democratisation; within the framework set by their existing constitutions, which confer responsibilities on an elaborate network of committees composed of academic staff (particularly senior staff) and laymen (in the universities other than Oxford and Cambridge), they have been prepared to give students a voice, and sometimes a vote, but never a preponderant vote; inevitably, therefore, there is the possibility of conflict—and the likelihood when the concerns and purposes of the average academic are compared with those of the militant students; in this context it is noteworthy that despite the conflicts of interest which can occur between professorial and non-professorial staff there has been little sympathy amongst the latter for student agitation against decisions made by committees dominated by the former; although in some places constitutional revision has been undertaken in response to pressures from students and non-professorial staff it can hardly be said that they are an alliance of workers and poor peasants against the professorial kulaks—if a political analogy of that kind is wanted it might be sought in the relationship between blacks and poor whites, but to search for it is to ignore the fundamental facts that all junior academic staff have had a good chance of being promoted and that there has been a general trend (stimulated by the national and local Associations of University Teachers and associations of non-professorial staff) towards an increase in the influence of non-professorial staff at departmental and higher levels; it is, however, possible that in the later 1970s diminishing opportunities for promotion and the inevitable increase in the proportion of academic staff recruited from the militant generations of students will cause a serious change in the relationship between future student militants and non-professorial staff.[12]

The second principal reason for the frustrating outcome of student representation has been that the internal government of British universities operates mainly by a network of committees which are responsible for different sectors, services or functions, which are semi-autonomous rather than hierarchically arranged, and whose members—whether *ex officio* or elected by other bodies within the university or outside it (e.g. local authorities 'represented' on the university council or court)—are expected more often to act as trustees for the university than to act as agents of the categories from which they come.[13] Although not created to inhibit change it tends to have that effect, particularly as those who man it naturally tend to be concerned with maintaining the system so that members of the university can get on with study, teaching and research rather than with transforming it. Moreover, its ramifications provide its more permanent participants (particularly the vice-chancellor, registrar, bursar and lay officers) with too many temptations to play the committee game with each generation of students by transferring certain responsibilities from one committee on which students have been put to another on which they have not or by shunting difficult business from one committee to another until a more propitious moment arrives. (These tactics can, of course, sometimes be used against non-professorial staff, professors, and deans serving for limited periods on committees.)

Third, there has been a tendency for students on central bodies to be officers of the students' union or elected by ballot or general meeting of the union. In principal this should ensure that they are representative but in practice the union is often too volatile an organisation to be a very satisfactory source of student representatives on university bodies. Officers and special representatives elected by ballot tend to be more moderate in their opinions and less outrageous in their methods than the majority of those who attend general meetings of the union, and are liable to be overthrown by them; in so far as officers and other representatives are representative of the general meeting they are likely to be keener on exploiting—or even manufacturing—political issues and on demanding concessions which neither academics as such nor trustees as such would make than on reaching compromises and are unlikely to be much concerned with ordinary humdrum business. In any event, of course, they and their constituents are short-lived members of the community and even their immediate successors may have different attitudes on important issues. No city State of antiquity or trade union of today has so transient a membership and so kaleidoscopic a political record as a students' union. Attempts to bypass the union and to have special electorates or a hierarchy of indirectly elected representatives have not been very successful, for, imperfect though it is, the union seems in most universities to have more legitimacy and vitality than the alternatives. Unfortunately neither the House of Commons committee in 1968–69 nor the Department of Education and Science in the winter of 1971–72 made very satisfactory proposals about unions.[14] The former worried unnecessarily about constitutional propriety and too little about political practicalities and the latter would have involved the university in frequent conflict-provoking intervention in the life of the union. It is increasingly tempting to envisage either the complete disestablishment of unions (which would become social clubs dependent on voluntary membership and no longer responsible for subsidising other clubs and societies, which would also rely on subscriptions) or at least the transfer of financial responsibility from the local authorities to the individual students, who would therefore have more incentive to take part in decision-making. The first course would probably decrease the legitimacy of unions and leave a political vacuum which might or might not be filled, while the second would increase the likelihood of students taking part in their union's business and therefore making it more representative (but not necessarily more pacific).

What seems to have emerged from the experience of the last seven years is a somewhat precarious combination of consultation, representation, negotiation and insurrection. On many matters—particularly academic ones—there are consultative bodies. On certain committees which make or prepare decisions—particularly council, senate and bodies concerned with welfare, residence and common services—students serve as full members or in attendance for items other than reserved business; matters of minor or medium importance can be settled at the committee but major matters are likely to be also the object of negotiation between the students' union and the appropriate spokesmen of the university. Some matters, which may or may not be within the scope of a committee attended by students, may arouse such dispute that they result in insurrection, which has virtually become an integral part of the political system.

Universities are ill equipped to deal with insurrectionary activities by their students (or, indeed, with disruption by intruders). Internally, they cannot afford adequate security forces (which would need to be very well trained if ugly incidents were to be avoided); for good and bad reasons their academic staff tend to be reluctant to act as policemen or informers; their disciplinary processes are so scrupulously elaborate in order to achieve fairness and legitimacy that they offer considerable scope for students (financed by their local union) to have recourse to litigation, of which the cost seems to be more daunting to universities than to their students' unions; most of their students are paid three months in advance, and (despite occasional mutterings) local authorities have been unwilling to co-operate with universities in using their grant-awarding powers as a means of disciplining students (even those who refuse to pay the universities the hall fees which grants are intended to pay) that they have virtually renounced the intention of doing so. Externally, universities suffer from the present state of the law regarding trespass, the attitudes of the courts towards institutions seeking injunctions, the reluctance of the police to intervene unless there is a clear danger of a breach of the peace, and the readiness of many trade unionists to treat student pickets as they would the pickets of a trade union on strike (even although the TUC has rejected the application of the NUS for membership).

The recent experience is discouraging and the prospects are bleak. Higher education in general and universities in particular will be seriously affected by the state of the economy. The material conditions and the careers opportunities for both staff and students are likely to worsen even if student members do not rise as much as was envisaged in 1972: resources will be insufficient to maintain standards in libraries, laboratories and offices; promotion blocks are likely to be serious as a result of the great expansion of the middle 1960s being followed by a lengthening period in which new and vacated senior posts will be fairly rare (a position made unnecessarily bad by the failure of universities and the AUT to press ahead with revising the career structure); the financial situation of students is unlikely to improve to the level of the Anderson principle; and the market for graduates is unlikely to be welcoming. Industrial unrest and political frustration are likely to provide a context favourable to student militancy. Although some of the expressions of the self-consciousness of adolescents and young adults have changed, the campaigns of the winter of 1973–74 seem to show that the causes of past turbulence are no weaker than before. As has been implied at various points in this essay, little has been done to put universities in a better posture for defence. Perhaps, however, the resilient suppleness they showed in 1968–74 will be enough.

Notes

[1] B. Wilson, *The Youth Culture and the Universities*, London, 1970, contains some prophetic essays from the early 1960s about the impact which youth culture would have on British universities as they expanded; see particularly ch. 5. See also D. Martin (ed.), *Anarchy and Culture*, A. Cockburn and R. Blackburn (ed.) *Student Power*, London, 1969, and J. Nagel, *Student Power*, London, 1969. The international literature is now immense. In their different ways T. Roszak, *The Making of a Counterculture*, London, 1970, and J. Searle, *The Campus War*, are particularly helpful.

[2] For evidence see such surveys as those cited by the House of Commons Select Committee on Students and the Relations with Universities and Colleges, session 1968–69, H.C. 449–IV, pp. 395, 412–17, and v, pp.

299–310. See also T. Blackstone *et al.*, *Students in Conflict: LSE in 1967*, London, 1970.

[3] The examples given below—confined to some of the most dramatic encounters in universities and other institutions—is based partly on my own records and partly on C. Crouch's invaluable *The Student Revolt*, London, 1970; see also M. A. Rooke, *Anarchy and Apathy*, London, 1971. The development of militancy in the NUS is considered by Sir E. Ashby and M. Anderson, *The Rise of the Student Estate*, London, 1970.

[4] For the most sustained and radical of these conflicts see Students and Staff of Hornsey College of Art, *The Hornsey Affair*, London, 1969. See also T. Fawthrop, *Education or Examination?*, London, 1968; Cockburn and Blackburn, *op. cit.*, Nagel, *op. cit.*; and 'Socialist education and the university', *Focus*, 30, University of Sussex, May 1973, for examples of radical critiques of English university education.

[5] From a certain standpoint the publications of the Campaign for Academic Freedom and Democracy provide essential information about a number of cases of this kind.

[6] Some ironic diplomatic revolutions have occurred; for example, in summer 1972 Kent students staged a sit-in protest against schemes for reducing service staff as an economy measure but in February 1972 service staff at Kent were planning to strike against the disruption caused by a sit-in on behalf of a student threatened with dismissal because of his academic record.

[7] For an interesting account of this incident and the public presentation of it see E. C. Wright, *Participation, Disruption and Moderation*, University of Bristol, 1969.

[8] See E. P. Thompson, *Warwick University Ltd*, London, 1970.

[9] D. Adelstein, *Teach yourself Student Power*, London, 1968, p. 19, reprinted in Cockburn and R. Blackburn, *op. cit.*, p. 77.

[10] Based on information kindly supplied by the Committee of Vice-Chancellors and Principals.

[11] For an example of vehemently expressed frustration see J. Straw *et al.*, *Universities: Boundaries of Change*, London, 1970, pp. 7–27.

[12] See Martin, *op. cit.*, pp. 77–84 and 200–5, and A. H. Halsey and M. A. Trow, *The British Academics*, London, 1971.

[13] On university government in general the book by G. Moodie and R. Eustace is eagerly awaited. See meanwhile the articles by R. Eustace in D. Martin, *op. cit*, pp. 51–64, and by both authors, 'British universities as political systems', *Political Studies*, XIX, 3 September 1971. For a daunting survey of how Birmingham is governed see Sir R. Aitken, *Administration of a University*, London, 1966; after it one can read the Grimond report—*Report of the Review Body appointed by the Council of the University of Birmingham*, Birmingham, 1972, and G. Ostergaard, *Gelding the Grimond*, Birmingham, 1973. See also Sir S. Caine, *British Universities*, London, 1969.

[14] Grimond report, *op. cit.*, and Department of Education and Science, *The Financing of Student Unions*, 1971.

David Donnison

4

Social policy and administration

I came to Magdalen College during the war to take the scholarship examinations as a seventeen-year-old with a foggy conviction that the world could be much improved if we learned to understand it better. At twenty-one I was back, writing my first essays for Bill Mackenzie, whom I followed to Manchester three years later, there to become one of his assistant lecturers in social administration. This seems a fitting moment to report on the progress I have made in thinking about the subject to which he introduced me.

I will not describe what is taught in universities and colleges under the title of Social Administration: it includes almost anything that deals with social services and the social policies of government.[1] It is the purpose of this work I want to discuss here, and the scope it affords for making the world a better place. *Why* study social administration? The answer to that question depends on your views about the functions of social services and social policies. What scope do *they* afford for making the world a better place? I shall explore that problem by outlining four different views about the social services, briefly contrasting their implications for students of social administration, and finally drawing some provisional conclusions. No one who has read *Politics and Social Science*[2] would suggest these are the only feasible approaches to the study of government, but together they pose most of the questions to be considered. Summarising each in a couple of words, I would list them as: (1) philanthropic or residual, (2) neo-Marxist or structuralist, (3) programmatic or managerial, and (4) pluralist or incremental.

1. *A philanthropic or residual approach*

It used to be widely held that the social services were typically founded by philanthropic pioneers and later extended on a national scale by the State to help the relatively poor at the expense of the relatively rich. 'The generally accepted hallmark of social service is that of direct concern with the personal well-being of the individual,' says one of the most widely used textbooks on the subject, and its 'basis ... is ... to be found in the obligation a person feels to help another in distress'.[3] The most influential Conservative statement of the 1950s began with the assertion that

The essential marks of a social service are:

- (a) that it is rendered by, or on behalf of, the community *to an individual* or at most *to a family*, and appropriated to his or its exclusive use; and
- (b) that it contains an element of redistribution, i.e. that the majority of the individuals or families who avail themselves of it are receiving more than they give.[4]

This philanthropic approach to the subject was to be found on the right and left, both among people who regarded the social services as a burden upon productive enterprise and among those who welcomed them as a benign and growing feature of a progressive society. 'Why should any social service be provided *without* test of need?'[5] Do these services produce a 'decline in initiative and repudiation of personal and family responsibility'?[6] Such were the questions posed by this approach to the subject, and they still appear in the examination papers.

These are not trivial questions; in the right context they deserve to be taken seriously. But the concerns that prompt them now seem archaic. They spring from grossly unhistorical assumptions about the origin and development of the social services. Industrial and military pressures, working-class traditions of mutal aid, professional training and aspirations, and the attempts of governments to contain social conflicts—these and many other factors play a part in the story.[7] Some of the most expensive social programmes—for education, medical care and social insurance, for example—were never intended to be redistributive. Meanwhile fiscal procedures, policies for town planning and economic development, occupational welfare services provided by employers and other programmes not traditionally regarded as social services often do more to advance human welfare and to redistribute resources—progressively or regressively.[8]

Social policies cannot be understood if they are treated as a separate sphere to be studied in isolation from the rest of society, or as a residual activity—a frill upon the fabric of the productive economy—which we can choose to have or do without. Social policies deal with many institutions and programmes to be found both in the public and the private sectors of every urban, industrial society, and their history is an integral part of the development of such societies. That is certainly the assumption of the next approach to be considered.

2. *A neo-Marxist or structuralist approach*

The political science of Marx and his successors begins from the observation that 'The executive of the modern State is but a committee for managing the common affairs of the whole bourgeoisie.'[9] The State's social policies are therefore designed to maintain the existing social order and to protect the interests of its ruling class. Social services institutionalise and legitimise social injustice, conferring their most generous benefits on the bourgeoisie, and keeping the working class in subjection.[10] The 'welfare State' is a sham; the social problems it purports to resolve are a product of the capitalist system. They can be solved only—and then readily—when that system is destroyed.

In the principal Marxist text on housing Engels dismissed liberal social policies with contempt: '... it does not occur to me to try to solve the so-called housing *question* any more than I can occupy myself with the details of the still more important *food question*. I am satisfied if I can prove ... that there are houses enough in existence to provide the working masses for the time being with roomy and healthy living accommodation. To speculate as to how a future society would organise the distribution ... of dwellings leads directly to Utopia.'[11]

According to this view, scholars in the field of social administration may pursue knowledge in order to open their students' eyes to the iniquities of the world they live in. But within a bourgeois democracy they can make few practical contributions to the development of the social services unless they are content to be docile servants of the existing order.[12]

That is why, in its purer forms, this view is found not in university departments of social administration but in neighbouring disciplines—sociology and political science, for example. It furnishes its exponents with a very comfortable intellectual posture, for they are burdened neither with the philanthropic duties of conservative *noblesse oblige*, nor with the social democratic obligation to soil their hands with the compromises of reformist politics, while—in Britain at least—they are spared the dangers of real revolution. Their comfort, of course, is no proof of error.

We should beware of saying that Marxism is simply wrong, for the propositions of this doctrine—like those of religion and Freudian psychology—can be interpreted to furnish an explanation of almost any outcome. Manual workers and their children, it is said, rarely achieve 'the big leap into higher business and independent professional occupations'; but if they do, 'it is all but inevitable that recruits from the subordinate classes into the upper reaches of the State system should, by the very fact of their entry into it, become part of the class which continues to dominate it'; and if, against all odds, 'a dramatic extension of the system of welfare' is brought about, we can be sure that 'it did not, for all its importance, constitute any threat to the existing system of power or privilege', because reform, once it has occurred, must by definition accord with the ideas of the ruling class.[13]

It would be more accurate to say that traditional Marxist assumptions are likely to mislead us. They suggest that conflict between the ruling class and the workers is the dominant theme of history and the principal motor of social change, in the social services as in everything else. But there are many other important conflicts which must be understood—conflicts between religions, sexes and regions for example—and they are not all instances of submerged class conflict (although we shall often understand them better if we are alert to the class composition of the groups concerned).

Many of the larger problems to which social policies are addressed—problems of medical care and mental illness, for example—cannot be adequately explained or resolved with the language of class war. Differences between countries in the distribution of incomes and opportunities cannot be explained in this language either. If you want to know how equally a country's incomes are distributed it is generally more useful to ask about the extent and pace of urbanisation and industrialisation than to ask whether the regime is capitalist or communist.[14] (If you want to know about the distribution of *wealth* the colour of the regime is more important.)

The plight of the poorest people in urban societies is recorded in statistics (published by reformist organisations such as Shelter and the Child Poverty Action Group) which are often quoted by Marxist

critics of the 'welfare State'. But the homeless, the long-term un-
employed, the disorganised and 'feckless' are often neglected by
social programmes of the Labour movement, introduced at the
behest of the broad mass of working people; indeed their plight is
partly due to such programmes, which stigmatise them as outcasts.
Charles Booth glimpsed this conflict long ago. 'To the rich the
very poor are a sentimental interest: to the poor they are a crushing
load. The poverty of the poor is mainly the result of the competition
of the very poor.'[15]

Fundamentalist Marxists are now a dying breed. They have paid
the basic political penalty of their failure to understand urban,
industrial societies: few people vote for them, even when they
resort to explicitly parliamentary tactics. But many who would
accept the criticisms of a literal Marxism outlined in the previous
paragraphs would argue that neo-Marxist formulations nevertheless
offer us revealing metaphors. (And that is all we can get from most
social theories. They provide 'as if' explanations. Economists who
formulated the theory of the firm do not argue that individual
entrepreneurs actually equate—or even know—their marginal
revenues and costs, only that the market as a whole tends to behave
as if they did, because those who persistently fail to do so are eventually excluded from it.)

Neo-Marxists, or 'structuralists', as they might better be described,
argue that the metaphors of class conflict prove revealing if you
want to predict who will benefit most from a new social programme
(the current expansion of nursery education, for example), who will
come off worst when restrictions are imposed (under the next phase
of Britain's incomes policies, for example) and why egalitarian reforms do not quickly or radically change the distribution of rewards
and opportunities (why the national health service has not equalised
the life expectations of different classes, and why the reorganisation
of secondary education will not equalise their educational attain-
ments, for example). And they are often right. Without anyone
plotting the subjection of the workers or the protection of privilege,
society tends to evolve as if the ruling class were following strategies
of that kind, and those who persistently and aggressively pursue the
opposite policies tend to be excluded from power. Inequality is
complex, pervasive and deeply rooted in the political, economic and
psychological mechanisms of our kind of social order.

In the field of social policy the Marxist metaphor has too much predictive power to be treated with anything but respect—critical respect, naturally. But we must wonder whether the messianic figure who gave his name to it had discovered the key to a final solution of social conflict and injustice, or whether he had merely made some revealing observations about urban, industrial bureaucratic societies. In his day such societies were capitalist—what else could they be?— but now that we have a larger array of examples to study we may agree with Ralf Dahrendorf that 'the abolition of property merely replaces the old classes with new ones . . .'. 'The origin of inequality is . . . to be found in . . . norms of behaviour to which sanctions are attached.' For '. . . all men are equal *before* the law but they are no longer equal *after* it . . .'. In any society 'the system of inequality that we call social stratification is only a secondary consequence of the social structure of power'.[16]

Frank Parkin, one of the very few neo-Marxists to give as critical attention to eastern Europe as he gives to the West, argues that the communist countries have made some progress towards economic and social equality, but points out the horrifying price they have paid for this in lost liberties of many sorts.[17] Anyone who wants to journey towards a more equal society should be suspicious of those who find it necessary to scrap constitutional government and civil rights on the way. The price of liberty has not fallen since it was noted, nearly two centuries ago, to be eternal vigilance. The 'negative features' of Soviet communism, its 'democratic centralism' and the 'catastrophic ideological impoverishment' which so soon pervaded the world-wide communist movement were no historical accident.[18] They were an inevitable result of the rejection of older liberal traditions.

At the start of this section I recalled Engels' classic work on housing, which Lenin read and annotated during the months before the October revolution. Between 1923 and 1950 the urban population of the Soviet Union grew from 21·6 to 74·5 millions, and urban dwelling space grew from 139 to 297 million square metres. Space per head fell from 6·4 to 4·0 square metres. Although the war played a part in this story, the decline continued throughout the period, with no intervals of improvement. A radical change of policy followed after 1952: none too soon—for by then there had been a reduction of nearly 40 per cent in the housing space available for urban workers.[19] Such a social disaster could not have occurred in a parliamentary democracy.

3. *A programmatic or managerial approach*

'Structuralists' are apt to dismiss those who adopt a managerial approach to the social services as loyal servants of the existing social order. Although that would gravely underestimate the intelligence and critical capacity of some of the people involved, it is true that a programmatic approach is best suited to situations in which there are many organisations with different and occasionally conflicting jobs to do, but no irreconcilable social cleavages.

Beady-eyed social scientists, trained to identify conflicts and dilemmas, should not scorn this approach. Practical men know that the intellectual habits of the seminar are ill suited to the world of action, where conflicts may not be irreconcilable and should not be needlessly provoked. Professor John Stewart is speaking to them when he commends the following strategy to those who manage local government services.

(a) The organisation identifies certain needs, present and foreseen, in its environment.
(b) It sets objectives in relation to those needs, i.e. the extent to which it will plan to meet those needs.
(c) It considers alternative ways of achieving those objectives.
(d) It evaluates those alternatives in terms of their use of resources and of their effects.
(e) Decisions are made in the light of that evalution.
(f) Those decisions are translated into management action.
(g) The results of the action taken are monitored and fed back to modify the continuing process; by altering the perception of needs, the objectives set, the alternatives considered, the evaluation, the decision made or the action taken.[20]

In recent years a whole armoury of new techniques has been assembled to put this approach into practice. Systems analyses of various kinds are brought to bear when general strategies have to be formulated and aims are ill-specified. Cost–benefit analyses help decision-makers to choose between different programmes of action when broad objectives have been agreed. At a smaller scale, operational research suggests the best techniques for attaining clearly specified objectives. These and other procedures (social accounting, zero budgeting, PPBS, management by objectives, AIDA . . .) have been entitled 'programmatic analysis' in a recent review of policy analysis by Hugh Heclo.[21]

Now that the first excessive enthusiasm for this approach is giving way to a more cautious realism, it is clear that we have a lot to learn from it. At its best it offers far more than technocratic procedures for clarifying objectives and organising the means to attain them: it is a democratic attempt to put the reins back into the hands of elected representatives. Recent reorganisations in some of our town halls were intended to give councillors and their policy committees greater power and more opportunities for making effective policy choices.[22]

But the limitations of this school of thought must be recognised. It is best suited to occasions when objectives can be clearly defined. Its procedures tend to give most effective expression to the values of the existing social order and the regime that governs it. The 'externalities' which are not reflected in market transactions, and the values of the unpaid and the low-paid, tend to be underemphasised. The managerial approach has been most successful where a consensus can be achieved and performance can be clearly measured. It is not surprising that Professor Stewart's list of the most urgent problems facing local government begins with 'the impact of the car; new patterns of transportation; the transformation of rural life ...'[23]—all of them important issues, but perhaps not the most contentious of those debated in our town halls. Many problems of social administration, however, are unavoidably contentious, and there are often good reasons why social objectives cannot be clearly defined and must remain vague, unexplicit or unresolved.[24] It was for situations such as these that a fourth approach was formulated.

4. A pluralist or incremental approach

Philanthropists and neo-Marxists see the world through ideological spectacles of contrasting hues, each trying to remake it in their own ways. Those who adopt a managerial approach assume that social conflicts can be resolved, and concentrate instead on seeking more efficient ways to attain agreed ends.

Representatives of a fourth school of thought would reject all three views. We live, they argue, in a plural society in which there can be no lasting consensus. Social policies evolve piecemeal as the outcome of decisions made in different places by different elites under pressures from different quarters. A practical politics cannot be founded either on comprehensive, rational planning or on the

consistent pursuit of ideological objectives, for both are precluded by
the dizzying variety of choices open to policy makers, the profusion
of unpredictable primary, secondary and further repercussions, and
the conflicting political pressures which must be accommodated
every time something has to be done. Put another way, the costs of
gathering and interpreting all the information required to formulate
and implement consistent policies are too high for anyone to attempt
the task. Moreover the clarification of goals—the essential starting
point for programmatic or ideological strategies—tends in practice
to be counter-productive: people who might agree about the immediate action to be taken fall out as their longer-term differences
are revealed, while others who can at length be induced to adopt
similar aims may not agree about immediate action.

In practice, therefore, social administrators, like other decision
makers, do not clarify long-term aims or pursue them consistently.
They compare the immediate, known implications of a few marginal
adjustments to present programmes, and choose the course of action
which maximises political support and secures the assent of those
who must collaborate in implementing the next few decisions.

This 'strategy of disjointed incrementalism' (or 'the science of
muddling through') is an attempt to 'satisfice' rather than to
'optimise'. It avoids the risks inherent in comprehensive or doctrinaire policies. A marginal change can be tried, its practical outcome
examined and modifications made before the next step is taken.
Relying as it does on political bargaining for its decisions, the
strategy can also be defended as a democratc learning process.[25]

This is indeed the way things often are, and have to be. Practical
men have for too long been sneered at by academics for apparently
crude decision-making procedures which they have no reason to be
ashamed of. But although this pluralist account of government 'as
she is spoke' provides a healthy antidote for naive rationalists and
over-enthusiastic ideologues, it is vulnerable on each of the two
fronts its advocates are committed to defend. On the managerial
front they reject programmatic styles of government too in-
discriminately. On the structuralist front they are over-eager to hail
the end of ideology. On both fronts they are too ready to assume
that we do actually live in a genuinely plural society.

There is no scarcity of cautionary tales about the failure of
rational, comprehensive or synoptic planning (all boo words to
dedicated pluralists). Such failures occur when the scale of the

decision makers' powers, knowledge and resources does not match the scale of the problems they are dealing with. If the two sides of the equation can be brought into balance by tackling smaller problems or by extending the powers, knowledge and resources available to solve them, a rational or managerial approach to social policy can be made to work. (Whether it would work *best* in any particular situation is a different question.)

The point can be briefly illustrated—first with a problem which matches the means available for solving it. If a city authority knows all about the volume of its domestic refuse, the location of sites for disposing of it and the means of transport for doing the job, if it has the necessary legal powers, staff and equipment, and if there is general agreement about the standards of service which are at current costs worth maintaining, then its problem is capable of solution in a managerial or programmatic fashion. That is the sort of problem the Local Government Operational Research Unit solves every week.[26]

But the problem may be enlarged to a scale which no longer matches the means for resolving it. As local tips are filled up, the city fathers start dumping their refuse in the territory of neighbouring authorities, which bitterly resist this invasion; strong local pressure groups complain that the city's dustcarts endanger their children and pollute the streets with noise and smells; the treasurer reports that alternative procedures for incinerating refuse would save staff but entail unacceptable capital expenditure for which the central government refuses to give loan sanction; and the dustmen threaten to go on strike if labour-saving equipment is installed. Decision makers may now be compelled to adopt disjointedly incremental strategies as they strive to attain multiple, conflicting objectives in a decidedly plural society.

Operational researchers prefer to work in the former kind of situation; social scientists find the latter more interesting. But which kind of situation we are dealing with on any particular occasion can be determined by empirical study, and we are not obliged passively to accept either. A technical problem can be 'enlarged' into a political one (a problem, that is, which can be resolved only by an exercise of power). And a political problem can be converted into a technical one by restricting the criteria for its solution, or by extending the powers, knowledge and resources available for solving it. The pluralists are too apt to make a virtue of disjointedly incremental strategies which would not be required if more imaginative and effective political leadership was brought to bear.

On their other front, when dealing with ideologues, the prophets of the plural society have been too ready to hail the end of ideology and too complacent about the politics of urban, industrial societies. As a strategy, disjointed incrementalism best suits governments which are opposed to radically progressive (or radically reactionary) policies and content to move gently with the political tide. It works best in a reasonably well informed, tolerant and robust democracy, and attracts those who believe they inhabit one.

Offering what some would regard as a political scientist's version of the 'liberal' economist's obeisance to the free market, Lindblom asserts that 'almost every interest has its watchdog. Without claiming that every interest has a sufficiently powerful watchdog, it can be argued that our system often can assure a more comprehensive regard for the values of the whole society than any attempt at intellectual comprehensiveness.'[27] This is not the place to question his celebration of the American constitution, but most Englishmen would be less confident that every majority can get a hearing in their own political market places—and less confident, too, that those most often heard are competing, circulating elites: they look suspiciously like a dominant class. The pluralistic stance, moreover, is not neutral in the influence it exerts on the distribution of power. The societies which have given manual workers and people of working-class origins the largest representation in their political systems (among their elected city councillors, for example) seem to be those with labour movements and strong socialist traditions—those, that is, with explicitly ideological rather than pluralist political cultures.[28]

Pluralists have tended to assume that ideological styles of politics are on the wane. But the death of ideology has been greatly exaggerated. I recently contrasted two styles of urban management: one at Milton Keynes, which was intended to be planned in a comprehensive and programmatic fashion to realise specific aims and values, and the other in a town as nearly as possible unplanned.[29] In Houston, Texas (no mean city, with its population of 1,200,000) you might expect no ideologies, no goals, no PPBS—just market forces and a bit of healthy incremental politics. That, roughly, is the view of Bernard Siegan, upon whose account I mainly rely.[30]

Yet Houston's growth reflects clear and distinctive aims and assumptions about urban development; a sort of ideology, in fact. Land use controls are imposed by developers through restrictive covenants which 'will remain in force for long periods. They may be as effective as zoning (by planners) in maintaining single-family homogeneity' (i.e. in keeping out apartment blocks and the poorer households who subdivide houses). In ' "deluxe" sub-divisions catering to the wealthy ... covenants have provided an exclusivity that the most restrictive zoning code could not achieve ...' Lest property owners and their legal advisers become careless about their rights, the city administration is itself prepared 'to enforce residential restrictive covenants' and, in effect, to extend them beyond their normal terminal date. The administration also imposes minimum sizes on residential lots—'5000 square feet where sewer and water services are available and 7000 where they are not'—along with other standards which together must go far to determine, through prices, who has an opportunity of getting a new house. Siegan commends this system because it is less restrictive than the usual zoning regulations and therefore encourages more 'non-home construction' —possibly $11 million more in 1968, which would produce over $175,000 annually in taxes. 'Non-home construction,' Siegan points out, 'is even more profitable for schools, since it results in considerably less children per tax dollar than results from home.' He urges all cities to adopt similar arrangements.

I do not want the political overtones of this account to confuse the argument. My intention is neither to condemn nor to applaud the government of Houston or its apologists, but to show that they express a pattern of aims and assumptions about the 'good' city, its development and administration, which are about as ideological as Milton Keynes's. Central to this ideology are the individual property owner's rights to secure for himself as much, or as little, as he can buy, his right to exclude citizens with less money or different life styles from his neighbourhood, and the community's obligation to compete, in business terms, with other cities by promoting investment which generates more revenue than expenditure.

The city fathers of Houston do not lack goals, or ideologies, although they probably do lack Milton Keynes's procedures for making such ideas explicit and exposing them to criticism. Houston may therefore be in less danger of bureacratic paralysis, but in greater danger of error: certainly it has no better evidence to justify its determination to preserve economic, social (and therefore racial) segregation than Milton Keynes has for following the opposite policies.

Conclusion

The purpose of this essay is neither to prescribe social policies nor to define the content of social administration as a subject of study, but to clarify the character and purpose of academic work in this field. Can it help to make the world a better place? And if so, how?

I briefly sketched—caricatured, some would say—four views of the world which I described as philanthropic, neo-Marxist, pro-grammatic and pluralist, and outlined some of the answers which exponents of each would give to these questions. Real life is not so simple. Each approach—along with others which I have not explored—suits different situations. Moreover a scholar may examine a situation for different purposes, asking questions which therefore start from different assumptions. The point is well made by Martin Rein, using three somewhat different categories. 'A *consensual* approach proceeds from agreed-upon aims; it asks whether policies, and the specific programs that implement them, work as intended . . . A *contentious* approach proceeds in a more disputatious manner, searching for the very areas in society where our social ideals are not honored, not because we try and fail but because we do not make an effort in the first instance. A *paradigm challenge* occurs when the validity of a theory of intervention is brought under scrutiny.'[31] But I cannot conclude my discussion by saying only that you pays your money and you takes your choice, for the different approaches which I have outlined are not just interestingly varied; they express conflicting assumptions about the world. While there is something to be learnt from each, at a particular time and place (Britain in 1973, for instance) they cannot all be generally and equally valid. So where do I stand?

Britain, like other countries which can be described as urban, in-dustrial and bureaucratic, provides a distribution of opportunities and rewards which is profoundly unequal and unfair. Most of the problems to which social policies are directed are related in various ways to those inequalities—inequalities which are very difficult to change because they are the product of a power structure that is deeply rooted in the country's economic, social and cultural institu-tions. As a metaphor, theories of class conflict often provide revealing insights and valid predictions. But evicting the current ruling class does not fundamentally change the structure of society or the institutions and technologies in which its culture is rooted. Indeed, it would be very unmarxist, scientifically speaking, to assume that it would do.)

Revolution makes some problems easier to solve and others harder. Communist countries which share our urban, industrial and bureaucratic character have made considerable progress in remedying some inequalities, particularly in the distribution of wealth, at the cost of disastrous setbacks in other directions, particularly in the distributions of power, and opportunities for social comment and innovation. When they set about longer-term reforms they turn, like us, to organising pension schemes,[32] reorganising secondary education on comprehensive lines,[33] introducing new (and higher) house rents,[34] subsidising public transport, and grappling with many other familiar problems in familiar ways. Anyone who follows this path of reform is soon confronted with multiple and conflicting needs and demands, both amongst the public and within the bureaucracy—a pluralist world, in fact. But in Britain the social policies hammered out through incremental political processes must ultimately be defended before, and approved by, central and local authorities accountable in principle to the whole electorate of their territory. Whatever the practical failings of democratic procedure (and they are too glaring to enumerate) that means there is usually an 'authority' responsible for the continuing development of the policies and programmes of particular groups of social services. Even if that authority appears to be little more than a legal fiction, it is nevertheless a useful fiction which repeatedly re-creates some sense of the public interest and a confused, intermittent yet continuing debate about social policies which is more than the hubbub of trade-offs negotiated in the political market places of a plural society.[35]

Debates about general concepts, codes and principles have exerted enormous influence on the development of the social services and socal policies of this country, and—for better or worse—academic research, fact-gathering and teaching have from time to time made important contributions to those debates. A history of British social policies could not be written without mentioning Booth, Rowntree, Keynes, Titmuss, Bowlby and many others who had no votes to deliver and nothing to offer but ideas and evidence.

Empirically tested ideologies help to shape the world, and not only on this broad national scale. The initiative for new developments within local units of the social services generally comes from their staff, though many others outside the organisation help to shape the directions in which innovations ultimately lead. There are many different policies for which the staff of a particular agency might secure assent. In choosing between them '. . . their perceptions of the needs to be met and the standards of service they regard as fitting are crucial. These perceptions depend largely on the education and previous experience of the staff, and the climate of opinion they establish amongst themselves.'[36]

What scope there is for a more rigorous, programmatic approach to social administration depends not only on the training of the people concerned but on the assembly of powers, knowledge and a budget adequate for the task. (Adding a computer and a systems analyst to an organisation which is powerless, ignorant or grossly impoverished will not do much good to anyone.) If they are backed by resources sufficient to match the problems to be solved, the new managerial techniques can be used to considerable effect, provided it is recognised that they are not a 'black box' which can be fed with data and programmed to produce solutions but an additional way of learning about the factors in play—a means of clarifying and testing ideologies, not replacing them.

I will try to sum up this rambling conclusion. Urban industrial societies suffer from profound structural inequalities which are very difficult to change. But those problems are not unique to the capitalist versions of such societies. In Britain amelioration of the system is possible, and here—as elsewhere—social policies and programmes play an important part in ameliorating things. Innovations of this sort evolve gradually, shaped by pressures of many kinds. But their development cannot be understood if it is envisaged only as the outcome of a political market place: it owes a lot to interaction between them; and to ideologies at both scales the work of researchers, teachers and writers on social administration makes an important and continuing contribution. More systematic managerial procedures can clarify these developments, but they cannot replace judgement and leadership, or change the fundamentally political character of the process. That, it may be said, is a conventional, liberal, Fabian view. But then, the Fabians were often right.

Notes

1 The content of the subject has not changed radically since the analysis I made with the help of the Joint University Council for Social and Public Administration a dozen years ago. 'The teaching of social administration', *British Journal of Sociology*, xiii, 3, September 1961. For a more recent discussion see Joyce Warham, 'Social administration and sociology', *Journal of Social Policy*, ii, 3, July 1973, p. 193.

2 W. J. M. Mackenzie, *Politics and Social Science*, Penguin Books, Harmondsworth, 1967.

3 Penelope Hall, *The Social Services of Modern England*, Routledge & Kegan Paul, London, 1959, pp. 3–4.

4 Iain McLeod and Enoch Powell, *The Social Services: Needs and Means*, Conservative Political Centre, second edition, 1954, p. 5.

5 McLeod and Powell, *op. cit.*, p. 9.

6 Hall, *op. cit.*, p. 7.

7 I have briefly traced some of these influences in *The Development of Social Administration: an Inaugural Lecture*, London School of Economics and Political Science, 1962.

8 Richard Titmuss's essay on *The Social Division of Welfare* (Eleanor Rathbone memorial lecture, Liverpool University Press, 1956) did a great deal to open people's eyes to these things and thus to extend the scope of the subject.

9 *Communist Manifesto.*

10 Although he himself does not belong to this school of thought, Brian Abel-Smith's exposé of the inequitable effects of social policies, 'Whose Welfare State?' (in Norman Mackenzie (ed.), *Conviction*, McGibbon & Kee, London, 1958) remains the best thing of its kind.

11 Frederick Engels, *The Housing Question*, Lawrence & Wishart, London, 1936, p. 98.

12 Professor Ray Pahl made this point vividly about town planners, whom he described as 'estate managers to capitalism'. 'Social processes and urban change' in Richard Rose (ed.), *The Management of Urban Change in Britain and Germany*, Sage Publications, Beverly Hills, 1974.

13 The quotations are from Ralph Miliband, *The State in Capitalist Society*, Basic Books, New York, 1973, pp. 37, 60, 99.

14 Harold Lydall, *The Structure of Earnings*, Oxford University Press, London, 1968; e.g. p. 157.

15 Charles Booth, *Life and Labour of the People of London*, i, ch. v, p. 154.

16 *Essays in the Theory of Society*, Routledge & Kegan Paul, London, 1968, pp. 160n and 169.

17 *Class Inequality and Political Order*, MacGibbon & Kee, London, 1971, pp. 171–83.

18 Ralph Miliband, who uses these phrases (*The State in Capitalist Society*, pp. 177–8), implies that the movement might have developed in quite different ways.

[19] Timothy Sosnovy, *The Housing Problem in the Soviet Union*, Research Programme on the USSR, New York, 1954.

[20] J. D. Stewart, *Management in Local Government: a Viewpoint*, Knight, London, 1971, pp. viii–ix.

[21] *British Journal of Political Science*, II, 1973, p. 83.

[22] For an example of one such attempt, in Kingston upon Hull, see *New Directions for Local Government*, McKinsey, London, 1971.

[23] Stewart, *op. cit.*, p. 179.

[24] See D. V. Donnison *et al.*, *Social Policy and Administration*, Allen & Unwin, London, 1965, p. 240–1, for a discussion of this point.

[25] Contributions to this line of argument can be culled from Sir Karl Popper, Herbert A. Simon, Martin Meyerson, Aaron Wildavsky and others: a formidable crew. They are well summarised by an opponent, Charles L. Schultze, in *The Politics and Economics of Public Spending*, Brookings Institution, Washington, D.C. 1968, but their fullest expression is probably in David Braybrook and Charles E. Lindblom, *A Strategy of Decision*, Free Press of Glencoe, New York, 1963, and their most condensed in Charles E. Lindblom, "The science of muddling through", *Public Administration Review*, XIX, 1959, pp. 79–88.

[26] It tackles more interesting problems too.

[27] 'The science of muddling through', p. 85.

[28] L. J. Sharpe, 'American democracy reconsidered', *British Journal of Political Science*, January 1973, part I, pp. 1–28; April 1973, part II, pp. 129–67.

[29] *Journal of Social Policy*, I, 2.

[30] Bernard H. Siegan, 'The Houston solution: the case for removing public land-use controls', *Land-use Controls Quarterly*, IV, 3, summer 1970.

[31] *Values, Social Science and Social Policy*, Joint Center for Urban Studies of the Massachusetts Institute of Technology and Harvard University, working paper No. 21, June 1973, pp. 38–9.

[32] US Department of Health, Education and Welfare, *Social Security Programs throughout the World*, 1964.

[33] W. Kenneth Richmond, *Educational Planning: Old and New Perspectives*, Joseph, London, 1966.

[34] D. V. Donnison, *The Government of Housing*, Penguin Books, Harmondsworth, 1967, ch. 4.

[35] The American 'pluralists' who are sceptical about this view of Britain and their colleagues who are over-enthusiastic about the virtues of British government both tend to forget that this island is roughly the size of California, produces a roughly similar gross income, and has less ethnic and cultural diversity than that state. Rational, liberal government is much easier in this small island than in their enormously vaster and more contentious federal country.

[36] Donnison *et al.*, *Social Policy and Administration*, p. 238.

Dorothy Emmet

5

Three strands in morality

There are political scientists who try to see politics as an autonomous domain, defined by a single interest. Thus Kurt Loewenstein opens his book *Political Power and the Governmental Process* (Chicago, 1957) by saying 'the basic urges that dominate man's life in society ... are threefold: love, faith and power. They are mysteriously intertwined and interwoven.' Yet he continues, 'Politics is *nothing else* but the struggle for power' (italics mine). Bill Mackenzie has never been so restrictive. He knows that politics is much too deeply involved in the ways in which people try to live for most of their main interests—even 'urges'—not to come into it at some time or another. For him the units which pass in and out of the systems with which political science is concerned are 'men socially in movement', and while it may be possible in the perspective of a special enquiry to consider 'social man', 'specified by characteristics relevant to the enquiry', the real unit in the background is 'natural man', who 'exists unspecified, bearing an unexplored reserve of latent characteristics' (*Politics and Social Science*, p. 354). And for man in the round, not just man as maximiser or manipulator, there is a moral dimension to be taken into account.

This is not to be an essay on 'Morals and politics', a theme on which a great deal has been said and will continue to be said. It will simply be an attempt to say something about the character of morality which I believe needs to be said if we are to reckon with its public face as well as its private and personal face.

Mackenzie seldom talks or writes directly about morality. He probably shares the British embarrassment (not always so noticeable in North Britons) about getting into a kind of talk which can easily look like preaching. But the damped down fire is there, and every now and then it shoots out; and in thinking about political studies he knows that 'this sort of theorizing requires an ethical anchorage

or at least an ethical area of concern' (ibid., p. 355). Moral philosophers have tried to map this area of concern, and it is their job
to do so even at the cost of some embarrassment. I hope that if I
try to do a bit of such mapping, Bill Mackenzie may see the effort
as part of one of the ploys we have shared together.

There is another link which he may recognise. What I shall
try to say about personal and social morality is in some respects a
variation on a theme played by A. D. Lindsay.[1] Lindsay distinguished
two kinds of morality, the morality of social norms on which we
should be able to count, and personal morality, which goes beyond
this in ways which can be gladly received but cannot be demanded
or expected as of right. Here my main difference is that I see
morality as a *three*-stranded cord in which each strand needs the
others rather than as distinguishable into two types. But Lindsay is
certainly there in the background. He started me off in these matters
as his undergraduate pupil, and he was a power in Mackenzie's
Balliol. We both came out of his stable, though we have both
wandered a good way off from it.

'Three strands in morality' suggests intertwining and not just
triple threads. A threefold cord is not easily broken: and if morality
is to stand the strains of actual life in societies I believe it will need
to be made out of these three strands, though sociologists and moral
philosophers have all too often tried to unravel them, and talk about
morality as if a sufficient account could be given in terms of one of
them, while the others can be discarded as matters of some other
concern.

I shall call the first strand 'Custom' and the second 'Reciprocity'.
There is no obvious name for the third. I shall call it 'Grace'
(following Lindsay here), though I shall not be using the word with
the technical theological associations which will be familiar to Bill
Mackenzie from his Presbyterian background, and to me to a lesser
extent from my Anglican one. I shall use it to refer to a generous
spirit in personal actions, which may, but need not necessarily, have
a religious root. I shall label these three strands A, B and C, not as
an order of grading (they are *strands*, not streams), but simply
for convenience of reference. From time to time I shall talk about
A, B and C types of moral behaviour, because people can predominantly show one rather than the others. But this must not be
taken to mean that an all-round working morality can fall into one
of these types as if it were self-sufficient. They need each other, just

as the people who clearly 'major' in one of them will need people who 'major' in one of the others. And though people may 'major' in one, I doubt whether anyone's morality can belong *solely* to one type. Sociologists have tried to talk about morality purely in A terms, Kantian and moral philosophers in B terms, Existentialists in C terms, but this is abstraction, not life in the round.

First, then, A—Custom. 'Custom' stands broadly for the *mores*, the morality which is a going—or not so going—concern in any society. It is a mixture of rules of thumb, wisdom of experience, and taboos whose original point, if any, may have been forgotten. It may not fit well into existing situations, especially when times are changing. But whether we conform or whether we revolt, we all depend more than we like to own on there being some customs which keep going, and which will give us reasonably stable expectations as to how other people are likely to behave, saving us from always having to think out how we ourselves would behave all along the line. We need to be able to take a good deal for granted on some occasions if we are to have the energy to think, criticise and innovate on others. So we need Custom as well as spontaneity; this can be seen even in the 'alternative societies' set up by people who repudiate the existing *mores*. They very soon have to produce *mores* of their own, or else their communes peter out in uncertainty and instability. In any case, they count on some fairly constant framework being kept going in the wider society from which they have partially contracted out—at any rate, they expect to find road and rail transport and telephone communications.

It may be said that all this is sociologically interesting; that 'Custom is king' may even be part of what is meant by a society. But what has it to do with morality? Morality should be a matter of people's free personal decisions on what they think right or wrong: the *mores* are moral only where they are deliberately accepted. This is partly a matter of definition. We can, if we like, reserve 'morality' for people's deliberate decisions about what they ought to do, and call the customary element just 'social behaviour'. What is not a matter of definition, but of fact, is that first-hand decisions are exacting and often time-consuming. We often have to act off the cuff, falling back on built-in dispositions which have been formed out of intuitively absorbed social training as well as out of our own conscious decisions. Existentialists speak as though morality should consist in agonising choices, where there are no guidelines and where we must act in absolute freedom. So indeed it sometimes does; but it can hardly do so all the time. There are too many decisions to be made in the course of the day. If in most of them we fall back on customary guidelines, the Existentialists will call this 'mauvaise foi'. If it is, we must carry a great load of inevitable guilt feelings along with us, and this is a grim prospect. We can, of course, give general assent to some of the rules we find round us in the *mores* (though 'general assent' would not satisfy an Existentialist). An instance might be the obligation to return borrowed books, which figured so large in the moral philosophy lectures of Prichard and Ross in Mackenzie's and my Oxford days as the paradigm of a self-evident moral intuition. (How self-evident? My present impression is that it is even ceasing to be part of the *mores*.) But can we even give (or withhold) general assent in personal reflection all along the line? Often the best we can hope for is that the parts of the *mores* which we still take for granted will not be too indefensible, and that our failure to be self-conscious about them will not land us into serious *mauvaise foi*. But I am not happy about excluding from our definition of morality even the parts of the *mores* which we have not examined and consented to, because if we do exclude them we may well not have the honesty and humility to acknowledge how often we depend on them. So it may be better to bring this above board, and allow Custom (whether consciously or tacitly accepted) to be one strand—though only one—in our actual working morality. Some customs are not just what we ourselves would have prescribed if we had thought them up. But I do not see how a society can cohere without a good deal that can be taken for granted in this way. Sir Karl Popper's open society inhabited by pure critical rationalists would not, I suspect, be coherent for very long. Social morality runs a good deal on Custom; and we are being less than candid about our own personal behaviour unless we own that we rely to a very considerable extent on rules of thumb to which we give little or no critical attention.

For this very reason the customary side of morality can let us down. For we can be faced with situations to which the *mores* have not been tailored; even parts of them thought to be 'self-evident' institutions may turn out not so self-evident to a later generation. Also the *mores* are a mixed bag, some of whose contents got there through good sense born of experience, and some in much more chancy ways. How do we sort the contents out?

We can try to do so by using our wits, critically as to consequences, and with a sense of fairness as a guiding light as to principle. This brings us to B, the second strand, which I have labelled Reciprocity. Broadly this attempts to bring some rationality into customary morality. As one of our strands I do not believe it is totally lacking even in what are thought of as traditional 'closed' societies. A good deal of shrewd comment goes on in such societies.[2] But of course it is more noticeable in societies where people are learning to think critically, and where traditional moral sanctions are loosened. It is therefore the approach distinctive of liberal moral reformers. This may be why most moral philosophers in our culture usually take this as what 'ethics' is about. (If it serves any useful purpose to distinguish 'ethics' from morality, this distinction might consist in using 'ethics' for this kind of rational effort, and, theoretically, for the meta-ethical discussions which go on among moral philosophers about what it is like, and to use the term 'morality' for the amalgam of less clearly defined guides which we follow in deciding what we ought to do in practice.) As I think that the B strand with its liberal principles is only one strand, along with the A strand of Custom (and a further C strand which will come in later), I am here talking about 'morality', and not 'ethics' in the more restricted sense, and in any case 'ethics' in the more restricted sense need to live with these other elements if it is to get off the ground.

The B strand in morality, then, is spun out of reflection on the mixed set of customs which make up the A strand. If reflection is to be critical it needs a guiding light, and here the main guiding light is Reciprocity. This can cover both a sense of fairness and mutual respect for interests and obligations. If being 'reasonable' is not to be defined only in prudential terms, as maximising one's own interest on a cost–benefit basis, it can be extended into seeing that if one expects other people to keep a rule it is only fair to be prepared to do so oneself. 'What is sauce for the goose is sauce for the gander.' This rationality of consistency can, of course, go along with a conservative view of the rules. It doesn't matter what kind of sauce is being served, provided we are prepared to spread it on both dishes alike. But even this tells us not to cheat over the rules in our own favour—a first step into rational objectivity, and one not to be despised. Taken along with mutual respect for interests, this minimum fairness can grow beyond merely seeing that we should not make exceptions in our own favour into a more imaginative kind of Reciprocity, a capacity to think of oneself as in the other man's shoes, and see how the situation would look if the roles were reversed (especially in a non-symmetrical transaction where one of the parties is the under-dog at the receiving end). Reciprocity, then, points not only to 'sauce for the goose is sauce for the gander' morality but to Golden Rule morality.

Consistency and mutual respect: this sounds very Kantian, and indeed Kant might be taken as the paradigm philosopher of B morality. But even Kant, when he is talking *morality* and not just doing meta-ethics, brings in some actual notions of right and wrong taken out of the *mores* of the Protestant Christianity in which he was brought up. And he has hints about the perfection of the Good Will when it becomes a Holy Will which, if they were pressed, would lead on to the C strand. Nevertheless, broadly speaking, Kant's morality is B type, a morality of rational beings, treating each other as such with impartial natural justice. It is the kind of morality that, we hold, should underlie uncorrupt administrative and judicial procedures. It operates without 'respect of persons' but with respect *for* persons, an essential distinction where impersonal decisions are called for.

This impersonality may be why it has a bad press in some contemporary circles, notably those connected with the 'counter-culture', where 'bureaucrat' has become a dirty word, with 'soulless' as something of an inseparable prefix. Here not only the A type morality of the *mores* is under fire but also the B type, with its liberal effort after fairness and rationality. But not so the C type; that which, for want of a better name, I have called the morality of Grace. This stands partly for the quest for an elusive ideal good which cannot be contained in any set of rules. Rules, if they are not just arbitrarily imposed by some people on other people, go with the morality of Reciprocity. You accept the fact that if you expect other people to keep them, then you should do so too in cases when they apply to you. And correspondingly, if you are to be expected to keep them, then you most certainly hold that other people ought to do so too. Otherwise your readiness to keep them will become strained, to say the least; in any case Reciprocity embraces a morality of give and take.

The C type, the morality of Grace, is not thus calculating, how-ever fair and reasonable such calculations may be. Miss Iris Murdoch has written persuasively about this, where it is the quest after an ultimate Good, in her Leslie Stephen lecture 'The sovereignty of good over other concepts'[3]—and so much more persuasively than anything I could write that I will just gratefully refer to her lecture. She has brought a latter-day Platonic Idea of the Good back into the centre of ethics.

But my present concern is with C-type morality as it enters into our relations with one another, rather than with how it may inform the flight of the alone to the alone. Here the morality of Grace stands for a highly personal kind of behaviour, which certainly cannot be prescribed in any set of rules, or be expected as of right. At one end of the scale this is the morality of saints and heroes; but there is a scale and there are points all up the scale where it comes out in the behaviour of all sorts of people, in uncovenanted, 'gracious' acts of kindness where people are prepared, freely and ungrudgingly, not always to stand on their rights.

How does this connect with institutional morality? In institutional behaviour we need to know more or less where we stand and what we can reasonably expect and fairly demand of each other. The Sermon on the Mount contains sayings which are paradigmatic pieces of C morality. But 'Give hoping for nothing again' is hardly a principle on which a joint stock bank could be run; nor could 'Judge not that ye be not judged' be the appropriate maxim for members of appointments committees. The drop-out who wants all our transactions to be directly personal and spontaneous overlooks the fact that many of them involve a range of obligations to others besides immediate face-to-face individuals; and some of these transactions—appointing to a job, for instance—call for attempts at impartial assessing of relevant qualities, if justice is to be done both to the candidates who do not get the job and to those who are going to have to live with the candidate who does. This does not mean that the qualities so estimated are necessarily the most important, though it is hoped that they are the ones which are relevant to the situation. In any case, behind and beyond them stands the actual man, who, as Mackenzie says in another connection, 'exists unspecified, bearing an unexplored reserve of latent characteristics'.[4] And confronted with him, 'Judge not' may strike the appropriate note. Yet since we are involved in innumerable transactions in multiple relations, most of which have to be indirect, we depend on some framework through which they can be steered, and which have procedures that do not have to be called up *ad hoc* for each situation. And if there must be some institutional order, it is surely preferable to try to bring B principles to bear on it—reciprocity tempered by reason—rather than just to trust to the folkways, which, left to themselves, can well be custom tempered by corruption.

This does not mean that people with roles in institutions in which they try to behave in a B-like way can have no time for the C kind of behaviour. Just as C cannot stand by itself as a social morality, because it would produce anarchy,[5] so the B spirit needs a touch of inspired innovation as well as compassion from the C spirit if it is not to lead to the 'soulless bureaucracy' which the drop-out thinks it is. This is not just a way of saying that soulless bureaucrats may after all have a soul in their off-duty moments. It is to say that even in their on-duty moments there is a difference between knowing and not knowing, when making decisions according to rules and precedents, that they are also doing things with people's lives. And many of them do know it. A wise administrator knows that any set of rules needs loopholes. But they must be loopholes. The drop-out who repudiates institutional decisions sometimes seems to be asking for the loophole to be made into a new rule. But if what is done through the loophole is made into a new rule, it may be still less workable than the old one. It is broadly true that hard cases make bad laws. In any case, the genius of the C kind of morality lies in seeing when the rule is no longer the guide.

Less drastic than finding loopholes, there is also the fact that no system of rules can be administered without some place for discretion, and a C attitude can come out in the use of discretion. I remember an occasion when I was on the State Studentships Committee of what was then the Ministry of Education; a great deal of trouble was being taken by the officials administering the scheme where a holder of a studentship had got into prison (a less common occurrence in student life then than it has since become). They were leaning over backwards to see that he was supplied with books and to see how his studentship could be held open for him for when he came out. I once considered dedicating something I wrote remotely connected with the theme of this paper to 'administrators whose hearts are with the anarchists, and to anarchists who have a heart for the administrators'. I do not think that the former at any rate form a null class. The pure Weberian model of impersonal, rule-governed rational bureaucracy is far too pure to exist. In any case, if it did exist it would soon be strangled in its own red tape.

For the role of administrator, like all roles, is not simply a matter of applying rules. Cases are too varied for all decisions to be so programmed. There is the question of which rule applies and how; there are exceptional circumstances; there is the penumbra of personal relationship which surrounds even rather formal kinds of transaction. There has to be a margin for discretion, and the individual plays his role in his own style, more and less humanely.

This gives a foothold for C qualities even in quite routine kinds of transaction. At a simple level they can come out in courtesy and patience, which indeed can come to be expected in a civilised society. I was in a small branch post office in Manchester when an old age pensioner in front of me was drawing his pension and getting into muddles which the woman behind the counter was gently sorting out for him. This much might be expected from a post office employee, and the public might well complain if they were treated brusquely. But it was not all. After the old man had gone, the woman behind the counter said to me, 'They do get into muddles. But we know our old age pensioners, and if they haven't been in for three weeks one of us slips round to where they live to see if they are all right.' Note 'our old age pensioners'. And since some of them might well be living alone, and not able to get out if they were ill, I should not be surprised if the woman from the post office not only took along their pension but did a bit of clearing up and shopping for them as well—an unobtrusive bit of C action beyond the duties of her role.

But even within the duties of the role there is the place for the attitude of mind in which the role player carries them out more and less considerately. This, as I have said, comes out in administration even at a simple level. The higher the level the more necessary it may be that the people who have these responsibilities should be able to feel the pull of the C strand of morality, even if their job mainly asks them to keep the B strand in repair.

Similarly if those who run their lives mainly on the A strand of Custom are not just to turn into programmed conformists, they will need the occasional inspired innovation and the far less occasional touch of spontaneous generosity which comes from the spirit of C. Beyond these again are the heroic, sacrificial kinds of C action. But C also may go to the bad if it is taken as self-sufficient. The horrible possibilities of what might happen here were borne in on me at an early age when I came across a Victorian children's book that had belonged to my mother. It was about two little girls who never quarrelled except about which of them should give up. They were obviously each wanting to be in the superior moral position of the giver-up, and the book showed me that it was much better for most of family life to run on principles of give and take and fair shares. Most, but not all; sometimes people indeed need to be prepared to give and not take. The hopeless thing about the little girls in the story was that they wanted to make this into a rule, and since it was a rule that *both* of them could not keep at the same time, they had to quarrel over it.

There is another reason why there are dangers in trying to run life on C considerations alone, and this is connected with where the morality of Grace goes along with aspiration after an extreme ideal. Seekers after an extreme ideal will be exasperated by the compromises of give and take. And when they are exasperated, the sacrificial drive in their morality can turn to violence. For violence can also be sacrificial, since those who take to it know they are as likely—often more likely—to be killed as to kill. Violence is the dark shadow of the morality of Grace, which may be why people who live by the morality of Grace are more able to talk to the violent than are the liberal people who live by the B principles of Reciprocity.

I have talked about A, B and C type people because people's morality can predominantly belong to one of these types rather than the others. But I come back to questioning whether any one of them can exist on its own. The C type saint or hero needs some customs to fall back on; and if he is not prepared to run some of his transactions on the reciprocity of give and take, he will wear us all out and end up as a fanatic. And I have spoken of how A and B types need the touch of C to give them creative imagination and personal compassion, to counter the drag to complacency and conformity.

Bill Mackenzie's writings on politics and administration show the realistic good sense of someone who thoroughly understands the need for B morality, yet at the same time, generally without letting on, puts a C kind of personal caring into it. Sometimes he shows his sympathies overtly. In the course of writing about the job of a teacher of politics he makes some remarks on Michael Oakshott's views. Michael Oakshott talks as though the teaching of politics should just be done in A terms, following the 'intimations' of a tradi-

tion; though in fact he turns it into a poetic kind of C. For
Mackenzie this doesn't solve the problem of what the person on the
job has got to do. 'There is a lot of sordid business with syllabuses,
and local government promotion examinations, and the pass mark
of 40 per cent, and the selection, pay and careers of university
teachers and other honest persons. The system in its nature stan-
dardises and conscripts; things distasteful and to be resisted. But
are they best resisted by ignoring them? or is it best to accept, study
and mitigate? This is an open choice, but my own inclination is to
face the problem rather than to evade it.'⁶

As Bill Mackenzie and I both started out from Greats, it may be
appropriate to end on a reference to the Greeks. In Plato's *Protagoras* there is a myth about how men acquired *politike techne*—
the art of political life. 'They sought to assemble together and save
their lives by founding cities. But often as they assembled they
injured one another, for lack of the political art; so again they dispersed and were perishing. Zeus therefore, fearing that our race
would be quite destroyed, sent Hermes to take to men justice (*dike*)
and reverence (*aidos*) that there might be orderers of cities and links
bringing them together in friendship' (*Protagoras* 322 b–c). *Aidos*
and *dike*. It is not easy to translate *aidos*. *Dike*—justice—is easier.
'Reverence' is not very satisfactory, but I think the Greek word
suggests ingrained scruples which include respect for moral traditions. It was used in the contexts of moral discussion, where it was
said that the best recipe for being a good man was to have taken the
precaution of being born of parents who lived in a city with good
customs. So *aidos* may be the virtue characteristic of the A strand
in morality, as *dike* is clearly characteristic of the B strand. The
Greeks had no name that I know for a virtue especially characteristic of the C strand. There is *charis*, but this is 'grace', a name
for this whole aspect of morality rather than its virtue. The New
Testament has a name, *agape*, for the kind of outgoing love which
seems to be characteristic of the unscripted C strand in morality. So
we may add *agape* to *aidos* and *dike* as the gifts Hermes needed to
take to men as means of ordering cities and forging links of friendship. Hermes was also a trickster, and when he gave men *aidos* he
no doubt did not expect them always to treat the *mores* with un-
mitigated solemnity. We can respect some customs better when
we can also turn a critical eye on others in the name of fairness:
and if the perfection of fairness, which is equity, needs imaginative

understanding of the particular individual case, this surely also needs agapeistic sympathy.

So we come back to morality as a three-stranded cord, where Custom, Reciprocity and Grace, with the qualities that inform them, intertwine with each other as 'orderers of cities and links which bring people together in friendship'.

For Bill Mackenzie 'political art' is surely concerned not only with ordering cities but also with bringing people together in friendship. While I have been writing this, from time to time I have thought I heard a grunt, I hope of interest, perhaps even of agreement. And sometimes I have thought I heard 'But that's *hopeless*.' And then I have tried again.

Notes

[1] See especially his *The Two Moralities*, London, Eyre & Spottiswoode, 1940.

[2] On this, see Paul Radin, *Primitive Man as Philosopher*, Dover Publications, New York, 1972.

[3] Cambridge, 1967. Reprinted in I. Murdoch, *The Sovereignty of Good*, Routledge & Kegan Paul, London, 1970.

[4] See above, p. 69.

[5] I suspect anarchists assume, without owning it, that someone is going to keep some sort of order going. If what they want is confined to spontaneous order in a small group, even this is probably not all that spontaneous. Decisions have to be talked over, and there will need to be some presumption that they will be carried out.

[6] 'Political theory and political education', *Universities Quarterly*, IX, 4, August 1955, p. 360.

John Erickson

6

The air defence problem, 1939-40: British and
Soviet roads to radar compared

The processes by which science came to the aid of air defence in
Great Britain in the 1930s, resulting in the development and
operational application of RDF (better known as radar), have
received more than adequate coverage in both memoir and monograph literature, with Sir Charles Snow providing in his celebrated
work *Science and Government* a dramatic exposition of the Lindemann–Tizard vendetta which formed an integral part of this
venture.[1] These pyrotechnics of personality undoubtedly exercise a
fascination all their own, but the real burden of Sir Charles Snow's
work is an examination of 'cardinal choices'—'... those which
determine in the crudest sense whether we live or die'—and, in
particular, 'secret scientific choices', including technical choices:
the net result is to furnish a simple model of the interaction between
science and government, though at the outset Sir Charles specifically
eschews 'models' and insists that the mould of accepted models
and the like must be broken to arrive at something like the true
nature of these operations. Leaving aside the niceties of a model
and its properties, the questions remain: what is 'scientific choice'
and to what degree do men who start out as 'scientists' but who
engage increasingly in bureaucratic battles to implement these
'choices' still remain scientists in the accepted, professional sense,
or else suffer some irreversible sea change? Admitting that 'secret
scientific choices' imply a highly restricted circulation of vital information and a narrowly constricted decision-making circle, what
is the real effect of such 'closed politics' and what form do such
politics assume? In sum, Sir Charles is asking how decisions are
really made.

Several of the assumptions, propositions and hypotheses advanced
in *Science and Government* did not go unchallenged, as might be
expected, though an opportunity to review their general validity

comes from an unexpected and hitherto unexplored quarter, no less a person than one of the key 'scientist–managers' of the Soviet radar programme in the 1930s, Lieutenant-General M. M. Lobanov, who in 1962 produced a startling and highly original essay on the origins of Soviet research on radar:[2] seven years later—and the time lag is significant in view of the cautious editorial comment which accompanied that initial essay—General Lobanov published a substantial monograph. *Iz proshlogo radiolokatsii*, dealing with the development of radar in the Soviet Union.[3] The very existence of indigenous and extensive Soviet research on radar may well come as a surprise to many, bred on tales that radar was virtually unknown in the Soviet Union and that only wartime lend–lease remedied this state of scientific and technical ignorance, but any blow to British *amour propre* is readily offset by the utility and the uniqueness of this newer evidence.

At least there is no difficulty in explaining the communality of the problem facing both Great Britain and the Soviet Union in the 1930s: the fast, high-flying bomber posed a formidable threat, and prevailing air defence measures were manifestly inadequate to deal with it. The Soviet air defence command—Voiska protivo-voz-dushnoi oborony: PVO—learned this in dramatic fashion in March 1932, when the latest combined searchlight and sound locator system (designated Prozhzvuk, from *prozhektor*, 'searchlight', and *zvuk*, sound locator), showed that maximum success in searching for and locating a hostile aircraft was only in the order of 50–60 per cent, and even that was achieved under artificially ideal conditions (lack of wind, no evasive action by the target and only one target to track).[4] The Prozhzvuk system was nonetheless adopted, for the simple reason that there was nothing better: even the use of blind persons as operators, with their heightened sense of hearing, failed to improve performance to any appreciable degree. Two years later, in 1934, major British air defence exercises demonstrated the hapless-ness of the defence: the giant sound locator at Romney Marsh, designed to give warning of hostile aircraft approaching from the Channel, could provide only the rough bearing of a target at a distance of some eight miles, but without any indication of either height or range.[5] Aircraft which approached at an acute angle to the locator escaped detection entirely. The 'enemy' bomber force simulating the attack and composed of Vickers Virginias, which cruised at a mere 73 m.p.h., with a full-load ceiling of only 7,000 ft, went largely undetected and 48 per cent reached their 'targets', even as head-winds still further reduced their speed. Like their British counterparts, the Soviet command realised the implications of this vulnerability, which could only worsen as more modern aircraft came into service, and therefore searched not altogether hopefully for some new solution to their dilemma.

1. *The problem and the initial approach*

At the end of 1932 in the Soviet Union the Main Artillery Administration (Glavnoe artilleriiskoe upravlenie: GAU), the engineering brain of the Red Army, realised abruptly that 'acoustical methods' alone would not solve the air defence problem, if only because they could not furnish that range of observation which would facilitate the effective use of fighter aircraft and AA guns. Having exhausted its own resources, GAU looked for outside help and seemed to have found a promising solution in the work of Professor V. L. Granovskii, who had been investigating the significance of thermal energy emitted by aircraft in flight. In pursuit of this 'infra-red solution' (which was, incidentally, a line of research passionately espoused by Professor Lindemann, who pressed it on the Tizard committee), Professor Granovskii developed a 'receiver–indicator/detector' using an anti-aircraft searchlight with a heat element at its centre: General Lobanov conducted the early tests of this equipment, which could detect an aircraft at a distance of some 10–12 km, but this method could be used only at night and in the absence of cloud, which produced its own thermal radiation. Aircraft flying above thick cloud remained undetected by Granovskii's *teplopelengator* ('thermal course and bearing indicator'): only the Red fleet enjoyed an unexpected bonus from this new infra-red technology, which proved to be useful in detecting surface targets, but in 1935 the infra-red programme was halted (save for some special work with the navy).[6]

'Acoustical means' were severely limited, the 'infra-red solution' failed to live up to its promise, whereupon the GAU sought for some 'engineering' or 'radio technical solution'. Mention of radio meant turning to the Scientific Research Experimental Institute of Red Army Signals (NIIS KA), only to receive the frosty answer that radio meant essentially radio communications: as for any scheme of 'radio-technical' detector stations, the massive sources of power so essential for any widespread deployment virtually ruled out this idea. Thus rebuffed, the GAU decided to push the infra-red programme to the limit, while contacting a number of prominent Soviet radiophysicists. In August 1933 the GAU held a conference at the Central Radio Laboratory (TsRL), whose director, D. N. Rumyantsev, agreed to look into 'radio detection'—*radioobnaruzhenie*, as it was termed—and set Engineer Yu. K. Korovin's section to work: on 1 January 1934 a formal contract committed Korovin to investigating the reflection of electro-magnetic waves from the surface area of an aircraft, using the apparatus for geodesic radio measurement developed by N. D. Papaleksi. In a deliberate duplication of effort the GAU also signed up the Leningrad Electrophysics Institute (LEFI) to work on 'radiodetection': Engineer B. K. Shembel' had immediate responsibility for this work.[7]

At this juncture, and apparently coincidentally, the air defence forces—the PVO—entered the 'radio detection' stakes, seeking to a means to extend the range of observation beyond its audio and visual systems (organised into VNOS, the Soviet equivalent of the Observer Corps). Here PVO and GAU interests diverged, for the latter wanted 'radio detection' for accurate gun-laying and the direction of AA searchlights—and here lay an unsuspected problem of much complexity, since it required a good deal of time and effort later in the programme to disentangle the requirements for early-warning and gun-laying radar. Only future disappointments and frustrations would reveal this, but in August 1933 E. P. K. Oshchepkov, a promising young engineer working within the PVO, sounded out the views of the Soviet Academy of Sciences at a meeting in Leningrad.[8] The Academy did not disparage the idea of 'radio detection', and in October 1933, with the backing of the Defence Commissariat itself (and the cognisance of the Defence Commissar, K. E. Voroshilov), with a separate budgetary allocation for research and with the full encouragement of none other than Tukhachevskii (at that time Chief of Ordnance: *Nachal'nik vooruzheniya*), a 'special construction office' (SKB) was set up under the direction of Engineer Oshchepkov. The first experimental programme involved a 'panoramic' type of radio detection apparatus which was provisionally named Elektrovizor. In fact, the Interdepartmental Commission for Scientific Research Work attached to Tukhachevskii's office (which supervised military R & D) had already accepted the PVO submission for the development of a 'VNOS reconnaissance electromagnetic station'.[9]

For all the rush of activity and the grandiose names, much of this smacked of pie in the sky, in the literal and figurative sense. The point was made with some acerbity at the special conference arranged between the air defence forces and prominent Soviet radio physicists and radio specialists, who met together on 16 January 1934. The talent assembled here was formidable, including several Academicians, opitical and acoustics experts, physicists and engineers. Academician A. F. Ioffe, who was by no means unsympathetic to the idea of 'radio detection' and who had lent his considerable aid in bringing this conference together, asserted from the outset that he saw a future only for long waves, as opposed to notions of centimetric and decimetric wavelengths—Academician Ioffe was arguing by way of analogy with the laws of optics. In what was obviously a lively and wide-ranging debate, the idea of 'radio detection' was adjudged to be feasible in principle, but the dispute broke out over how it was to be managed in practice: the 'technical means' were simply not to hand, and it was open to question whether the amount of electro-magnetic energy reflected from an aircraft would be significant enough to facilitate 'detection'. The proponents of sound location, with N. N. Andreyev in the lead, urged this solution to the air defence problem, for all the talk about 'radio detection', while from their camp the exponents of infra-red technology exhorted the conference to back further work on detecting the exhausts of aircraft engines. In the end, however, the 'radio detection' lobby won the day, at least to judge by the final minute of the conference—a document entitled '... on the question of investigating means to detect aircraft at night, in conditions of poor visibility and at great height for purposes of national air defence'— which asserted that the most promising 'instruments' were those designed 'on the principle of the use of electro-magnetic waves of *sufficiently short wavelengths* (decimetric and centimetric waves)'.[10]

This was certainly no hazardous leap in the dark. Academician Ioffe with his own hand struck out the phrase 'sufficiently short wavelengths' and deleted 'decimetric and centimetric waves': the conference as a whole accepted the idea of equipment designed to produce the necessary electro-magnetic radiation and receivers able to pick up the reflected beam, but the patent novelty of the whole idea caused the conference to insist on a 'belt and braces' approach, with further development of optical instruments, sound-ranging and infra-red technology. Undeterred by this formidable opposition, the

PVO engineers publicly restated their faith in the principles of 'radio detection' in the February (1934) issue of their own professional *Air Defence Journal (Sbornik PVO)*: '... if there is a source of generating for ultra-short or decimetric waves or even centimetric electro-magnetic waves and the emission of these waves from the source of their generation is directed into space, then, with such a beam of electro-magnetic waves directed towards any object, it is *always possible* to pick up the reflected electro-magnetic beam'.[11] Thus it would be possible 'with great exactitude' to determine both the direction of the body emitting such reflections and the place in which it is located. (In November of that same year, 1934, Mr Wimperis—Director of Scientific Research—proposed in Great Britain the creation of a committee designed to undertake a scientific survey of air defence problems, thus bringing the 'Tizard committee' to eventual life; Mr Wimperis also enlisted the aid of Mr (later Sir) Robert Watson-Watt of the Radio Research Station, the result of which was the famous paper 'Detection and location of aircraft by radio methods', submitted to the Air Ministry on 12 February 1935.)[12]

Seized with its own ideas, the PVO at once set about trying to realise the technology of 'radio detection': on 19 February 1934 the air defence forces signed a contract with the Leningrad Electrophysics Institute to develop a transmitter and receiver for conducting tests on the detection of an aircraft by picking up reflected signals. The result was the 'Rapid' apparatus, compromising a transmitter with an output of 150–200 W, operating on a wavelength of 4·7 m with a frequency modulation of 1,000 Hz: the receiver was of the 'super regenerator type', with one horizontal vibrator acting as an antenna positioned in the centre of the zone of observation. Tests in the summer of 1934 established that the presence of an aircraft could be indicated in an area with a radius of some three kilometres from the receiver and up to heights of 1,000 m: further tests confirmed that a range of 75 km from the transmitter (given the level of power and the height of the transmitter and receiving antennae) was more or less the operational limit. Five such sets were ordered for experimental production, but in spite of the understandable elation of the PVO engineers the 'Rapid' set could give no indication of the range of an aircraft, although it might indicate its presence.[13] The battle had only just begun.

2. *Technical choices and Soviet 'Radio location equipment'*

For all the initial excitements and the flurry of conferences and meetings, the prime 'secret scientific choice' had not yet been made, not even in that intuitive sense which Sir Charles Snow suggested was part of the British decision. Though very eminent Soviet scientists had been approached and even involved, there was nothing comparable in the Soviet Union to the 'Tizard committee'—nor was there ever to be such a body. Certainly the air defence forces, the PVO, had made their point with 'Rapid': in October 1934 Tuk-hachevskii wrote to Sergei Kirov in Leningrad, impressing him with the importance of the current research and experimental pro-gramme and urging him to expedite the work of the several Lenin-grad institutes and factories engaged on this special work. At the end of 1934 there were two institutes—the Central Radio Labora-tory and the Leningrad Electro-physics Institute—working on *radiolokatory*, 'radio location equipment', but they had to straddle the differing requirements of the PVO and the GAU: the PVO thought in terms of a 'linear radio technical system', nothing less than an 'electro-magnetic screen' along the Soviet frontiers and reaching a height of 10,000 m, indicating penetration by hostile air-craft but without any effective measure of height, range or speed, while the GAU needed precisely that information to direct its AA guns and to co-ordinate the fighter forces.[14]

Nor could these two Soviet institutes—the TsRL and LEFI—draw any appreciable degree on the resources of the Soviet radio industry. The radio industry was concerned chiefly with long and short waves, whereas *radiolokatsiya*—'radio location'—involved exploiting ultra-short waves, thus necessitating new electro-vacuum equipment and magnetrons in order to generate electro-magnetic waves of decimetric length. This, together with research into ariels and antennae, power supply and the means to display information, proved to be a formidable task, but the real obstacle to success arose from one of the fundamental technical choices selected by LEFI and TsRL—the continuous wave solution, which led only to relatively poor results. LEFI pushed on with its programme nonetheless, though in 1935 it ceased to enjoy an independent existence and was absorbed into the Television Institute: within this orbit LEFI became NII–9 and fell under the direction of a very renowned Soviet radio en-gineer, Professor M. A. Bonch-Bruevich, aided by talented radio engineers and radio physicists such as A. A. Slutskin, D. S. Shteinberg and B. A. Vvedenskii.[15]

Mention of Shteinberg and Slutskin brings in yet another major research centre, the Physico-technical Institute of the Ukrainian Academy of Sciences (UFTI). These two men had worked under Professor D. A. Rozhanskii at UFTI on a programme of research dealing with magnetronic methods of generating electro-magnetic oscillation: in 1932 UFTI had produced a magnetron with an oscillating capacity of 100–300 W operating on a wavelength of between 80 and 20 cm. At the end of 1936 UFTI succeeded in producing decimetric waves with a power of up to 1 kW, thus opening a whole new range of possibilities. Meanwhile NII–9 (the erstwhile *LEFI*), working for the Artillery Administration (GAU) produced its first prototype of a search and tracking radar, code-named 'Burya' ('Storm'): 'Burya' operated on an 18 cm wavelength at a power of 6–7 W (continuous wave), fitted with two parabolic aerials, one for transmitting and one for receiving. The results of field tests showed this set to be too unreliable for use with AA guns, since the range (10–11 km) and the accuracy of definition (angular co-ordinates) of 3–4° fell short of operational requirements: the chief difficulty seemed to lie with the narrowness of the polar diagram. Increasing the range did not present insuperable problems, for this was a matter of improving the transmitter output and the sensitivity of the receiver: accuracy and reliability were, however, quite a different matter.[16] Improvements to the power output were incorporated into the development plan for 1937, and at the same conference Professor Bonch-Bruevich suggested an antenna arrangement with a flat polar diagram, thereby contributing to solving the problem of accurate search and closer angular co-ordinates. The same meeting also decided on equi-signal contours to increase accuracy in determining angular co-ordinates.[17]

The 'Burya' continuous wave set had been produced for the GAU as a result of work begun under that preliminary contact with LEFI (now NII–9). Meanwhile the air defence forces, the PVO, worked with Academician Ioffe's Physico-technical Institute (FTI) in Leningrad and drew in Rozhanskii and the UFTI: both of these institutes, the FTI and the UFTI, came under the control of the Research Sector of the People's Commissariat for Heavy Industry, in spite of their apparent connections with Academicians and the Academy of Sciences. In addition, the PVO operated its own electro-vacuum laboratories, though again these worked in close association with Academician Ioffe's FTI. The technical solution adopted here proved to be much more fortunate, for Engineer V. V. Tsimbalin was developing an impulse generator valve with a wavelength of 4 m and a power of 40–50 W, resulting in the development of a prototype pulse radar set: tested in 1936, this early model—designed for use with the VNOS system—had a range of 7 km, increased to $12\frac{1}{2}$–17 km by stepping up the power output and installing the receiver in a wider radius from the transmitter. An aircraft could be located at a height of some 1,500 m with this same set—a modest result, but the real significance lay in the definite start on the pulse method.[18]

Amidst all this technical and scientific travail the fortunes of the entire 'radio location' programme continued to see-saw. From the outset the Red Army Signals command had expressed its scepticism of and its opposition to 'detection by radio means', and in 1935 mounted a full-scale attack in a report submitted in the name of the Signals command research organisation—NIIIS KA—to Tukhachevskii, demanding that an end be put to this useless research and that the GAU disengage from it at once.[19] The technical reasons for this opposition are far from clear, but to judge from subsequent events and the role which NIIIS KA ultimately came to play, it would appear that sheer pique had much to do with this stubborn opposition. At no distant date, but in somewhat melancholy circumstances, these scientific storm-troopers of the Signals command made their triumphant entry on the scene and ruthlessly took advantage of the situation, abruptly reversing their negative attitude. Fortunately, the GAU could show some preliminary results from its 'radio location' programme, and Tukhachevskii was persuaded to allow the research to continue.

During this phase fortune seemed to favour the PVO, for the death in 1936 of the chief of the air defence forces, Army Commander S. S. Kamenev, brought Army Commander (Second Grade) A. I. Sedyakin to this post, and he turned a more than sympathetic ear to the cause of 'radio location'. It was Sedyakin who, in 1937, initiated the first large-scale air defence exercises in the history of the air defence forces in an attempt to lay down firm operational procedures for using AA guns in conjunction with sound locators and deploying fighter aircraft to engage hostile bombers in 'illumination zones' provided by searchlights. The results were on a par with the British exercises of 1934, demonstrating once again that sound location was wholly inadequate in directing the fire of AA guns and the effective use of searchlights.[20]

During one of the interludes in the exercises Sedyakin was told of the work at NII–9 to develop 'radio detection'. Evidently impressed, he asked the director of NII–9 and Professor Bonch-Bruevich to prepare specific proposals which Sedyakin might present formally to 'the government'—presumably Stalin himself—with the object of speeding up the whole programme. In a 'semi-official' talk with Sedyakin, M. M. Lobanov provided details of the state of the art and plans for the future, presenting at the same time Professor Bonch-Bruevich's appraisal of the obstacles which had to be faced. Sedyakin at once took the point about improving range and accuracy, asking at the same time about the role of possible radio counter-measures which an enemy might employ, a point which had not escaped the attentions of the NII–9 scientists. All in all, despite the catalogue of technical problems facing the radio location programme, it seemed in the winter of 1936–37 that it had survived to the point of demonstrating real feasibility, and here was a basis for 'going to the government', which would have meant upgrading the programme to one of 'State significance' rather than simply another military research programme. And already the odds seemed to favour the PVO, for its less exacting tactical technical requirements for use with its visual observations system (VNOS) meant that only two co-ordinates were required, whereas the GAU needed three—azimuth, angle of elevation and range—for an effective gun-laying radar. Moreover, PVO engineers had turned to the pulse method, which certainly increased the range and the accuracy of determining it, whereas the GAU's scientific collaborators adhered to continuous wave, which presented the major disadvantage of the transmitter inhibiting the receiver. But at least the case for 'radio detection' was proven, certainly in principle and not a little in practice.

3. Closed politics, hierarchical politics and 'court politics'

Though Sir Charles Snow is at pains to make a dramatic distinction between 'closed politics' and 'open politics' for the purposes of his narrative about the British radar programme, this contrast has little or no relevance to the Soviet scene, where 'closed politics' predominated and was given a horrific significance all its own by the Stalinist purges: party men, administrators, scientists and the military became hopelessly trapped within the labyrinthine processes of this terror, first unleashed in the wake of the assassination of Kirov in 1934—the man to whom Tukhachevskii himself, followed by Sedyakin and a whole segment of the Soviet high command, went to the wall in June 1937: not only Red Army commanders, but also the military technical research institutes and design centres working for or with them were also decimated. The radio location programme was no exception, and indeed its losses were especially severe, since it depended on so small a group of highly specialised scientists and engineers. Oshchepkov, who deserves to be recognised as one of the brilliant innovators of the Soviet programme, suffered at once: arrested in 1937, he spent the next ten years in prison, a grim existence relieved only by the personal decency of Academician Ioffe in sending him parcels and letters.[21]

Obviously, with such murderous irrationality abroad, it is impossible to arrive at a neat verdict on cause and effect. But what is clear, in the case of the Soviet radar programme, is that personal and professional feuds were pressed under cover of the main and massive purge, though where one leaves off and the other begins— feud or purge—is a moot point. Suffice it is to say that the Red Army Signals command and the directors of the Signals research institute—NIIIS KA—saw their chance and seized it in avid, if ugly, fashion. NII–9, the old LEFI, which had worked under contract for the Main Artillery Administration, was 'investigated' by a special commission, which included officers from the Signals command. Inevitably heads rolled, including those of Engineer Shembel' and the director of NII–9, Smirnov. The new head of the GAU, Kulik (and a crony of Stalin's) turned a deaf ear to pleas about the plight of NII–9, and it seemed that this institute was finally doomed. At this juncture Professor Bonch-Bruevich and the secretary of the party organisation within NII–9 itself appealed direct to A. A. Zhdanov, the powerful party boss in Leningrad. Zhdanov ordered his own enquiry, and the secretary of the party committee for industry in Leningrad investigated the situation personally, finally submitting a report (compiled with the staff of NII–9) which brought a reprieve. The research on radar was given heavy emphasis, and the future work programme recommended for NII–9 included *radiolokatsiya* as well as television and the hardening of armour plate with high voltage.[22] Zhdanov accepted these recommendations, and NII–9 as an institute was saved, if only by the skin of its teeth.

One of the effects of the purge in terms of 'closed politics' and 'secret choices', even allowing for the previous style of closed and high compartmentalised decision-making, was to make such choices even more constricted within a smaller circle and one demonstrably eccentric. Stalin himself took detailed and complicated technical decisions—witness his personal preference for a large and powerful surface navy, his intervention to secure more advanced Soviet fighters and improved aero-engines, his initiation of a new artillery programme and his own personal interpretation of the military experience of the Spanish civil war, which resulted in the disbanding of large, independent Soviet armoured formations and the distribution of the tanks to infantry divisions.[23] This is not to say that all these decisions were wrong or ill-advised (though some were), but rather that they hung on the whim of one man.

Hierarchical politics received a new twist, if only because so many hierarchies had been smashed, or connections between institutes and the military left in utter disarray. The radar programme was a case in point. Though the Signals command and NIIIS KA had evinced nothing but implacable hostility towards *radiolokatsiya* and anything to do with it, the result of the purge was to place NIIIS KA in undisputed control of radar research—and, *mirabile dictu*, opposition vanished overnight, to be replaced by ruthless energy to see the programme through to a successful conclusion. NIIIS KA took over the research contracts, laid hands on Oshchepkov's research laboratory and assumed responsibility for the production contracts originally placed by the PVO, though the experimental test sector of the PVO was finally closed down. No trace of Engineer Oshchepkov was left. None can deny the disreputable and even odious tactics of NIIIS KA at this time, but the total effect on the radar programme was far from ruinous, allowing for the fact that NII–9 had been saved from premature extinction: there was still no co-ordinating committee on the British lines, but NIIIS KA made it its business to infuse new vigour into the Soviet programme and did contribute to cutting through the coils of separate research undertakings, ironically enough pushing Oshchepkov's earlier programme on to a successful conclusion.[24]

By 'court politics' Sir Charles Snow understands 'attempts to exert power through a man who possesses a concentration of power'.

In the early stages of the radar programme such 'court politics' were played through the person of Tukhachevskii, whose support was indispensable, but during and after 1937, once the military purge had bitten so deep, there could be only one meaning to court politics, and that meant influence with Stalin, or at best with his minions and cronies. With the latter the protagonists of the Soviet radar programme were by no means unsuccessful, as we shall shortly see, but this was almost entirely offset by the effect of the military purge *in toto*, which not only culled men but also drained professional competence from the Soviet officer corps. Put briefly, this post-purge command embraced in all too simplistic fashion the doctrine of the offensive as well as uncritically gulping down the notion of Soviet 'invincibility'. Interest in defensive systems and weaponry dwindled to vanishing point. The primacy of the offensive was everything and not only radar was ignored: Marshal Kulik, who had been prepared in 1937 to see NII–9 axed down, disparaged the machine pistol as a 'policeman's weapon' and demanded ever more rifles for staunch, attacking Soviet infantry. No amount of 'court politics' could change this climate of opinion, for it stemmed directly from the 'secret choices' made by none but Stalin himself. Courtiers there were, but their prime concern was keeping a whole skin, not challenging 'the boss'.

4. *The radar programme and military scientific judgement, 1938–1940*

It is to the credit of NIIIS KA and the Signals command that they did not waste the opportunity they had so viciously manufactured. Oshchepkov's work on a search radar now came under Engineer D. S. Stogov of the NIIIS: the result was a limited production order towards the end of 1938 for the 'Reven' set (General Lobanov printed the specifications issued to the radio factories for this continuous wave set). In the following year (1939) the Chief of the General Staff, Marshal B. M. Shaposhnikov, approved field trials, Engineer Stogov supervised these tests in the Kiev special military district, and in September 1939 the Defence Commissariat officially accepted the 'Reven' search radar—redesignated 'RUS–1'—into the military inventory. In all, some forty-five RUS–1 sets were produced, with a number of the early models going to the Soviet Far East and the Transcaucasus.[25]

Engineer A. I. Shestakov, also of NIIIS, scored an undeniable success with the impulse set developed by Ioffe's FTI, operating on a wavelength of 3·7 m using two G–165 valves and two 'Uda–Yagi' aerials. The first tests in 1937 showed that this equipment could detect an aircraft at a range of 50 km and at heights of up to 1,500 m: the improved model prepared by FTI in the summer of 1938 used Tsimablin's IG–8 valve in the generator and the G–3000 valve as modulator. Tested in August 1938, this newer model could detect aircraft at the same range of 50 km—all confirming the absolute superiority of the impulse method and the advantage of utilising the Doppler effect. Soviet factories refused to conclude a contract, however, for what was essentially a prototype, whereupon NIIIS and FTI divided further development work between them: this equipment, designated 'Redut', used IG–8 valves and developed a power of 50 kW. Tested again, 'Redut' demonstrated that its range might well attain 100 km and would serve satisfactorily as a long-range search radar for use with the PVO. (General Lobanov again reprints the technical specifications of 'Redut' and the provisional contract for a mobile version of this equipment.) 'Redut' finally went into service with the PVO after official acceptance on 26 July 1942, though the subsequent improved models were designated 'RUS–2'.[26]

Gun-laying radar, however, posed seemingly intractable problems. The metric wavelengths used in search radar for the air defence forces utilised techniques not wholly unfamiliar to the radio industry, but the 'centrimetric revolution'—Oshchepkov, like Mr Robert Watson-Watt, pressed for short-wave radar at an early stage—meant breaking wholly new ground in generating a powerful source of such waves. Both UFTI and NII–9 had laboured on this problem for the Main Artillery Administration and its search for an effective gun-laying radar. UFTI in 1937 produced one model operating on a wavelength of 60–65 cm: the test model used a magnetron generator with an impulse power of up to 1 kW and a wavelength of 68 cm. Designated 'Zenit', this equipment could pick up an SB bomber at a range of 3 km. 'Zenit' was superior to NII–9's 'Burya', but in spite of increasing its range up to 25–30 km the apparatus could deliver target co-ordinates only at intervals—seventeen seconds for azimuth, thirteen seconds for angular co-ordinates and thirty-eight seconds for all three co-ordinates (azimuth, angle of elevation and range). Thus it could not be used with the current automatic fire control system for AA guns (Puazo). Lengthy improvements to 'Zenit' resulted in a much modified piece of equipment, 'Rubin', though the outbreak of war in 1941 seriously disrupted this programme.[27]

It was apparently gun-laying radar which really concerned the Soviet command, and here the GAU put the pressure on. Prompted by the military commissar attached to the GAU, G. K. Savchenko, the influential chairman of the artillery committee of the GAU, Colonel-General V. D. Grendal', wrote to the director of NII–9, asking him to do everything possible to speed up the work on GL radar. In September 1938 a 'scientific technical conference' on radar convened, followed by an immediate appeal by the GAU to the Defence Committee (Komitet Oborony: a defence co-ordinating body at a high level) to instruct the Commissariat of Defence Industry and NII–9 to develop three experimental prototypes of gun-laying radar.[28] The result was three variations of the 'Burya' model, one ('B–2') with a cone-shaped polar diagram and two (designated 'B–3') with flat polar diagrams: it was the latter which proved on test to be the most reliable, with a high degree of accuracy in defining angular co-ordinates (1°) and a range of 17·5 km. This far outstripped sound location equipment, even if the B–2 and B–3 sets were far from ideal as GL radars: nevertheless, the detection range had doubled. The immediate task was to ensure that the B–2 and B–3 sets could effect reliable detection at heights in excess of 4,000 m.

NII–9 was also deeply involved in the 'centimetric revolution'. Both NII–9 and UFTI had pioneered work on new sources of power for centimetric waves, and N. D. Devyatkov in NII–9 had developed a series of magnetrons operating on 12–90 cm and with an output of 7–9 W to 15–20 kW. Working under Professor Bonch-Bruevich, two engineers, N. F. Alekseyev and E. D. Malyarov, had by 1938 produced multi-segment magnetrons for impulse and continuous wave generators.[29] It was also in 1938 that NII–9 took up the pulse method in all earnestness: Yu. N. Shein's laboratory developed an impulse magnetron operating on a wavelength of 25 cm and Devyatkov produced the valve amplifiers. A real breakthrough was provided by A. E. Suzant's research group, which developed a prototype impulse radio rangefinder—*radiodal'nomer*—code-named 'Strelets' which worked on a wavelength of 80 cm with a power of 16 kW: capable of locating an aircraft at a range of 20 km to an

accuracy of 160 m 'Strelets' obtained also an accuracy of some 3°
in an angle of elevation of the target.[30] The 'tactical technical
specifications' for GL radar laid down in 1939—together with a
major research plan for NII–9—envisaged a range of 30–35 km, an
accuracy of angular co-ordination in the order of 0.6° and 100 per
cent reliability in detecting the target. The end product of this
research, for which an initial contract was placed in 1940, was the
'Luna' anti-aircraft radar with an azimuth setting based on the
latest NII–9 model and an improved radio rangefinder based on
'Strelets' to establish the range, height and angle of elevation of the
target: the azimuth setting utilised the continuous wave regime
of the B–3 set, operating on a wavelength of 15–16 cm, with an
output of 20 W. The tests of the prototype in November 1940
demonstrated that 'Luna' could pick up a target at a range of
30 km, and the accuracy of angular co-ordination fell within the
margin of 0·6 per cent—all to the satisfaction of the GAU. In 1941
NII–9 and the radio factories proposed further refinements, but war
itself intervened: the factories were hastily evacuated to the east,
and the strange story of NII–9 finally ended when it was blown to
pieces by German guns in the fight for Leningrad in 1941.[31]

It was all the more surprising in view of these obvious successes
that the 'acoustics lobby' was able to mount a heavy attack on
'radio detection methods'. In the summer of 1940, at the instigation
of the staff of the Acoustics Department of the Dzerzhinskii Artillery
Academy, a conference was summoned to appraise the radar programme: the real object, however, was to take the GAU to task for
its support of the 'radio technical' research programme. Amidst a
distinguished gathering, including Professor N. D. Papaleksi and
Professor of Acoustics N. N. Andreyev, the head of the Acoustics
Department of the Academy, complained bitterly about the 'gloomy
picture' painted of the future of acoustics, and argued rather that
it was 'radio detection' which had no future. Both Papaleksi and
Andreyev ridiculed this idea as being scientifically quite baseless,
whereupon the conference seems to have abruptly terminated its
proceedings and closed its doors without adopting any kind of
resolution.[32]

Yet it was not the opposition but what General Lobanov calls 'the
neutrals'—*neutral'naya storona*—which formed the greatest threat
to the efficient use of radar. The scientific research institutes and
the higher technical centres of the Soviet air force and the Soviet

navy paid little or no heed to this new development: it is possible
that this was due to the close secrecy which surrounded the project,
to the aura of 'gadgetry' with which it was associated, to the
diminished professional and engineering competence within the
Soviet military—for example, it required herculean efforts to obtain
proper use of ordinary radio sets—and, finally if not fatally, to that
penchant for offensive weapons to fit the accepted dogma about the
offensive. From that point of view there is absolutely no comparison
with the British programme, which hinged on arguments about
air attack and national survival—correctly, as it proved: what
did as much as anything to save the Soviet Union after 1941 was the
T–34 medium tank, not radar. It is indicative also that the most
purposeful exploitation of the radar programme was its use as an
adjunct to another 'main' weapons system, artillery. Not until 1943
did radar acquire the status of 'State significance', when in June
1943 the Sovet po radiolokatsii pri GOKO (Radio Location/Radar
Council attached to the State Defence Committee) was set up,
thanks again largely to the 'radar lobby', which numbered General
Lobanov within its ranks.[33] The very technical and scientific complexity of the radar programme also militated against its full significance being recognised, save by a few officers in specialised posts
or with specialist knowledge: there was nothing comparable to
Tizard persuading 'the [Royal] Air Force to base their defensive
planning on the assumption that radar would work...', for there
was no Soviet Tizard and under no circumstances—whether offensive
or defensive—was the Soviet air force even remotely considered to
be a 'war-winning' weapon.

Notes

[1] C. P. Snow, *Science and Government*, Harvard University Press,
Cambridge, Mass., 1961; see also Sir Robert Watson-Watt, *Three Steps
to Victory*, London, 1958; Robert M. Page, *The Origins of Radar*, Garden
City, 1962; Ronald W. Clark, *The Rise of the Boffins*, London, 1962; Earl
of Birkenhead, *The Prof. in Two Worlds*, London, 1961; Ronald W.
Clark, *Tizard*, London, 1965; see also J. D. Scott, 'The development of
radar' in M. M. Postan *et al.*, *Design and Development of Weapons*,
Studies in Government and Industrial Organisation, HMSO, London,
1964, part III, ch. XV.

[2] Lieutenant-General (Reserve) M. M. Lobanov, 'K voprosu voznik-
noveniya i razvitiya otechestvennoi radiolokatsii' in *Voenno-istoricheskii
Zhurnal*, Voenizdat, Moscow, 1962, vol. 4, No. 8, pp. 13–29; on this earlier

study see my own paper in *Science Studies*, University of Edinburgh, 1972, II, pp. 241–63.

[3] M. M. Lobanov, *Iz proshlogo radiolokatsii. Kratkii ocherk*, Voenizdat, Moscow, 1969. In spite of being subtitled 'A short outline' (*Kratkii ocherk*), this is an extensive treatment of the subject, complete with photographs of early Soviet equipment and technical/operating specifications where relevant. In addition, this volume also goes into some detail on war-time (post-1941) developments, though the small edition by Soviet standards—6,500 copies—suggests that this is a specialised work intended only for libraries, research institutes and research workers.

[4] See Lobanov, *Iz proshlogo radiolokatsii*, ch. 1, pp. 5–14, under 'Akusticheskie sredstva obnaruzheniya samoletov' ('Acoustic detection of aircraft'); on the Prozhzvuk system and its details see pp. 12–14. (To distinguish General Lobanov's earlier article and this later monograph, the latter will be cited as 'Lobanov monograph, *I.P.R.*', with the requisite page reference.)

[5] See account in Derek Wood with Derek Dempster, *The Narrow Margin: the Battle of Britain and the Rise of Air Power, 1939–40*, 1969 edition, London, Arrow Books, p. 55.

[6] Lobanov monograph, *I.P.R.*, pp. 14–20: see p. 16 for photograph of 'heat detector' (*teploobnaruzhitel*) from adapted searchlight equipment.

[7] *Ibid.*, pp. 25–37, for details of contracts (with photostat reproductions) and of technical specifications of equipment.

[8] For Oshchepkov's own account of these meetings and exchanges see his autobiography, P. K. Oshchepkov, *Zhizn' mechta*, Zapiski inzhenera-izobretatelyi, konstruktora i uchennogogo, Moscow, first edition, 1965, and second edition, 1967, here second edition, pp. 65–6.

[9] Oshchepkov, *op. cit.*, pp. 57–8.

[10] Oshchepkov, *op. cit.*, pp. 71–2, for documentation: this comprised the record of the meeting, *Protokol soveshchaniya u Akademika A. F. Ioffe ot 16.1.1934 g.*

[11] Oshchepkov, *op. cit.*, pp. 56–7, quoting from the original paper entitled 'Sovremennye problemy razvitiya tekhniki protivovozdushnoi oborony', published in two parts.

[12] See Scott, 'The development of radar', pp. 373–5.

[13] Lobanov monograph, *I.P.R.*, pp. 93–6: the operating specifications are set out on p. 94. Oshchepkov, *op. cit.*, prints the early test reports on 'Rapid'.

[14] On Oshchepkov's plans for his detection system—Elektrovizor—see Lobanov monograph, *I.P.R.*, pp. 97–101 (which also includes details of two other experimental devices, 'Vega' and 'Konus'): see a comparable discussion of similar problems in Scott, *loc. cit.*, pp. 374–6 and 381–2 (under 'Aiding the guns').

[15] Lobanov monograph, *I.P.R.*, pp. 41–2.

[16] *Ibid.*, pp. 45–55 for technical details: there is a photograph of the 'Burya' apparatus supplied on p. 44.

[17] *Ibid.*, pp. 45–6.

[18] *Ibid.*, pp. 106–7.

[19] This is mentioned specifically in General Lobanov's article in *Voenno-istoricheskii Zhurnal, loc. cit.,* p. 28, though it is given less prominence in his monograph: at the same time, the monograph *I.P.R.,* p. 108, briefly mentions another crisis at the end of 1936, when it was clear that the 'experimental and test sector' of the PVO could carry out all its tasks and was abruptly subordinated to the technical administration of the Red Army.

[20] Lobanov monograph, *I.P.R.,* pp. 47–8.

[21] General Lobanov's article in *Voenno-istoricheskii Zhurnal* mentions this arrest in stark terms (p. 28), but again his monograph refers only to Oshchepkov's removal from his directing post early in 1937.

[22] Lobanov article, *Voenno-istoricheskii Zhurnal, loc. cit.,* p. 28.

[23] The best guide through a voluminous Soviet literature on this theme is Seweryn Bialer (ed.), *Stalin and his Generals,* New York, Pegasus, 1969, which consists of translations from Soviet military memoirs, with careful and extensive notation supplied by Dr Bialer.

[24] This change was already ushered in by the reorganisation begun at the end of 1936: the Red Army technical administration, under Divisional Engineer S. V. Bordovskii, was nominally in charge of the radar programme in 1937, but Oshchepkov's old experimental unit was rapidly transformed into the Sixth Department of the NIIS, thus placing it at the heart of the programme.

[25] Lobanov monograph, *I.P.R.,* pp. 111–14; see p. 113 for photograph of RUS–1 installation and equipment.

[26] *Ibid.,* pp. 115–25, for technical details and test results.

[27] *Ibid.,* pp. 72–82, for details of Zenit and Rubin.

[28] *Ibid.,* pp. 57–62; photographs of B–2 and B–3 are supplied on p. 58 and p. 60 respectively.

[29] *Ibid.,* p. 52.

[30] *Ibid.,* pp. 62–4, for technical details.

[31] *Ibid.,* pp. 65–7.

[32] Lobanov article, *Voenno-istoricheskii Zhurnal, loc. cit.,* pp. 28–9.

[33] Lobanov monograph, *I.P.R.,* pp. 166–78.

Max Gluckman

7

Spouse, child, parent or sibling—who should be saved? The disputed passage in Sophocles' *Antigone*

My interests in studying African societies, both in their traditional forms and in how they have changed since they were brought into the political and economic field of Europe, were mainly in politics and law. They coincided largely with Bill Mackenzie's interests, particularly after he started research in Tanganyika and Kenya. I benefited greatly, as did many of my social anthropological colleagues and pupils, from discussions with him, both privately and in seminars in our respective departments, as well as from the generosity with which he gave his time to commenting on our manuscripts. Our debt to him is manifest in our published work. But I was also often most encouraged by the way in which, out of his wide knowledge in many other fields, he would suggest that an anthropological finding or analysis might be used to throw light on some quite different problem or puzzle. In my 1952 Frazer lecture on 'Rituals of rebellion in south-east Africa' (published 1954) I tried to show how their setting in particular forms of socio-political organisation might explain forms of ritual behaviour in which, for example, subjects openly expressed their resentment against the authority of their leaders, and princes openly demonstrated that they were potential aggressors against and assassins of the king. These statements of societal strife and conflict were not uncontrolled out-bursts but were, on the contrary, compelled by the ritual in order to achieve fertility, victory, and other blessings for the political groups involved. When Mackenzie read my lecture in draft he urged me (on the grounds that Sir James Frazer was a classicist who started his great work on classical rituals) to insert a reference to what Mackenzie saw as a parallel argument: Aristotle's thesis that tragedy purges through the emotions of pity and terror which it excites in its audience. Though I had at one stage in my career as a student studied Aristotle on tragedy, I must admit that it had not occurred to me that I was dealing with the same problem; and for lack of time, I inserted only a brief reference. Unhappily for my argument, I did not expand on my borrowed scholarship when the lecture was published. In the result, because I used Aristotle's word 'catharsis', many of my readers (see Gluckman 1963, pp. 24 f.) were led to fancy that I was trying, and failing, to make a psychological analysis, despite my immediate disclaimer, after the citation, that I was not competent to do so, but was essaying a sociological–anthropological analysis.

What I failed to do at the time, because it would have involved a searching look at Greek tragedy and I was otherwise engaged, was to develop the point that just as African 'rituals of rebellion' (as I termed them) were 'religious', so were presentations of Greek tragedies, and hence the comparison might be furthered by someone with the appropriate scholarship.

I start with this small piece of history, which shows how Mackenzie could open our eyes to wider views, because in this tributary essay to him I take up a problem he set me in a letter he wrote after reading another of my public lectures—for he was wont to take the extra trouble to set his views down on paper, and not merely to make his points over lunch. At the time when I was invited to contribute to this *Festschrift* I was sorting my papers, and I came again on his letter. My lecture, delivered shortly after I arrived in Manchester to the Manchester Literary and Philosophical Society, was on 'Social beliefs and individual thinking in primitive society' (Gluckman, 1950a). I discussed the manner in which patterns of 'love' between spouses and among kinsfolk were determined by the culture of a society, and in particular forms of social organisation influenced the behaviour of individuals. He commented on a passage in which I wrote that the individual family in tribal societies was less important, compared with groups of kinsfolk, than in our society:

A man's strongest attachments are those to his blood-kin reckoned to many degrees, and all marriages tend to be marriages of state with other groups of blood-kin. Therefore Lozi [of Zambia] say: 'Do not confide in your wife, confide in your sister. Tomorrow she may be someone else's wife; your sister is always your sister.' One observer [Culwick, 1943, p. 36] has even said in summary on Africa, 'a man sleeps with his wife, loves his sister, and seeks companionship with other men'. [Gluckman, 1950a, p. 3.]

Mackenzie's comment on this passage was: 'Have you ever come on this strange textual crux in Sophocles (*Antigone*, line 904—and see Jebb's appendix); and a famous passage in Herodotus, book III? What worries the scholars is that what seems a strange piece of pedantic sophistry is struck into the middle of a play the theme of which is (in most modern terms) eternal law versus State law. But perhaps the scholars are just wrong about Greek psychology—or anthropology?' At the time, I read the passages, but had no chance to write about them, though the passage which troubled scholars, according to Jebb, in *Antigone* seemed to me most appropriate in so far as I could react in the same way that the African people I had studied intensively might have reacted to it. I have just re-read the play and Herodotus (right through, compulsively, not book III alone), and in taking up this theme I am thanking Mackenzie for the deep pleasure his letter led me to, yet again.

I hope that Mackenzie will not mind my citing verbatim from a handwritten letter, which was written twenty-three years ago, and in which he presumably did not ponder carefully over his wording. He knew too that Jebb's edition of *Antigone* was first published in 1888, when the passage was a centre of lively debate. I have consulted Professor G. B. Kerferd, our Hulme Professor of Greek. He drew my attention to a citation from, and brief discussion of, the passage by Aristotle in his treatise on *The 'art' of rhetoric* (about 335–330 B.C.), where though Aristotle changes one word (see Cope translation, 1877, p. 194), he quotes thus: '... of this Sophocles gives an example where his Antigone says that she cared more for her brother than for husband or children ...' (Freese translation, 1947, pp. 448–9). Aristotle thus clearly thought the passage was written by Sophocles himself. Though this treatise was written probably between 335 and 330 B.C., and Sophocles died in 406 B.C., Aristotle was born in 384 B.C., and may well have become acquainted with the passage within some forty-five years after Sophocles' death. Towards the end of this essay I shall examine Aristotle's discussion in detail, but I must note here that he clearly considered Antigone's reasoning would be 'incredible' to most people; and this runs against at least a large part of my argument.

Furthermore, Professor Kerferd says that modern opinion about this passage has changed to some extent since Jebb wrote, and that its authenticity would now be accepted without difficulty by many scholars,[1] perhaps partly because Greek tragedies are now seen as essentially dramatic confrontations between the central characters rather than as philosophical debates. Nevertheless, there should still be value in my discussing the problem as seen by Jebb and his contemporaries, and as set me by Mackenzie. An anthropologist's view from an African background may bring evidence about, and set the social context for, how people reacted in personal confrontations, when faced with conflicts of duty, in societies organised in extended groups of kin, as ancient Greece probably was. Thus an African view may deepen our understanding of Antigone's dilemma. That is, while my superficial knowledge of Greek culture and thought, and hence of Greek 'psychology and anthropology' (Mackenzie), fills me with trepidation, I can suggest how the troublesome passage might appear to a traditional African audience at a similar tragic, ritual performance of an Antigone condemned to miserable death for burying her last surviving brother in defiance of a royal edict that he be not buried. If my analysis, using the Greek examples as though they were African, is any help towards solving the classical controversy, as Mackenzie hoped, perhaps some classical scholar could take it up. But I must first put the problem to readers who (like myself before being inspired by Mackenzie) do not know Herodotus' *Histories* and Sophocles' tragedy, and the details of the controversy over the passage in *Antigone*.

I begin with the earlier, Herodotus (book III, 119). Darius was one of seven conspirators who successfully revolted against the Magus family, which had in effect seized the Persian throne while King Cambyses was in Egypt, by one of them pretending to be the king's elder brother (slaughtered at Cambyses' order). After Cambyses' death the conspirators discovered the imposture and killed the Magus. They debated whether to set up a democratic, oligarchical or monarchical government—a debate which, as reported by Herodotus, raises many of the central controversies in modern social science. Darius persuaded the others that a monarchy was best, and, according to Herodotus, they decided to select the king from among themselves, by means of an 'oracle'—whose horse should neigh first after the sun was up. Darius ensured by trickery that he would win. But before the test, from which the initiator of the conspiracy withdrew on condition that he and his descendants would not be forced to submit to the king's rule, though they would obey the law, the conspirators further agreed that any of the seven should be allowed 'to enter the palace unannounced, except when the king was in bed with a woman'. A short time afterwards one of them, Intaphrenes, wished to enter the palace to transact business with Darius. He claimed his right to enter unannounced; but he was stopped by the king's chamberlain and the sentry at the gate, who told him that Darius had a woman with him. Thinking this was a trumped-up excuse, Intaphrenes 'drew his scimitar and cut off their ears and noses, strung them on the horse's bridle, tied the bridle round their necks, and sent them packing. The poor fellows showed themselves to Darius and explained the reason for their plight, which at once suggested to the king the alarming possibility of a fresh conspiracy.' He sent for each of the conspirators in turn, and found that none of them approved of what Intaphrenes had done. He was satisfied that Intaphrenes had acted on his own initiative, so he had Intaphrenes arrested, together with his children and all his near relations, on the strong suspicion that

he and his family were about to raise a revolt. All the prisoners were then chained, as condemned criminals. After his arrest, Intaphrenes' wife came to the palace and began to weep and lament outside the door, and continued so long to do so that Darius, moved to pity by her incessant tears, sent someone to speak to her. 'Lady', the message ran, 'the king is willing to spare the life of one member of your family—choose which of the prisoners you wish to save.' Having thought this offer over, the woman answered that, if the king granted the life of one of her family, she would choose her brother. The answer surprised Darius, and he sent again and asked why it was that she rejected her husband and children, and preferred to save her brother, who was neither so near to her as her children, nor so dear as her husband. 'My lord,' she replied, 'God willing, I may get another husband, and other children when these are gone. But as my father and mother are both dead, I can never possibly have another brother. That was the reason for what I said.' Darius appreciated the lady's good sense, and, to mark his pleasure, granted her not only the life she asked, but also that of her eldest son. The rest of the family were all put to death.[2]

One of my intensive studies of an African people was made among the Lozi (Barotse) nation of what is now Zambia. To some extent, I concentrated on a study of trials in court; and one day when there were no cases to be heard at the northern tribal capital (see Gluckman, 1955a), one of the clerks asked the judges a riddle. This set them off on further riddles, and then on posing social dilemmas involving difficult choices. One dilemma, which I later found to be standard among the Lozi, was: 'if you saw your mother, your sister, your wife, and your child drowning, and you could save only one, whom would you save?' Those present, both judges and onlookers in the court, agreed that it was a terrible choice to face. They discussed how a man must feel 'in his heart' about each of the women, and how deeply a man was attached to his children. Clearly, they considered that it was one of those moral problems which, as Aristotle said, no individual can solve. They conned a man's obligations to his mother, who gave birth to him and nurtured and comforted him; the strength of his bonds with his sister, to whom also he might be obliged for nurturance and comfort in childhood and for advice and support in adulthood; his debt to his wife, who gave him pleasure at night, helped produce his food, provided his domestic comforts and gave him children—this despite the fact that the Lozi have a very high rate of divorce (see Gluckman, 1950b). Finally, they dwelt on the delight they got from a child, and how they looked to a child to care for them in old age. The man who proposed the problem insisted that a choice be made; and almost all of them in the end said they would save their sisters. Dear as a mother was, she was likely to die before too long, in the course of life; but the sister might live as long as, or longer than, oneself. Dear and valuable as a wife might be, one might divorce, or be divorced by, her: and as I have already noted, the divorce rate among the Lozi is high. One could always marry another wife: one could not replace a sister. And dearly as one loved a child, one could hope, if God were agreeable, to have another child. The sister was seen as unique among women; and when I asked about a brother, they said that they would save a sister before a brother, a brother before a wife, a child before a brother.

I put the problem that evening, substituting husband for wife and brother for sister, to the few women in our camp—wives of my servants and attendants. Their choice, made painfully, was sibling, child, parent, spouse, for much the same reasons as the men's.[3]

I note, with reference to my later argument, that the Lozi do not emphasise descent in one line (as did Zulu and probably Greek and Persians—see below): Lozi groupings of kindred in villages were drawn from all lines.

I realise now, of course, that I should have posed the problem of this critical choice among relatives to many more Lozi, in a line of research that has developed since I worked among the Lozi in the 1940s. But thirty men participated in the discussion, and the drift of choice among them was in itself illuminating. I repeat, they all saw the choice involved as agonising, and only made it when pressed to do so. It is clear from Herodotus' story that the choice of Intaphrenes' wife was also very difficult: she thought the offer over, according to the story he was told, before making her decision. Nor was it the obvious choice: her answer 'surprised Darius', who thought she would choose her husband or a child. Of course, with the spouse there is always the possibility that he or she is disliked or even hated, and his or her death may be regarded as liberation which sets one free to find another partner, though this is not relevant for Lozi and Zulu *men*, who may be polygynous and can in effect divorce a wife at will. But the choice of a woman or brother before child is striking; and despite his surprise and astonishment, Darius appreciated 'the good sense' of the Persian lady's reasoning. This at least implies that this form of reasoning would seem reasonable to Persians telling the story to Herodotus, and possibly to Herodotus when he reported the story.

I wonder what answer would be given by modern European or American men and women if they were set this cruel problem. We know that such problems, perhaps not of saving from death but certainly of choice between obligations to relatives, are a constant theme of novels and plays (one has only to think of Romeo and Juliet or of Cordelia and Desdemona). But increasingly, I think, the cultural pattern of ideals, as these references show, has emphasised the bond to beloved or spouse, rather than to parents and sibling.[4] This is shown in a divorce case in Britain, reported in the press some years ago, where a brother and sister married a sister and brother respectively. One pair fell out and the wife sued for divorce. Her brother then initiated divorce proceedings against his wife, and persisted in his demand for a divorce even after the first pair were reconciled. When the judge remonstrated with him that his sister had made things up with her husband, he said, 'That's because, my lord, you think a wife is more important than a sister, when a sister is more important than a wife.' Most people today are likely to feel that that is not a correct assessment of ideals, even if the judge was merely emphasising that it was silly to continue a quarrel arising out of a quarrel now settled. But clearly this kind of problem in actual behaviour continues to beset many people. I had heard that there has been research by sociologists on the kind of choice posed by Herodotus, but when I consulted some of my sociological colleagues the research they put me on to was not on all fours: it was mostly exercises in game theory. I scrutinised the essays, and the reviews, in a few standard sociological journals, back to 1900, and came on nothing that seemed relevant.

I consider that it was relatively easy for the Lozi to put the spouse last, since, as stated twice above, their rate of divorce and of remarriage is high. In the lecture on which Mackenzie was commenting I was stressing that the sentiments of love, of intense emotional mutual involvement, and of close companionship, which are now, according to some of our ideals, appropriate to the marital relationship, are part of our culture, and the cultural development of these sentiments has been traced. But in fact later research on British families has shown that there is considerable variation in the actual patterns of marital activities and sentiments; and that these variations can be related to the pattern of the network of social relationships that contain each family; and that the shape of this network is related ultimately to stability of residence or mobility, both geographical and in social status. This was first clearly demonstrated by Bott in a path-breaking book on *Family and Social Network* (1957). She has considered later research on the problem, largely inspired by her book, in an additional initial chapter to the second edition (1971).[5] There is also more variation in the patterns of marital relationships in African society, within a standard difference from many of our modern families, than we once thought (see, for example, Colson, 1958). It is certain too that there are variations around the central pattern in any one society—variations which, I believe, with adequate research could be related to the factors selected by Bott as significant in her study of British families. Nevertheless, the conception of what we might call 'romantic love' is not well developed in tribal culture. This is clearly brought out in an illuminating story by Richards, in her study of *Bemba Marriage and Modern Economic Conditions* (1940, p. 22, note):

I [Richards] once amazed a group of elderly Bemba [of what is now Zambia] by telling them an English folk-tale about the difficulties experienced by a Prince in winning the hand of his bride—glassy mountains, chasms, dragons, giants and the like. An old chief present was genuinely astonished. 'Why not take another girl?' he said.

The same sentiment was expressed by some old Fingo in South Africa when they complained to the members of the Cape of Good Hope government's Commission on Native Law and Custom (1883: minutes of evidence, p. 303, q. 5, 5479–80) about the increasing number of illegitimate births and runaway marriages: 'The trouble

arises through a thing called love. We do not comprehend this at
all ... This thing called love has been introduced.' In short, the
cultural pattern of sexual mating and marital life in traditional
Africa differed radically from that which cries out to us from our
fairy-tales and novels and plays, and from advertisements—the idea
that each of us has somewhere an ideal mate. This is not to deny that
African men and women are mutually attracted to one another in
pairs, who, so to speak, fall in love with each other. But the
standardised expected sentiments do differ, though they are changing—as those old Fingo complained as far back as the 1880s.
Richards reported from the matrilineal Bemba, among whom the
rate of divorce was also high (*loc. cit.*), and I observed among the
Lozi, as others have elsewhere in Africa, that when a husband, in
despite of the cultural pattern, is too attached to his wife, is extrava-
gantly jealous of her, or spends too much time with her, his fellows
shake their heads and fear she has seduced him from his senses with
strong magic (see, for example, Kuper on Swazi, 1970, p. 44).
As I have cited from Culwick, a man sleeps with his wife, loves his
sister, and seeks companionship with other men, mainly his kinsmen.

In these terms, the fact that Intaphrenes' wife did not choose to
succour him before her brother makes sense to me, if ancient Greek
society (as Fustel de Coulanges, 1884, argued) and ancient Persian
society were organised in extended groups of kin, and each marital
pair tended to be surrounded by a network of close kin, allegiance
to whom tended to pull the spouses apart (see Bott, 1957, 1971;
Gluckman, 1955b, chapter III). Her choice of brother before child
has a compelling logic if she were young enough to hope to bear
more children; but it is perhaps worth considering whether, if
ancient Persian society, like ancient Greek society in at least
historical times, was organised in terms of agnatic (patrilineal)
lineages, a woman's child belonged to her husband's agnatic lineage,
and not to her natal lineage. This might have affected maternal sentiments through a childhood idoctrination in loyalty to the natal
agnatic lineage. But individual reaction must have been significant.

Here the viewpoints of a man and a woman might differ radically.
In a society of agnatic lineages such as ancient Greek and Persian
societies appear to have been, a woman expects that her life will be
devoted to producing and rearing children for her husband's lineage
and not for her own. I studied such a society in the Zulu of South
Africa, and though my observations on women's sentiments and

attitudes were restricted by Zulu suspicion and by the general South African colour bar, I formed the opinion that though girls are liable to pass through a severe trauma before they enter on marriage (see Bryant, 1911, p. 36; Gluckman, 1955a, chap. v; Lee, 1950, 1962), thereafter they sink their allegiances into the husband's lineage. I have suggested, following others, that in societies with strong agnatic lineages or strong affiliations to the father for jural purposes the rate of divorce tends to be low, and despite the fact that there are exceptions to this rule, I consider that anthropological research supports the hypothesis.[6] My own impression is that among the Zulu there was a much greater strength of relationship, based on probable common enduring interests, because divorce was very rare, than among the Lozi, with their high rate of divorce and hence the high possibility that their spouses would divorce: a fact vouched for by genealogies I collected and by contemporary records—though these may have been biased, since they were written by missionaries who stressed the immorality of the Lozi in order to justify further their evangelical mission. This was true also of the Bemba studied by Richards. Again, I report from the Lozi, as Richards did for the Bemba (1939), that there were many instances of middle-aged and elderly couples whose marriages had survived many years and who were close companions, as well as many instances of deep mutual affection both among them and in younger couples (see also Schapera, 1940). But one would expect that, in a society where marriage is for life, the ties between spouses would be stronger— though maybe more resented by some women, since men could escape, if they could afford it, into polygamy—than in societies where many marriages were unstable. For example, among some African matrilineal societies—but not the Bemba—most men move to their wives' villages after marriage, and the divorce rate tends to be very high: the men retain their homes in their natal villages, while their children grow up, and inherit and succeed, in the wives' (the children's mothers') villages. And in some matrilineal societies, even when a wife goes to her husband's home during her married life, and her children grow up there, when her sons become adult they move to her brother's (their maternal uncle's) village; and after her menopause the woman may leave her husband and follow them there, because she prefers to live with her brother and her sons in her old age, rather than with her aged husband (e.g. Turner, 1957; E. Goody, 1962).

There are many variations in the pattern; what I am trying to emphasise is that it is highly ethnocentric to approach the mores, and the stories and tragedies, and the moral arguments, of another society from the viewpoint of our own. I believe that members of most African societies, if told of the choice that Darius inflicted on Intaphrenes' wife, would have considered him to be a cruel tyrant for compelling her thus; but they might, like him, have considered her decision to be 'good sense', since she had to make some choice.

If ancient Persian and Greek societies were organised in extended groups of kin, related agnatically, as does seem probable, then we can narrow our comparison, and bring another set of social factors into consideration. While the theory of a society thus organised, as among Zulu and Tswana, emphasises that a man should not neglect looking after his agnatic kin in heaping goods on his wife, and that if he does the latter she may have bewitched him, there are socio-cultural goals, as well as developing sentiments of affection and attachment, which moved him in that direction. As a member of an agnatic group, a man's individuality is to a large extent submerged in his unity and indentification with his fellow agnates, his brothers and cousins in his generation, his father and uncles in the senior generation, and so forth. But he matures as an individual, and he himself may become the point of proliferation of a new section of the agnatic group, and ultimately the possible founder of a new, independent agnatic group, through his sons, born to him by his wife. Hence on top of the attachment to his wife which develops from their sexual relationship, and from her work for and care of him, and from her giving him much-desired children (as stated by the Lozi answering the problem), he depends on her if he is to fulfil his legitimate ambitions to become a fully mature adult, an independent man, and a procreator of sons whose own descendants may immortalise him socially through the formation of an agnatic group. I have argued elsewhere, with increasing strength in the light of new research Gluckman, 1955b, chapter v; 1965; 1972b), that in these societies an insoluble social conflict therefore focuses on a wife: her duty to the group of agnates, one of whose members she marries, is to produce sons to strengthen the group and ensure its powerful continuity. She is severely reprobated if she fails in this duty because she is barren, and even if she bears only girls and no boys. But in the very course of fulfilling her duty by bearing sons she produces competitors for the limited positions of authority and the material resources of the group, males who will compete with their fellow agnates. In addition, as stated, she may give rise, within the agnatic group, to a branch which will strive for independence. I have suggested further that this deep conflict, between demanded duty and the effects of fulfilling that duty, underlies the many more obvious reasons why there is serious strife in these societies between the mother-in-law, who represents the unity of a set of brothers, and the daughter-in-law, each of whom represents the potential independence, and competitiveness against his brothers, of each of the mother-in-law's sons. If a man has more than one wife, each wife strives for the interests of her own son(s) as against the interests of the sons of her co-wives, as well as for the favours of their husband to her personally. The wife who is too fertile may be suspected by her fellow wives of witchcraft, and the barren wife is feared lest she envy the fertile and bewitch them or their children.

Out of these deep conflicts I consider that we can also explain social beliefs which ascribe to women an inherent evil, manifested in many ways, such as attracting to their sexual appetites familiars who then demand the lives of their husband's kin. These beliefs cloak the fundamental conflict that resides in the society itself, since an agnatic lineage depends on the wives who marry into it to produce the male offspring who will weaken the group at the same time as they strengthen it (Gluckman, 1955, 1965, 1972b, *loc. cit.*). And in this situation, where a man comes to cherish his wife in despite of his agnatic allegiances, because she is the creator of his independence and his own full maturity, he may be torn by the conflict of his allegiances. If he too obviously loves his wife, she may be suspected of bewitching him (in our own phrase for a woman who makes a man 'lose his senses'): it is a sign of danger, as well as an indecency (see, for example, Kuper, 1970, p. 44).

It is little wonder, then, that Zulu girls, who are reared with marriage and children as their aim in life and their highest duties, nevertheless fear the approach of marriageable age, and are subject at that time to what seem to be forms of cultural hysteria, when they wander about, crying uncontrollably. These attacks are ascribed to the love magic which their would-be suitors, particularly if disappointed, employ to win them (Bryant, 1905, p. 220 (iHabiya); Lee, 1950). In sharp contrast stands the earlier relationship with the brother, which up to late adolescence seemed to me to be remarkably free and easy, even though in traditional times, and still when I was in Zululand in 1936–38, a girl's marriage might be required to bring in the cattle with which her brother could procure a bride (see Gluckman, 1955b, chap. v). In the 1930s, this conflict had eased, since many young men earned the cattle to marry by working in white enterprises. But, as I say, I observed how much easier were the relationships of Zulu girls with their brothers than they were with those in their married homes; and this ease of relationships persisted after the girl had married and settled in with her husband's family. She could come to her brother's home and make demands on him, and on his children, to help her (see, for example, Kuper, 1970, p. 53).

In this situation it is not surprising to find that in many respects it is women who have a deeper and more abiding interest in maintaining kinship morality and adherence to the demands of duty to kin than have men: for women are the meeting-points of diverse links of kinship and marital alliance (for a fine discussion of this point in an agnatically organised society see Peters, 1966, on the Bedouin of Cyrenaica). But they are also, as I have stressed, the meeting points of deep conflicts which lie outside personal relationships, in the structure of society itself. I would like to illustrate this from a tragic drama, such as *Antigone* was. I do so from the play written by Professor Hilda Kuper about Swazi, neighbours of the Zulu, called *A witch in my heart* (1970). It brings out the point clearly and it is authentic in depicting Swazi life and thought and drama. Having worked among the Zulu congeners of the Swazi, I myself can vouch for that; but more significantly, after it had been broadcast in South Africa in English it was not only dramatised in a Zulu translation (*Inhliziyo ngumthakathi*, 1962) but has also been used in this Zulu version in Swazi schools. I give only the main plot, not the play's dramatic quality.

The most beloved of the three wives of a young man is barren. Her co-wives, two sisters, envy her their husband's favour, and fear the favourite's envy and malice because one has had children and the other is pregnant, while she, despite the spending of many cattle on doctors, is sterile. Envy, of course, is one of the begetters of witchcraft. Her envy has been read into a remark the elder sister recounts to her younger sister co-wife: '... never will I forget the day my own child lay ill and that one found me weeping and said, "Why do you weep? You can bear others" ' (shades of Intaphrenes' wife and Antigone!). The country is afflicted with drought, and the homestead, ruled by the husband's father and father's elder brother, is short of food. The husband goes to seek work and money in Johannesburg, leaving his youngest wife, the younger of the two sisters married to him, pregnant, hopefully with a son, as the son of her elder sister had died, leaving only a daughter. After he has gone, the youngest wife gives birth to a still-born son. The husband's father and uncle go to a diviner, who finds that the favourite wife is a witch who killed the baby. The husband's father says he cannot kill her because of the foolish law of the white men, a law which protects witches, and sends her home. The husband learns of the child's death by letter, while he is drinking with friends, but before he can react is caught in a police raid and gaoled. When he comes home, and his banished favourite wife comes to welcome him, he learns that she has been driven out as a witch. His father attempts to beat her, and is restrained by his son, who then, because she has made him raise his hand against his father, refuses the favourite's plea that he take her back (*cf.* Haemon's suicide after he attacks his father in *Antigone*). But he finds his home dark now, and decides to go back to work in Johannesburg. The play takes its title from the penultimate line. The banished wife, left alone with her mother-in-law, appeals finally to her: 'Mother, pity me, I swear by my father I used no witchcraft. Can you not help me?'

Her mother-in-law: 'My child, I pity you, but for you there is no help.'

The wife (passionately [but seemingly aware of how she envied the other women their children]): 'The Diviner was right. I am a witch! In my heart.' She leaves, and the older woman, left alone, says, 'My child, that is the case with every woman.'

In this play the obverse of competition among women who have children in the interests of their children is shown: the barren wife, who may be cast away because she has failed in her duty (unless her husband is given a younger kinswoman of hers to bear children for her—another theme of the play), is seen not only as threatening her fruitful fellow wife and her children, but as threatening the whole agnatic lineage. The husband, deeply in love with her, nevertheless, in fear of witchcraft and shocked because she made him raise his hand against his father, drives her away. His father represents the agnatic lineage and interest in its future growth, beyond individual loves. The son yields to him, but leaves the homestead, now a sad place for him, to earn money in the town. Haemon in the end killed himself; the Swazi husband, given the modern situation, could go off to work for whites, as he could not have done in the past. Whatever the formal patterning of relationships (*cf.* Creon, who says of Haemon's losing Antigone, 'Is she the only woman he can bed with?' as Kitto translates; 'Nay, there are other fields for him to plough,' as Jebb does), personal bonds of affection and love may shatter the standardised framework of kinship morality, so that the strongly legitimated tie to wife, which should be weaker than the tie to kin, proves the stronger.

With this background summary of African, and particularly Zulu-Swazi, relationships among kinsfolk and spouses, I turn to the controversy posed by the passage, lines 904–20, in *Antigone*. It follows on Antigone's statement, when she is sentenced to be incarcerated in the cave, that she was impelled by the sacred duty, established by the gods, to perform the last rites for dead kin, instanced by her statement to the shades of her parents: 'when ye died, with mine own hands I washed and dressed you, and poured drink-offerings at your graves; and now [my brother] Polyneices, 'tis for tending thy corpse that I win such recompense as this'.[7]

The passage, which Jebb printed in square brackets, since it was regarded as such a fall in the tragic level of the play that it was thought to have been inserted after Sophocles' death[8] by his son, or by the actors, runs thus:

And yet I honoured thee, as the wise will deem, rightly. Never, had I been a mother of children, or if a husband had been mouldering in death, would I have taken this task upon me in the city's despite [using Ismene's phrase in the opening scene]. What law, ye ask, is my warrant for that word? The husband lost, another might have been found, and child from another, to replace the first-born, but, father and mother hidden in Hades, no brother's life could ever bloom for me again. Such was the law whereby I held thee first in honour; but Creon deemed me guilty of error therein, and of outrage, ah brother mine! And now he leads me thus, a captive in his hands; no bridal bed, no bridal song hath been mine, no joy of marriage, no portion in the nurture of children; but thus forlorn of friends, unhappy one, I go living to the vaults of death.

Jebb argued that, after Antigone has recounted how she performed her dutiful last rites for her parents, this passage can be excised without loss, and indeed with gain, by proceeding to line 921:

And what law of heaven have I transgressed? Why, hapless one, should I look to the gods any more—what ally should I invoke—when by piety I have earned the name of impious? Nay, then, if these things are pleasing to the gods, when I have suffered my doom, I shall come to know my sin; but if the sin is with my judges, I could wish them no fuller measure of evil than they, on their part, mete wrongfully to me.

Since I do not read Greek, I cannot say by my own judgement whether or not the original is not 'good', as Jebb judged it not to be. It may in the original lack the touch of the master. In English, perhaps because I am steeped to some extent in African ways of thinking and feeling, I find it moving. And of course, whether it was written by Sophocles himself, or inserted by his son or the actors when it was performed,[8] it was undoubtedly written by a Greek or Greeks of the period, so that it is likely to have come from some habit of Greek thought, even if not a widely dispersed one. Jebb points out that when Antigone describes how Polyneices was her last surviving brother (her parents and her other brother, Eteocles, being dead), and how hence he was a unique relative, she uses this as the basis of her argument why she owed him duties she might not have paid to her husband (had she had one) or her child (had she had one), her words 'are a tolerably close metrical version—and a very poor one, too—of the reason given by the wife of Intaphrenes for saving her brother rather than her husband or one of her children' (at his p. 260). Yet some Greek(s) drew on Herodotus, so it must have seemed to him (them) a credible sentiment, which would be appreciated by the audience.

Jebb opened (his p. 259) criticism of the disputed passage thus:

The first impression which the passage tends to produce is well described in the simple and direct words of Goethe, as reported by Eckermann. 'In the course of the piece, the heroine has given the most admirable reasons for her conduct, and has shown the noble courage of a stainless soul; but now, at the end, she puts forward a motive which is quite unworthy of her, ("ganz schlecht,") and which almost borders on the comic.' And then Goethe expresses the hope that scholars will prove the passage to be spurious.

Among those who think it is genuine, few, perhaps, would say that it is good. A large majority would allow that, at the best, it requires some apology. The question comes to this:—Can the faults of the passage, as they appear to a modern taste, be excused by a peculiarity in ancient modes of thought? Or are they such as to make it inconceivable that any great poet, ancient or modern, should have embodied the passage in a work of art? [Jebb, at p. 259].

The answer to the second question may be, on stylistic grounds, that the lines were not written by a great poet though, as Professor Kerferd tells me, at least most of the passage is now generally accepted as authentic Sophocles. But I consider that the sentiments expressed, and the point at which they are expressed, might well arise from 'a peculiarity in ancient modes of thought', and that in that sense the passage is not full of fault and needs no excuse. But here what Antigone says has to be seen together with her argument, in the very opening of the tragedy, with her sister Ismene, about whether they should bury Polyneices or obey the city's law: Ismene held they should not do so 'in the city's despite'. In short, through the course of the play a Greek audience was shown the problem of the two sisters torn between obedience to State law and defiance of that law to perform the sacred duty of giving the last rites to a beloved brother. And the fact that in the disputed passage Antigone repeats Ismene's words from the opening scene ('in the city's despite': see Jebb, p. 165) must be important. The situation is high drama: and even a modern audience is moved in the opening to sympathise with Antigone, on the grounds of her love for her brother, rather than because she is obeying the law of gods in whom they do not believe. During that first argument between Antigone and Ismene it seems to me that we are confronted with the same dramatic choice which Darius inflicted on the wife of Intaphrenes, and which (in theory) the questioner thrust upon the Lozi judges when he asked whom they would save: mother, sister, wife or child? Antigone later feels that Ismene's cowardice in refusing to help bury their brother justifies her rejecting Ismene's atoning attempt to share her fatal punishment. At this stage Ismene wishes to die with her sister: but Antigone seems to feel that one breach of the sibling duty is fatal to later loyalty to it.

The conflict of bonds is also brought out in Antigone's plaint that (though betrothed to Creon's son) she has had 'no joy of bridal bed, ... no joy of marriage, no portion in the nurture of children...' For shortly after she has slain herself after being incarcerated in the cave, the prophecy is given to King Creon that his son, Antigone's betrothed, Haemon, will also slay himself in despair at his beloved's cruel punishment and his father's injustice. This imminent death of a man for love of his wife-to-be brings out the strength of the bond between spouses, as Antigone's brave defiance of Creon's edict brings out the strength of the sibling bond, where

Ismene, admitting her cowardice, shows that courage is needed to fulfil its demands, to a sister, in the face of death.

The scene between Haemon and Creon is not only a conflict between justice and acknowledgement of the claims of the gods (*cf.* Tiresias' later statement that the corpse belonged neither to men nor to the gods above, but to the gods below) but also the conflict in the triangle of father to son (the agnatic bond) and son to wife-to-be (the bond that continues the agnatic lineage, for, as the Romans put it, *mulier et origo et finis familiae est*). Haemon cannot accept Creon's 'Nay, there are other fields for him to plough' (Jebb, line 569).

I venture that more could be made in regard to this passage of the obvious fact that there are two dramatic themes deeply interwoven in the plot. But the clash is not merely between duty to kin and the gods, and duty to obey municipal law: the clash also occurs among kin about who will fulfil duties to brother, to father, to betrothed, and, given a compelled choice, to which relative the duty will be discharged. There is indeed the problem of whether an edict of the State, against divine law, may be defied because no mortal 'could override the unwritten and unfailing statutes of heaven' when 'the justice that dwells with the gods below' requires that the living, and particularly kinsfolk, should perform the burial rites for the dead. In Antigone's words, 'Not through dread of any human pride could I answer to the gods for breaking these' (see Jebb's appendix at p. 259).

The second dramatic theme is, as in the Lozi dilemma, the working out of the deep conflicts that in such a society—and even in ours—afflict the complicated constellation of relationships involved between man or woman and the parents, siblings, spouse or spouse-to-be, and children or children-to-be. Ismene fails in her duty to their brother, where Antigone courts even death to fulfil hers: then Ismene tries to recover her identity by saying she will die with her sister, only to be spurned as no longer fit for sibling loyalty. In the course of Antigone's loyal conduct to the sibling bond she defies her betrothed's father, the king, and dooms her betrothed to strife with his father and (she might expect) to some period, at least, of misery and sadness. In fact, he goes to where she is entombed and embraces her hanging body when he finds she has killed herself. When his father, frightened into recanting the punishment by Tiresias' prophecy, arrives to release Antigone, Haemon attacks his father. Horrified, he then kills himself.

The problem of how to choose between fulfilling duties to several kinds of kin, and to spouse (and his or her kin), demonstrated as difficult and even agonising when posed in the sharp form 'Whom would you save from drowning?' is a persistent, constant one for Lozi, as many cases coming to the Barotse court showed. I quote only one moving passage from a judgement on a case in which a wife had sued her husband for divorce on the grounds that he neglected her kin:

You, woman, have astonished us by your suit. You thought you would shame your husband before the country which is us [the judges]. But you have instead brought honour to him, for we have never heard of so good a son-in-law. Your father told us the overcoat he wears is a present from your husband; see how your husband sits himself in a ragged jacket. He is not a rich man, but when he brought [from white country] an overcoat for his father, he brought one for your father; when he brought a dress for his mother, he brought one for your mother. He gave shawls to your unmarried sisters, and he built granaries for them and moved their harvest on the flood, not in the dug-out of your village but in his own dug-out. And so forth. You have not disgraced your husband before the Malozi, but you have brought fame to him, for none of us is as good a son in-law as he. You, my son, we admire what you have done, and we thank you. Do not cease to behave thus because your wife has brought you here: continue to look after your in-laws as you have done in the past. We thank you.

The judge, the senior in the court, then instructed his fellows and all in court to join him in saluting the husband (Gluckman, 1955a, p. 151).

In my Frazer lecture on 'Rituals of rebellion in south-east Africa' I argued that the polity of certain African States contained rebellion and civil war as endemic in the system. Civil wars were fought not as revolutions to change the political system or the types of person who would control power but to put into positions of power, within the same structure, similar types of, though other, persons (*cf.* Aristotle's *Politics*, books v and x, on different kinds of plot). There were, in short, rebellions, not revolutions. The attackers on the king followed, or induced to lead them, some prince: hence the rebellion was fought in the name of kingship, against an alleged tyrant or usurper or morally and ritually unworthy king, to defend the values of kingship, and the title of the extant royal family to it. (Polyneices had been engaged in that sort of revolt against Creon when Eteocles, the defender, and Polyneices, the attacker, slew each other.) In this type of State, in the Swazi instance I analysed (as reported by Kuper, 1947, chapter XIII, 'The drama of kingship'), subjects and princes at particular stages of the ritual, in complex patterns, were required to attack the king, in mime and in words, or by their absence from crucial rites, while the king's loneliness was sometimes emphasized. At other times subjects were required to act as if they were hostile to the royal family as a whole. In other rites the identification of king and princes, or of king and subjects, or of all, was stressed. Yet the aim of the ritual was to secure blessings for the nation: fertility of land and cattle and women, unity, peace and good order, victory in war, and so forth. In short, the prescribed, compelled acting of deep conflicts was believed to produce social good; and it did so in complicated ways into which I cannot here enter. We can say that the ritual emphasised communal unity and good in the teeth of deep endemic conflicts, acted in the ritual. The responses of individuals, as they acted their parts, must have been as varied and complex as are those of a church congregation to the service. In these circumstances, Mackenzie suggested, the ritual purged with pity and terror, as a tragedy does. Since Greek tragedies—and comedies—were performed on religious occasions, they presumably operated similarly: they embodied the deep conflicts, in terms of current beliefs, of the society, and on the whole, like those African rituals, they stressed the fundamental axioms of good conduct—though these were in conflict with one another. One might say that, in view of what happened to Creon and his family later, he was justified in honouring Eteocles for slaying Polyneices, but not in denying Polyneices the privilege of burial (as Tiresias warned him).

Yet Greek tragedies were dramas; though parts of religious festivals, they were not themselves ritual. Hence an intense personal dimension pervades them, as modern scholars say (see my statement from Professor Kerferd above). Ismene obeys the State and denies kinship bond and love; Antigone defies the State to obey the gods, and to discharge her duties to her brother, her kinsman. In psychological terms, the shaming discovery that she and her siblings were incestuous children, together with the tragic ends of her parents, Jocasta and Oedipus, on whom she tended, may, in Sophocles' view, have led to the intensity of her feeling for her brother, with whom she shared shame and, in a sense, guilt (see her remarks on her father's sin, the harsh fate of her race, the curse on brother and herself—Jebb, pp. 157–8; Kitto, p. 30). Ismene then felt it less, or not strongly enough to overcome her fears, until her last sibling, her sister, was threatened also with death. At least Aristotle regarded Antigone's reasoning as 'incredible' to ordinary men. This individual dimension is stressed by him in the 'art' of rhetoric (book III, xvi, 6–9: translation by Freese, 1947, pp. 447–8), where he cites Sophocles:

And the narrative should be of a moral character, and in fact it will be so, if we know what effects this. One thing is to make clear our moral purpose; for as is the moral purpose, so is the character, and as is the end, so is the moral purpose. For this reason mathematical treatises have no moral character, because neither have they moral purpose; for they have no moral end. But the Socratic dialogues have; for they discuss such questions. Other ethical indications are the accompanying peculiarities of each individual character . . . Nor should we speak as if from the intellect, but from moral purpose: 'But I wished it, and I preferred it; and even if I profited nothing, it is better.' The first statement indicates prudence, the second virtue; for prudence consists in the pursuit of what is useful, virtue in that of what is honourable. If anything of the kind seems incredible, then the reason must be added; of this Sophocles gives an example, where his Antigone says that she cared more for her brother than for her husband or children; for the latter can be replaced after they are gone,

> but when father and mother are in the grave, no brother can ever be born.

If you have no reason, you should at least say that you are aware that what you assert is incredible, but that it is your nature; for no one believes that a man ever does anything of his own free will except from motives of self-interest.

Thus Aristotle clearly felt that most people would find Antigone's reasoning here incredible, but that it was in her nature; and the whole discussion implies that he regarded it as virtuous and honourable. His main point is that it was individual, to be understood thus; and of course, though the Lozi were virtually unanimous in stating their solution to their horrible choice, individual Lozi have varied relationships in the balancing of claims.

It is notable that Aristotle puts the question as if Antigone was making a choice between husband and children as against brother, though her future husband-to-be, Haemon, and children she might have had by him, are in question. Jebb cited (p. 261) Bellerman as having said that Antigone, as yet unmarried, did not know how she would feel towards a husband or a child, when she said she would have left them unburied, while she knew (*verstehen*, not *kennen*) how she felt as a sister. Also, Bellerman argued, we are aware at any one moment of the duty which confronts us, and see it as more imperative than a duty not involved at the moment. Jebb regarded this, implying a sliding scale of religious duty, as 'a fallacy, from the Greek point of view'. I myself find that I respond to Bellerman's defence of the passage, for Antigone as an individual. But I still suggest that it has to be seen in the context of the opening argument with Ismene, and Antigone's hope of marriage and children with Creon's son: after stating how divine law compels her to disobey the king's edict, she turns, at the last moment, as Seyffert said (cited Jebb, p. 262), to the deep affection—perhaps at unconscious levels the sense of guilt (fate, or curse)—which bound her to her brother. This points the drama of the choice she made as against the choice Ismene made, the choice among duties, which is so severe in all societies, and which is more frequently confronted in societies organised in extended groups of kin. Sophocles may not himself have written the disputed passage: whoever did, I am sure that it has to be seen in contrast with the differing responses of the sisters to the demand of loyalty to the sibling, perhaps the agnatic, tie. Sophocles (or the interpolator(s)) may well have inserted the passage to bring out this contrast: hence Antigone repeats, at that crucial stage, Ismene's own phrase, 'in the city's despite'.[9] Loyalty to a brother, due from both sisters, stands against municipal law. I feel an African audience would have responded to it, as rightly set where it is. They would certainly not have responded as Goethe did—a motive 'ganz schlecht' . . . 'and which almost borders on the comic'.

References

Aristotle (335–330 B.C.), *On the 'art' of rhetoric*, translations by:
  (a) Buckley, T. (1872). London, Bell & Daldy.
  (b) Cope, E. M. (1877). Cambridge University Press.
  (c) Freese, J. H. (1926), Loeb Classical Library, London, Heinemann.
Bott, E. (1957) *Family and social network*. London, Tavistock.
—(1971), *Family and social network* (second edition). London, Tavistock.
Bryant, A. T. (1905), *A Zulu–English dictionary*. Pinetown, Natal, Marianhill Mission Press.
—(1911), 'Zulu medicine and medicine-men', *Annals of Natal Government Museum*, vol. 2, part 1.

Cape of Good Hope Government (1883), *Report and proceedings*, with appendices, of the Government Commission on Native Laws and Customs. Cape Town, W. A. Richards (Parliamentary Paper G.4–1883).

Colson, E. (1958), *Marriage and the family among the Plateau Tonga of Northern Rhodesia*. Manchester University Press for the Rhodes-Livingstone Institute, Northern Rhodesia.

Culwick, A. T. (1943), *Good out of Africa: a study in the relativity of morals*. Rhodes-Livingstone Paper No. 8.

de Sélincourt, A. (1954), English translation of Herodotus' *The Histories*. Harmondworth, Penguin Classics.

Fustel de Coulanges, N. D. (1884), cited from 1956, *The ancient city: a study of the religion, laws, and institutions of Greece and Rome*. Garden City, N.Y., Doubleday.

Gluckman, M. (1950a), 'Social beliefs and individual thinking in primitive society', *Memoirs and proceedings of the Manchester Literary and Philosophical Society*, vol. XCI, pp. 1–26. Reprinted in R. O. Manners and D. Kaplan (eds.), *Theory in anthropology*, pp. 453–64, Chicago, Aldine, 1968.

—(1950b), 'Kinship and marriage among the Lozi of Northern Rhodesia and the Zulu of Natal' in *African systems of kinship and marriage*, (eds.), A. R. Radcliffe-Brown and C. D. Forde, pp. 166–206, London, Oxford University Press for the International African Institute.

—(1954), *Rituals of rebellion in south-east Africa*. The Frazer lecture, 1952. Manchester University Press. Reprinted in Gluckman (1963).

—(1955a), *The judicial process among the Barotse of Northern Rhodesia*. Manchester University Press for the Rhodes-Livingstone Institute, Northern Rhodesia.

—(1955b), *Custom and conflict in Africa*. Oxford, Blackwell.

—(1963), *Order and rebellion in tribal Africa: collected essays, with an autobiographical introduction*. London, Cohen & West.

—(1965), *Politics, law and ritual in tribal society*. Oxford, Blackwell.

—(1972a), 'Postscript' to extract from Gluckman (1950b), reprinted in J. Goody (ed.), *Readings in kinship and marriage*. Harmondsworth, Penguin.

—(1972b), 'Moral crises: magical and secular solutions' in M. Gluckman (ed.), *The allocation of responsibility*. Manchester University Press.

—(1973), *The judicial process among the Barotse of Northern Rhodesia* (Zambia). Reprint, with new preface, of second, enlarged, edition (1967) of Gluckman (1955a). Manchester University Press for the Institute for African Studies, University of Zambia, Lusaka.

Goody, E. (1962), 'Conjugal separation and divorce among the Gonja of northern Ghana' in M. Fortes (ed.), *Marriage in tribal societies*, pp. 14–54. Cambridge University Press.

Goody, J., and Buckley, J. (1973), 'Inheritance and women's labour in Africa', *Africa*, vol. XLIII, No. 2 (April).

Jebb, R. (1888), *Sophocles: the plays and fragments* (with critical notes, commentary, and translation into English prose), third edition (1900). Cambridge University Press.

Kitto, H. D. F. (1962), *Sophocles: three tragedies* (translated into English verse). London, Oxford University Press.

Kuper, H. (1947), *An African aristocracy: rank among the Swazi of the Protectorate*. London, Oxford University Press for the International African Institute.

—(1962), *Inhliziyo ngumthakathi*. Translation of Kuper (1972) into Zulu by T. Cope. Pietermaritzburg, Shuter & Shooter.

—(1970), *A witch in my heart: a play*. London, Oxford University Press for the International African Institute.

Lee, S. G. (1950), 'Some Zulu concepts of psychogenic disorder', *Journal of Social Research* (South Africa), vol. I, pp. 9–18.

—(1962), *Stress and adaptation: an inaugural lecture*. Leicester University Press.

Mitchell, J. C. (1963), 'Marriage stability and social structure in Bantu Africa', *International population conference proceedings*, New York, 1961. London, vol. II, pp. 255–62.

Peters, E. L. (1966), 'Sex differentiation in two Arab societies', in J. Peristianis, *Masculine and feminine in the Mediterranean* (privately published: cyclostyled copies of this article from Professor E. L. Peters, University of Manchester).

Pickard-Cambridge, A. W. (1949), 'Sophocles' in *The Oxford classical dictionary*. Oxford, Clarendon Press.

Richards, A. I. (1939), *Land, labour and diet in Northern Rhodesia: an economic study of the Bemba tribe*. London: Oxford University Press for the International African Institute.

—(1940), *Bemba marriage and modern economic conditions*. Rhodes-Livingstone Papers, No. 4.

Schapera, I. (1940), *Married life in an African tribe*. London, Faber & Faber.

Turner, V. W. (1957), *Schism and continuity in an African society: a study of Ndembu village life*. Manchester University Press for the Rhodes-Livingstone Institute, Northern Rhodesia.

Notes

[1] E.g. Kitto (1962) translates the passage without comment, it is true in a book without detailed notes.

[2] Citations are from A. de Sélincourt's translations of *The Histories of Herodotus* in the Penguin Classics (1954).

[3] I have not seen in studies of African societies a record of a similar debate, but Dr B. Sansom tells me he heard Pedi men (Transvaal) debate whether one would save mother or wife: they always selected mother, on the grounds that one could get another wife. The Pedi are organised patrilineally. Professor J. Clyde Mitchell, who worked among the matrilineally organised Yao of Malawi, immediately responded when I described the problem: 'Of course you would save your sister.'

[4] According to Christ's reply to the Pharisees, a man shall leave his father and mother and shall cleave to his wife (Matthew XIX, 3–7).

[5] See also my 'Foreword' to her second edition, where I put my own reinterpretation of her hypothesis, and discuss how her hypothesis illuminates the relation between marital relationships and kinship relationships in tribal societies (see further Gluckman, 1955b, chapter III, 'Estrangements in the family').

[6] I was not the first to advance this hypothesis, as I made clear in my 1950b essay, but most recent research and criticism have centred on my formulation. I considered some of this more recent research in Gluckman (1972a), and it has been checked statistically and quantitatively by Mitchell (1963) (and reformulated) and by J. Goody and Buckley (1973).

[7] Citations are from Jebb's translation (1900).

[8] Sophocles is reputed to have died while reading *Antigone* aloud (406 B.C.).

[9] Perhaps the choice emerges more clearly in translations like Kitto's (1962) 'against the city's will' than in Jebb's 'in the city's despite'.

J. W. Grove

8

'Science policy' and the attack on science

The Romans were so afraid of disinterested research that they discouraged any investigation the utilitarian value of which was not obvious.—George Sarton, *The History of Science and the New Humanism.*

There is a phrase that has been much on people's lips in recent times to the effect that science is ethically neutral. It is, no doubt, possible to attach a meaning to this. But it is also surely the case that with regard to one at least of the cardinal virtues, science is not neutral. Science must be true.—Benjamin Farrington, *Prometheus Bound: Government and Science in Classical Antiquity.*

I

The great debate about science policy has been conducted on an international scale. Public interest in the question was first aroused by the sharply escalating cost of science, which resulted partly from the exponential growth of research and partly from the increasing scale and sophistication of the instrumentation required to do it. As costs increased, so did pressures for the setting of rational research priorities. This is the *scarce resources* argument for national science policy. But science also supports (in ways much studied but as yet not clearly understood) the technology that is essential to economic growth. The *economic growth* argument for national science policy has been vigorously fostered for a decade or more, especially by international agencies like OECD, for whom a rising GNP became a sacred cow, a cow that could be fattened by continuous and, if need be, force feeding of large quantities of top-quality research and development. Most recently the emphasis has shifted significantly, with rising concern about the unwanted consequences—social, environmental and ecological—of technology, towards a third argument, a *human welfare* argument for national science policy, an argument that has developed, interestingly enough, alongside the growing realisation by experts that the relationship of science to economic growth is much more complex than was originally perceived.

There has emerged in the course of this debate a strongly instrumental view of fundamental science: a belief that fundamental science is an *overhead* and is therefore to be judged primarily, and perhaps exclusively, by its direct contribution to the material welfare of society. At its most extreme this takes the form of the (mindless) contention that most of the money now spent on fundamental science is a waste of resources that should be diverted as quickly as possible to socially useful things. More commonly it is asserted that fundamental science is an expensive luxury that can be supported only if it promises a clearly foreseeable pay-off in terms of practical application for economic development, national identity, national security, social welfare or some other "national goal". In the words of a recent OECD report:[1]

Parliaments and public are increasingly questioning the present vast expenditure on research and the impact of science and technology on the life of the individual and society. There are many who argue that technology is producing conditions of life, especially in the cities, which are basically intolerable and which must therefore be rejected ... All this leads to the conclusion that the major need now is for deeper, wiser and more comprehensive consideration of the ways in which science can be harnessed to the common well-being.

The report continues:

... the centre of interest [is shifting] from science for its own sake, or as a national mystique, to the deliberate use of science as a means of achieving national goals. [This latest phase in] the development of national science policy ... lays the stress on the relationship of science to the whole spectrum of national policies rather than solely on policy for the management of science itself ... Science policy, if it is agreed that one of its most essential elements is national development *through* science and technology, is therefore ... much more important than has hitherto been realised.

It is apparent that this kind of language (with its offhand reference to fundamental science as 'a national mystique'), language that typifies much current thinking about science, constitutes a serious challenge to fundamental science and embodies a deep-seated misunderstanding of its proper place in a technological society. Little attention has so far been directed to this problem. It is important that it should be seriously studied, especially since the pressures for science policy have recently been reinforced by a mounting tide of anti-science sentiment and renewed demands for 'social responsibility'.

Anti-science is not, of course, new. On the contrary, it is as old as science itself (which means much older than the scientific revolution of the sixteenth and seventeenth centuries) and it has often been the stronger force. The role of a kind of resistance movement against secular and religious politics is not new to science. What is new about the contemporary current of anti-science (which, as Edward Shils has said,[2] is a confluence of various currents of opinion rather than a movement) is to be found, paradoxically, in the present state of science itself. Science has emerged in the twentieth century as a seemingly irresistible force, supremely confident of its powers and of the virtue of its characteristic modes of thought. It has advanced at a staggering rate and has been immensely successful in increasing our knowledge of the physical universe, of the origin and nature of life on earth, and even of man himself. On a more mundane level it has been strikingly successful, by comparison with former times, in persuading its chief patron, the State, to support the education and training of its practitioners and their support staff in ever-increasing numbers, and to provide the instruments for their work. Once an under-privileged minority, scientists now take their place as an influential force in society, with excellent access to governing circles.

But there is another side to the coin. It is now clear that the exponential growth of science can continue only on certain conditions that are rather unlikely to be realised;[3] that the information 'explosion' which the growth of science has triggered has become virtually unmanageable;[4] that scientific rationalism, for all its past triumphs, is even yet unable to persuade us conclusively that it constitutes the best hope for civilised men; and that the remarkable progress in understanding the universe we inhabit has, indeed, been bought at a price.

Part of the price to be paid is encapsulated in the current attack on science. Scientists have done very little, directly, to bring about the 'nationalisation' of science (the product, very largely, of war, the threat of war, and the conflict of ideologies), but they have profited from it mightily, and they have done very little to control it. The American space programme is technology rather than science: it was not dreamed up by scientists as an elaborate subterfuge for securing massive public support for fundamental research. Yet the fact remains that, a few years ago, the NASA budget for fundamental research was *six times* the total appropriation for the National Science Foundation, notionally (with the National Institutes of Health) the major supporter of fundamental science in the United States.[5]

There have always been scientists who worked for the State—for example, Archimedes or, eighteen centuries later, Leonardo, both of whom (as Russell said) "were granted permission to add to human knowledge on condition that they subtracted from human life". Modern war and modern technology have not changed the principle, but they have added a new dimension: in a world where governments claim their services more and more, where they claim a large share of available public funds to support their work—in a word, where science has been 'nationalised'—it has become increasingly difficult for scientists to stay unpoliticised, to resist the pressures of ideology and the demands of national security and well-being. It is commonly asserted that science lost its innocence (in secret) when the first nuclear device was successfully exploded in the desert at Alamogordo on 16 July 1945. In fact, if we need to identify a symbolic act, a better one would be the day in January 1943 when Goldschmidt and Auger received from American scientists in Chicago, on behalf of the British, French and Canadian team in Montreal, the basic data about the Fermi pile and 4 μg of the first man-made plutonium. The occasion was the threatened suspension of all further collaboration on the part of the American allies. As J. J. Salomon has said,[6] a few days later the same exchange of friendly services, traditional and characteristic of science though it was, would have constituted a treasonable act.

II

Contemporary anti-science is, as Shils suggests, a confluence of currents of opinion. To the more traditional humanist concerns (which have been given a modern twist by recent existentialist and 'hermeneutic' philosophies) there have been added more pragmatic considerations about the nature and effects of technological society, the outlines of which have become apparent only in the last thirty years. The arguments of anti-science are understandable, as is their popular appeal, but I believe that they are at bottom both confused and potentially dangerous. Modern anti-science reifies technology; it confuses technology as instrument with technology as ideology; and (most particularly) it exhibits a profound misconception of the nature and inner dynamics of science and its relation to application (that is, it misinterprets the connections of scientific discovery to practice).

Science is a generalising activity. It is interested not in unique or single events but in whole classes of events. Or, to be more specific, it is interested only in single instances (for example, the results of an experiment or an observation) for the light they shed on whole classes of such instances. How this passion for generalisation came about in man is a fascinating anthropological problem. Until a culture possesses a language which contains words that express abstract ideas—universals—and some still existing cultures do not—it is impossible to arrive at the kind of generalised assertions that lie at the base of science.

The notion that there are classes of objects or events implies, of course, that there are regularities or uniformities in nature, and this is one of the assumptions of every science. Hence the assertion that science is interested in 'law-like' behaviour and in 'uncovering the laws of nature'. Thus science is *theoretical* both because it is abstract (i.e. it constructs abstractions or universal propositions about the world) and because it generalises.

Science is speculative and conjectural; but it is more than that. It is also *empirical*. It is speculative, but not purely speculative (though I believe that it is first and foremost speculative) because conjecture is supported by references to empirical evidence. Science is firmly rooted in an empirical base. The ancient Greeks (on the whole) were more interested in speculation (in theory) than they were in empirical evidence. Other civilisations—Islam, for example—have placed great emphasis on accurate observation and experiment but have given little attention to the development of theory. It was part of the achievement of the scientific revolution, begun by men like Galileo, to have succeeded in bringing theory and the search for supporting empirical evidence together in one undertaking. This, indeed, is perhaps the single most important fact about the scientific revolution. It is this particular conjunction of speculation and empiricism that distinguishes science from rational myth (e.g. much of the speculative thought of the Pre-Socratics, African witchcraft, psycho-analytic theory) and from purely empirical doctrines such as astrology and alchemy. It is interesting, and highly significant, that part of the current reaction against science takes the form of a growing interest on the part of intellectuals—including, sad to say, some scientists—in astrology,[7] and some (North American) colleges have actually begun to provide courses in astrology and alchemy.

Science not only postulates the existence of a knowable external world (that is, is basically *realist*, the quantum physicists notwithstanding), it also postulates a particular way of knowing the external world. It postulates the existence of a world about which it is possible to have public (or, as is sometimes said, inter-subjectively transmissible) knowledge. It deals very little in private knowledge such as a mystic or an intuitionist philosopher might claim to have, but in *directly communicable* knowledge. This is one of the things (but only one) that is meant when people talk about science as 'objective'. The mystic may say, 'Under my guidance you can attain to a knowledge of the inner—or true—meaning of things such as I possess'; but the knowledge so attained still remains—and must remain—private to the experiencing person. The scientist assumes that the world he experiences is *exactly the same world* as other scientists experience.

A further important characteristic of science is the manner in which it relates to commonsense knowledge. In particular, it is profoundly sceptical of common sense and continually challenges it. (One of the truly revolutionary metaphysical features of Einstein's work was his demonstration that our long-held commonsense notions about absolute space must be wrong). The beliefs that knowledge rests, in the final analysis, on the immediate apprehension of things through our senses, that error is 'subjective' (i.e. is the result of our own imperfections, possibly removable if we can purge ourselves and discover the right path to abiding truth), that knowledge is essentially *passive*, is forced upon us, so to speak, if our minds are open, by repetition and association—all these are rejected by modern physical science.

Perhaps the most important features of science from the point of view of the humanist critic, however, and the ones he finds it most difficult to accept, are its rejection of essentialism and of teleological explanation: what the philosopher G. H. von Wright[8] has called the 'aristotelian' tradition of knowledge. Modern science ('science since Galileo') is not concerned with attempting to find out what a thing 'really is', what its essence is, but with describing and explaining the way a thing behaves. In this (limited) sense, science is 'behavioural'; and it is especially concerned with regularities in the behaviour of classes of things. The scientist does not ask, 'What is energy?' but, rather, questions like 'How is genetic information conveyed in the cell?' or 'How did the moon get its craters?' He is not concerned with origins (except in the most general cosmological speculations), he is not concerned with purpose or in conceiving of physical systems as 'goal-seekers'; and if he appears sometimes to be asking questions of that form (e.g. 'What is a quasar?' or 'What function does RNA serve?' he is not asking them expecting an essentialist or teleological answer but rather an answer explaining behaviour in terms of physical laws.

In part, then, the humanist's concern about science involves a rejection as inadequate of much of the logic of scientific inquiry: its stress on regularity over uniqueness, its apparent refusal to admit speculative thought that is divorced from empirical test (or empirical test in principle), its limitation of discourse to the directly communicable, its rejection of design and purpose. But more is involved. Jacques Monod has suggested[9] that since the findings of modern science defy immediate understanding and intuitive grasp—are 'beyond the understanding of most men'—they 'represent a cause of permanent humiliation'. Or, as Nietzsche put it, 'All sciences today work for the destruction of man's ancient self-respect.'

The disquiet about the supposed implications of science for the life of man is reinforced by misunderstandings embodied in that peculiar complex of false ideas which is usually labelled 'scientism', a complex that is fed by many philosophers of science and sometimes, alas, by scientists themselves.[10]

There is no space for an adequate treatment of 'scientistic' ideas here, but one or two comments are in order.

1. A typical 'scientistic' claim is that science is a superior form of knowledge, a claim that derives partly from nineteenth-century positivism, partly from a misapplication of the Vienna Circle's (invalid) attempt to demarcate science from metaphysics, and partly from the confusion of science with technology (which I shall discuss later). This is nonesense: there are many ways of knowing the world, and the scientific way is an intellectually fruitful and powerful one. But it is impossible, in my opinion, to adjudge it superior in

any meaningful sense. The artist's vision and the poet's vision are at least as important, and I do not believe that there are many scientists of repute today who would assert that science is superior to either in any absolute sense; they would assert merely that it is obviously superior in that region of experience to which it relates.[11] In any event, although science contributes to knowledge, the notion that the only true or important knowledge is scientific knowledge is clearly false.

2. A related 'scientistic' misapprehension which has been very powerful has to do with the supposed infallibility of science: the notion that 'genuine' scientific statements must be unchallengeably true. This is a very old notion and it has strong roots, and science is supposed to derive its authority from this fact. Vulgar opinion is still, in this sense, Baconian: that the scientific method is a means of arriving at irrefutable knowledge about the world. But no reputable scientist any longer believes this. It is logically false, and all the practical history of science demonstrates that it is empirically false also. What is significant is the tentative nature of scientific discovery. (It has been well said[12] that 'the history of science is the history of human opinion on the question of certainty'.) When scientists are asked 'What is your warrant for believing such and such to be the case?' they reply, in effect, 'Our warrant for believing this is that all the available evidence (which to us is empirically based evidence) appears now to support it. We have been unable to refute it, but we are prepared to find at some point in the future, on the basis of new evidence, that it was not true after all.' But that kind of answer is not one, unfortunately, that philosophers have usually been willing to accept; the common man finds it exceedingly strange, and the opponents of science, failing to grasp that this critical attitude is precisely what has made science successful, look upon it as evidence of the bankruptcy of the scientific method.

3. The humanist distaste for science has derived much reinforcement from the curious philosophical strategems adopted by the quantum physicists, especially, of course, Bohr and Heisenberg. The proper interpretation of the philosophical import of quantum physics (which has generated a considerable literature) is a complex and still unresolved question. Yet many humanists speak as if the views of the Copenhagen school are beyond dispute.

Writing in *Daedalus* in 1958,[13] Heisenberg reiterated his position as follows:

... for the smallest building blocks of matter, every process of observation causes a major disturbance; it turns out that we can no longer talk of the behaviour of the particle apart from the process of observation ...

Two important conclusions follow. The first is that 'as Bohr has expressed it, we are not only spectators but also always participants on the stage of life';[14] the second is that 'we are finally led to believe that the laws of nature ... deal no longer with the particles themselves but with our knowledge of the particles'. Even the mathematics of quantum theory does not represent the behaviour of the particles, 'but rather our knowledge of this behaviour'.[15]

The conclusions drawn from such remarks by humanists (as well as by many social scientists and philosophers) are that science no longer deals with an objective reality, that theories are no more than prescriptions for making predictions (i.e. theories are operational rules), and that science is incapable of laying bare the reality that lies behind appearance. From these primary conclusions all kinds of corollaries, sometimes contradictory, have been held to follow.

One of the dangers of the 'quantum philosophy' which Einstein and others (such as Popper) clearly foresaw was the possibility it opened up for a retreat into irrationalism. The course of science (and especially physics) after Galileo was, in an important degree, a steady progression away from common sense, away from objects directly observable with the unaided senses. Yet it remained possible to express science in terms that the layman could at least partially grasp through the mediation of analogy and models based on familiar things. Electro-magnetism is still mysterious to the layman, though he can grasp something of its properties, for example through the analogy of water flowing through a pipe, physical feelings of attraction and repulsion, etc. But the quantum philosophical leap was a leap *into* the dark: it appeared that the ultimate building blocks of the world were to remain for ever wrapped in impenetrable mist.

4. Perhaps the most important 'scientistic' perversion (and certainly the most important for our purposes here) is to be found in the instrumentalist view of science. This view has been urged by many philosophers of science, who claim that it has received overwhelming support from quantum mechanics. It is also, incidentally, one of the strongest philosophical underpinnings of contemporary social science, particularly as developed in America under the influence of Deweian pragmatism (with which it shares many common features). Crudely

stated, instrumentalism asserts that we can never 'really know' the world; all that we can know is how to manipulate the world—how to calculate and predict it correctly. Whereas *realism* maintains that we can (albeit imperfectly and tentatively) know the real world, and *essentialism* maintains that knowledge of the world must describe real essences, *instrumentalism* maintains that all a scientific theory can do is to "represent" phenomena. This is a doctrine of utility rather than of truth; or, more precisely, in so far as it talks about truth at all, it is a doctrine that equates truth with utility. Scientific theories are instruments which are more or less useful, and in the now famous words of Heisenberg:

> It follows that we [physicists] do not say any longer that Newton's mechanics is false . . . Rather we may now use the following formulation— classical mechanics is everywhere exactly right—*where its concepts can be applied.*

The instrumentalist view has great attractions. It has proved attractive to the opponents of science since at least the time of Galileo. But it has not been acceptable within the Galilean tradition: in that tradition it is not sufficient that men accept the heliocentric theory because it is useful for making astronomical calculations while continuing to believe in the superior teaching of the Church for other purposes. Theory should not only be useful; it must also claim to be true.

Instrumentalism accords very well with behaviourism in the broadest sense[16] because it says, in effect, that all we can do is to measure the way bodies behave (thus gravitational force is dismissed as 'occult'). We can only observe things happening; all we can do in science is to compute and measure.[17] Hence Watsonian and Skinnerian psychology and indeed all behaviourist social science, is likely to be instrumentalist, and that is indeed what we find.

The second aspect of instrumentalism which is important for our purposes here is that, if it is accepted, fundamental science disappears as a separate kind of human endeavour *and all science becomes technology*—or the application of rules to the manipulation of nature. This notion—that all science is technology—is, in fact, now being quite openly asserted, and it fits very well both the pragmatist and the Marxist philosophies of science which underpin much of the contemporary discussion about the 'social responsibility of science'.[18]

The basic objection to instrumentalism, as I see it (though a more extended discussion would be needed to dispose of it finally) is that, although it fits technology very well—since technology is the application to the problems of altering the environment of rules relating to events of a kind that are already known (i.e. technology *is* manipulation)—it does not fit the major aim of fundamental science, which is the discovery of *new* kinds of knowledge. If a theory 'is everywhere exactly right—where its concepts can be applied' (i.e. if it is simply about known events), it can always be saved if it does not fit other facts by asserting that 'the theory does not apply here'. It is hard to believe that this kind of medieval ad-hocery could long persist in science. In other words, if instrumentalism were really, so to speak, practised by scientists, there would—probably in quite short order—be no more important discoveries. (This, basically, is what is wrong with Kuhn's conception of 'normal science'.)

III

Although it is true that science and technology have hitherto had largely separate histories;[19] that there have been technological societies which had little or no science (e.g. Rome and the 'hydraulic' societies of antiquity) and scientific societies that had little or no technology (e.g. ancient Greece); that science sometimes *follows* technology (e.g. the steam engine was invented before thermodynamics); even that technology may sometimes retard science (e.g. the explosion some years ago by the US of a nuclear device in inner space, between the Van Allen belts, which changed the earth's environment and hence the 'given' character of this aspect of nature that scientists study)—nevertheless it would be useless to deny that modern technological society does indeed typify a close marriage between the two. Indeed, it can be plausibly argued that societies today are only subsidiarily capitalist and non-capitalist; that the important distinction is between technological (and therefore science-based) societies (America and the USSR and their respective industrialised dependencies) and non-technological or not-yet-technological societies. But it is not only the vastness of the scale of the technology that is crucial; the *type* of technology—largely a technology of electronics and information; that is, a technology of manipulative rationality—is even more crucial.

It is not surprising that the critics see the new technological society as deriving its world view from an instrumentalist and behaviourist ontology that treats men as essentially *inert*, as passive receptors waiting to respond to stimuli. Men move, so to speak, with a uniform velocity (in 'traditional' ways, 'with false consciousness', etc.) until they are acted upon by some force. (Hence the complaint—voiced repeatedly by our more phenomenologically inclined students—that men have become 'the objects rather than the subjects of their own activity'.) Phrases like 'men have to learn how to *adapt* to the new technology' abound—even though technology is man-made, not something that is 'given'—while the pundits tell us that technology 'causes changes in societal values by creating new opportunities', that is, that it is not our values that govern what our opportunities shall be, but the other way round: in a word, that society is technology-driven.

But of course, values do determine opportunities. It is not 'technology' that causes changes in societal values by creating new opportunities but decision-making and manipulation by powerful groups exploiting technology. Emmanuel Mesthene[20] has argued that 'space technology makes it possible for the first time to go to the moon or to communicate by satellite, and thereby adds those two new options to the spectrum of choices available to society'. But surely this is literal nonsense? By what perverse logic can it possibly be argued that space technology *determined* the decisions to go to the moon and to build communication satellites? Space technology was *created* by the decision to go to the moon; it was the consequence of that decision, not the cause of it. The notion that a reified 'technology' *compels* us, or drives society, is as absurd as the contention that fundamental discoveries in science are 'bound' to be exploited in certain ways.

Similarly, it is not 'technology' that pollutes the environment but industrial enterprises, property developers, car manufacturers, oil companies. It is not 'technology' that 'damages the ecology of Spaceship Earth' but mining and lumbering operations, pulp and paper manufacturing, manufacturers of pesticides. And ourselves. In short, the explosive advance of technology in the past thirty years has added nothing—*except scale*—to what was already there before: namely, the innate potential destructiveness of economic and political institutions. As Whitehead said, 'The potter and not the pot is responsible for the shape of the pot.'

Of course, to say all this is to say nothing new. Nor does it even point towards any solution. But it does say something. It is no news to political scientists that 'virtually every possible extension of man's powers over nature and himself will almost certainly be made or not made, shaped in one direction or another, not by considerations of what is good for Man, but by what is good for some men'.[21] It is to this problem, as old as society, that we must direct our efforts, surely, not to an attack on science.

Yet the current demand for 'the social responsibility of science' (a phrase that now has a very different connotation from that which it had in the 1930s) constitutes such an attack because it insists on ignoring, or seeking to break down, precisely those things that distinguish science from technology. It is right to be disquieted about many of the implications and excesses of technological society and right to attack the use of new technologies to enhance the control of elites and to manipulate the masses. But it is in the highest degree irresponsible to attack the enterprise of science itself, which, properly understood, stands in frank opposition to technology on many issues.

It is now *de rigueur* to talk about the 'myth' of the neutrality of science, the phrase 'neutrality of science' being taken to mean that science is neutral as to the uses to which it is put. Of course the scientist and his community should not be 'neutral' (i.e. silent) about these uses when the uses are apparent; but one cannot work backwards from practical application to the original science, nor can we talk of the applications of the original science until the applications are known. In *that* sense, science *is* neutral. And so to argue, as do the Roses, that there is a 'myth of neutrality' and that this myth has been 'to a large degree *responsible* [my italics] for the anti-social applications—the non-human or inhuman uses—of science, which have strongly contributed to many of the world's major problems' is to take an extraordinarily muddled as well as a hopelessly biased view of the matter.

The progress of science is governed, in large measure, by its own internal dynamic, not by public demand. Some fundamental science, certainly, is done *in the knowledge that it will have an application:* but, even when that is the case, that is not the motive for doing it, and never has been. The motive is always curiosity, curiosity about 'the marvellous and gorgeous frame of the world'.[22] Of course, it is possible to forecast the *general directions* of scientific discovery, because 'frontier' work is usually concentrated in the scientifically most profitable fields (most profitable, that is, in terms of exciting problems and new 'breakthroughs'). But the practical applications of *particular* scientific discoveries are singularly hard to predict, and the reason is simple. It is that all the really great scientific discoveries have implications of which their discoverers are not aware. Thus if it were, so to speak, possible to reverse the arrow of time and work backwards from unwanted technological applications to the original science on which they came later to be based, hardly any science would be done at all. If we were seriously to argue that there are certain phenomena of nature that scientists should not be allowed to investigate because of the possible consequences, we would have a trivial science (and therefore one of limited practical utility also). Given Einstein, the atomic bomb was theoretically possible, but it could not be known to be feasible until 1938, when it was realised that what Otto Hahn had achieved in his laboratory was atomic fission. Only a few years earlier Rutherford had dismissed the prospect of 'atom-smashing' as a commercial source of power as 'moonshine'. It is now fashionable to see in this episode an illustration of how foolish and nearsighted even the very greatest scientists can sometimes be. On the contrary, the criticism itself illustrates how feebly people who think this way grasp the inner workings of science.

As has been well said,[23] there is no fundamental discovery that is free from risk; all new knowledge that is not trivial is potentially dangerous; and the only safe research is research that does not make discoveries. Moreover, 'a policy of selective suppression of research cannot work, because all scientific investigations are now so closely interdependent that one cannot suppress one field of investigation without damaging the prospects of success in others'. As Harvey Brooks has said,[24] 'It is one thing to deplore work on biological warfare which has little or no importance for the development of the conceptual structure of biology, and quite another to eschew work on molecular biology because it might be used for military or manipulative purposes. Yet the line between the two kinds of activities is increasingly difficult to draw in practice.' The 'social responsibilitists' would, in effect, draw the line and put everything on one side of it. One cannot divide the different branches of science into those that are important for practical application and those that are not, and to forbid work the practical effects of which are evident and considered potentially or actually harmful is to run the risk of banning work the ultimate applications of which are not evident and yet may be highly beneficial.[25]

According to André Gide, 'In nature there are no problems, there are only solutions.' But this looks at nature from the standpoint of technology, not science. Whereas technology is concerned with solutions, a true account of science would have to say, 'In nature there are no solutions, there are only problems,' for every scientific 'solution' generates a host of new problems to be solved. It is undeniable that there is feedback from technology to science; but science is concerned with theoretical problems, problems of discovery, not with practical ones.[26]

The logic of the science–technology distinction is simple, and has been clearly stated by Michael Polanyi.[27] Men have long known how to do things (technology), e.g. make fire, without understanding *why* they could do them (science). Science shares with technology a concern to accumulate knowledge, but unlike technology its major concern *is not simply knowledge but understanding*. As Polanyi has pointed out, a piece of science may lead to advances in our understanding even if it has no practical uses, whereas a piece of technology (e.g. the invention of a better form of lighting—say incandescent lighting) would have great practical value even if it added nothing at all to our understanding. In a general sense, science progresses by logical steps by a persistent unfolding of thought and error-correction, whereas technology consists of a series of logically disconnected or unconnected solutions to a progression of problems. There are no connecting principles in the (technological) progression: invention of the candle, the gas light, the neon tube, though all represent improvements in illumination. But there certainly are connecting principles in the progression: Kepler, Galileo, Newton, Einstein.

Mario Bunge has pointed out[28] that technology may work quite happily with long-outdated scientific theories. Thus the design of optical instruments makes use very largely of what was known about light in the middle of the seventeenth century (since 'ray' optics is sufficient, for the most part, for successful optical manufacture). 'The accuracy requirements in applied science and in practice are far below those prevailing in pure research.' Technology aims at typical values rather than at exact values, at maximal efficiency rather than truth. Great accuracy in technology may indeed be a disadvantage (like a hole in the head), since it may make

calculation too complicated. In real situations such as technology encounters the relevant variables are seldom all known and precisely
controlled. Bunge suggests that modern technology differs from the
older crafts (traditional technology) in that its rules are grounded
in scientific theory rather than in rules of thumb and that there is
a conscious attempt to give a technological twist to (some) scientific
laws. But the scientist's success depends on the *detachment* of
science—on the separation of scientist from object—on the location
of the *objects* of science in what Popper has called 'the Third World'
(or more recently, to avoid obvious confusion, 'world 3')[29]—whereas
the technologist's success depends precisely on his *commitment*.

IV

My question, therefore, is whether, or for how long, science can
survive in a technological society in which the stated aim is to tie
science ever more firmly to the search for technological solutions
and to 'national goals'; in which a vast amount of science is done
in support of missions or as 'free' research in mission-oriented
agencies; in which, in a word, science policy seeks to bind fundamental science to the immediately perceived needs of the State; and
where this policy draws its support (even in part) from currents of
opinion that attack science and tend to pervert and destroy the
scientific attitude through misunderstandings of its nature. The scientific attitude has always been precariously rooted in society, and
the fact that it is now becoming less firmly rooted among scientists
themselves is truly a danger signal. At the base of the scientific
attitude lies what Jacques Monod has called 'the most powerful
idea ever to have emerged in the nöosphere'—the idea of objective
knowledge. Destroy that idea, wilfully or by default, and you
destroy science.

A good example of the contemporary muddle is contained in an
article by a university chemist that appeared in *Science* a year or
two ago.[30] The author argues that the salient feature of the counter-
culture is its 'epistomology of direct sensuous experience, subjectivity,
and respect for intuition—especially intuitive knowledge based on
a "naive" openness to nature and to other people'. Science must
change because it is incomplete, and it is incomplete because it
fails to accommodate this epistemological mode. It is conceivable,
he says, that the notion of complementarity (deriving from the

Copenhagen school and especially from Bohr) affords a means of effecting this accommodation, since complementarity 'teaches' that a given phenomenon manifests itself to the observer in conflicting modes, neither of which can be subsumed in the other, but each of which is equally rational. There are three 'tenets of counter-cultural thought that [seem to the author to hold] great promise for the enrichment of scientific practice and, perhaps, for the improvement of scientific morality'. These are: that the most reliable and effective knowing follows from direct and open confrontation with phenomena ('nature's ways are open to direct intuitive, sensuous knowledge'); that since the self and the environment are inextricable, 'one can understand his surroundings by being sensitive to his own reactions to them'; and that 'because knowledge of nature is, in this way, equally open to all, the "expert" is highly suspect'. There appears to the author to be 'much of value in the mind-set that includes these ideas'. I have no doubt that these ideas were tremendously popular with his students; but it is inconceivable to me that anyone, let alone a scientist, could seriously think that science would be 'enriched' by their incorporation into scientific method. Indeed, 'enrichment' would be the very opposite of what one would expect from the operation of the complementarity principle in this (or any other) context, since what Bohr intended by 'complementarity' (though he may have muddied the waters when he extended his notion from its rather limited application in quantum physics to the wider world of thought) was, precisely, that each of a pair of complementary concepts *limits the simultaneous use of the other*.

The counter-culture is strongly egalitarian, conformist, and tribalistic. It is oriented to the present rather than to the future, and it places a high value on impulse, sensual enjoyment and immediate gratification. It is opposed in all these respects to science, which at once is 'elitist' (in the intellectual sense), is imbued with a sharply critical and competitive spirit (one really can't see Jim Watson in a commune), progresses through a rugged process of natural selection of ideas, is ascetic, and is prepared to have its servants wait (if need be for a lifetime) for results. In other words, it is everything that the counter-culture is not.

Lest it be thought that in my arguments against anti-science I have complacently avoided the real problems so conveniently hiding under the blanket called 'the social responsibility of science', let me end by saying that I believe that these problems need careful identification, analysis and thorough discussion. I would argue, however, that they are basically problems concerning the organisation of *scientists* rather than the character of *science*. Here I can only hint at what may be involved. For example, 'making scientific information openly available to the public at large' (which appears to be one of the 'grassroots' aims of the 'social responsibilists') is futile double-talk, since most if not all uninterpreted scientific information is not publicly comprehensible. Its 'meaning' and its significance for society (which is what is important) can be grasped by the public only if the information is already pre-digested and interpreted—which means interpreted by some group of scientists.

The 'social responsibility of science' means (or ought to mean) the growth of social responsibility *within* the scientific community itself. Thus, the impact on science of the 'professionalisation' and 'bureaucratisation' of scientists, the development of, and the growth in influence of, powerful scientific elites, the dubiously representative nature of the present system of 'science advisers' with special access to politics, the stifling of responsible discussion within learned societies, are all germane. Scientists as a group have to be honest with themselves, and much more honest than they have been lately with their political 'masters'; the method of rational critical discussion of the social issues raised by science has to be practised within the scientific community, beginning at the undergraduate level; 'sub-disciplinary' isolationism has to be broken down. The phenomenon of individual scientists (to adapt Ernest Bevin's famous phrase) 'hawking their consciences around in public' is a curious one, and probably does more harm than good. It is too late (and perhaps it was never possible) to 'disestablish' science, but that surely does not mean that scientists must continue indefinitely in an attitude of prudential acquiescence, whether to their own leaders or to the demands of the State? The Council for Science and Society (which was set up in July 1973 under the chairmanship of Sir Michael Swann) promises to be an interesting experiment in the responsible pursuit by scientists of the 'social responsibility of science'. Its progress will be watched with interest in many countries.[31]

Notes

1 OECD, *Reviews of National Science Policy, Canada,* Organisation for Economic Co-operation and Development, Paris, 1969.

2 'Anti-science', 'editorial comment in *Minerva*, October 1971. From here on, when I speak of 'science' without qualification, I mean fundamental science. By fundamental science I mean what philosophers of science, historians of science and sociologists of science mean: in fact what has usually been meant by the term until the science policy debate spawned innumerable fine distinctions. I mean the search for new kinds of facts about the universe we inhabit (scientific discovery) and the increase in our understanding of the nature of the world. This is done by probably no more than 5 per cent of all those who call themselves scientists, but it is basic to all the rest.

3 For the exponential growth of science, see Derek de Solla Price's numerous writings, especially *Little Science, Big Science,* Columbia University Press, New York, 1963; and for hints about the conditions for continued exponential growth, see W. J. M. Mackenzie, *Politics and Social Science,* Penguin Books, Harmondsworth, 1967, the concluding section of the book.

4 It is, of course, true in one important sense that we need new knowledge like, as Robert Oppenheimer put it on a famous occasion, 'a hole in the head'; but those who talk of a moratorium on scientific discovery (to allow time for society to absorb the applications of what is already known) are talking nonsense. A moratorium on scientific discovery would quickly destroy science.

5 I offer this as a rhetorical rather than an absolute statistic. It is entirely possible that the NASA figures heavily over-stated the amount actually spent on fundamental research, partly because of notorious difficulties in classification of types of research (which is always highly arbitrary) and partly because it was, *at that time* (it would not be now), clearly in NASA's political interests to make the amount spent on fundamental research look as big as possible.

6 Jean-Jacques Salomon, 'The mating of knowledge and power', *Impact,* XXII, 1–2, January–June 1972.

7 Harvey Brooks has pointed out that in America the national investment in astrology is 'between ten and twenty times' that in astronomy: 'Can science survive in the modern age?' *Science,* 1 October 1971.

8 *Explanation and Understanding,* Routledge & Kegan Paul, London, 1971. Von Wright says (p. 2), 'Two main traditions can be distinguished in the history of ideas, differing as to the conditions an explanation has to satisfy in order to be scientifically respectable. The one tradition is sometimes called *aristotelian,* the other *galilean.* The names suggest that the first has very ancient roots in the intellectual history of man, while the second is of relatively recent origin. There is some truth in this, but it should be taken with a grain of salt. What I call here the galilean tradition has an ancestry going back beyond Aristotle to Plato. *One should also*

beware of thinking that the aristotelian tradition today represents merely the fading survival of obsolete elements from which science is gradually becoming 'liberated'. (Italics added.)

[9] *From Biology to Ethics*, Salk Institute occasional papers, No. 1, 1969.

[10] Some of the recent statements of scientists and writers on science (some with scientific training), particularly but by no means exclusively those who incline towards the left, writing under the influence of the contemporary alarm about technology and the alleged seduction of science by 'the military–industrial complex', are quite extraordinary. The dismissal of the neutrality of science as a 'myth' (e.g. by the Roses, Stephen and Hilary, in *Science and Society*, Smith, Gloucester, Mass., 1970) has a respectable ancestry in Marxist thought and the sociology of knowledge. But Jerry Ravetz (*Scientific Knowledge and its Social Problems*, Oxford University Press, New York, 1971) now tells us that 'the conception of science as the pursuit of truth' is 'obsolete'; Kit Pedler (*New Scientist*, 5 November 1970) calls the 'duty of science to explore the unknown unhampered by any other considerations' a 'bankrupt and arrogant assumption'; and the editor of the *Spectator* (George Gale) tells us that few laymen would nowadays 'endorse the flattering version of science as scepticism postulated by Adam Smith. Were a new Adam Smith to write a new *Wealth of Nations* ... he would certainly not put forward so optimistic a view.'

[11] Distinguished and eccentric exceptions can always be found, of course; e.g. I. I. Rabi, who has described the arts as 'not the kind of thing that will inspire men to push on to new heights' and the works of Shakespeare as 'wonderful, glorified gossip'. But, on the whole, I think there are probably fewer daft statements by scientists about the humanities than there are by humanists about science.

[12] William S. Beck, *Modern Science and the Nature of Life*, Penguin Books, Harmondsworth, 1957.

[13] 'The representation of nature in contemporary physics', *Daedalus*, LXXXVII, summer 1958, pp. 95 ff.

[14] There is an amusing illustration of this in *Niels Bohr: his Life and Work as Seen by his Friends and Colleagues*, ed. S. Rozental, Interscience —John Wiley, New York, 1967. Commenting on a Tom Mix western movie, Bohr said, 'I didn't like the picture, it was too improbable. It's logical that the villain runs off with the girl, that always happens; it's unlikely that the bridge would collapse under their carriage, but I'm willing to accept it, and also that the heroine remains suspended in mid-air over a precipice. I am even willing to accept that at that very moment Tom Mix is coming by on his horse. But that at that very moment there should be a fellow with a motion picture camera to film the whole business, that is more than I am willing to believe.'

[15] Elsewhere in the same article Heisenberg says, 'When we speak of a picture of nature provided by contemporary exact science, we do not actually mean any longer a picture of nature, but rather a picture of our relation to nature' (i.e. 'exact' science is no longer exact). And again: 'Science is no longer in the position of an observer of nature, but rather

recognises itself as part of the interplay between man and nature' (i.e. what is said originally to hold only of particle physics is now extrapolated to include the whole of science).

[16] By 'behaviourism in the broadest sense' I mean the doctrine that holds: (a) that we can observe only behaviours, i.e. events external to the things observed, and (b) that only observables can enter into scientific discourse: nothing that is not observable may enter into the province of science (I follow J. O. Wisdom, 'Science versus the scientific revolution', *Philosophy of Social Science*, I, 1971, pp. 123 ff.).

[17] One of the earliest behaviourists in social science was Arthur F. Bentley, best known to political scientists as the author of *The Process of Government*, but closely associated with Dewey in some of his work. He attacked what he called 'feelings and faculties' as sources of social action on the ground that they were 'spooks'—i.e. occult.

[18] Since the authority of Francis Bacon is all too frequently brought in aid by 'social responsibilists', it is perhaps worth noting Bacon's point that God *first* made a Light to shine upon the World, i.e. knowledge came first, technology (improvements in the environment such as the creation of fowls of the air, creeping things, etc.) coming later in the week. Bacon never had any doubt that what he called Experiments of Light were prior to Experiments of Use. Deweian pragmatists, of course, hold the reverse: that our understanding of nature arises from our successful assumption of power over nature. But this is not what Bacon meant by Knowledge and Power.

[19] Art and technology have had separate histories too: e.g. magnificent art existed in the near absence of technology in the middle and late Paleolithic eras. But this is not to deny that art has in recent centuries, at least in many societies, notably our own, been much affected by technology.

[20] 'Some general implications of the research of the Harvard University program on technology and society', *Technology and Culture*, x, 4.

[21] Victor Ferkiss, *Technological Society*, Vintage Books, London, 1973.

[22] Thomas More, *Utopia*.

[23] Review of the Roses' *Science and Society* and Greenberg's *The Politics of American Science* in *The Times Literary Supplement*, 5 February 1970.

[24] 'Can science survive in the modern age?' *Science*, 1 October 1971, pp. 21 ff.

[25] It is worth remembering, too, that (as Brooks points out) fundamental science may, and often does, lead to a critique of technology: for example, the pesticide pollutant problem was first identified as an 'accidental' result of basic research in oceanography.

[26] There are, of course, a host of practical problems of *research design*, but that is another matter.

[27] E.g. in *The Logic of Liberty*, Routledge & Kegan Paul, London, 1951, ch. 5.

[28] 'Technology as applied science', *Technology and Culture*, VII, 1966, pp. 329 ff.

[29] World 1 is the world of physical objects and physical states, world 2 the world of mental states, and world 3 is the world of objective contents of thought. Objective *knowledge* exists in world 3 and as such is totally independent of any one person's claim to know or believe, disposition to assent, etc. Popper's formulation, to which it is impossible to do justice in a footnote, is fully consistent with his critical rationalism, realism, anti-psychologism, anti-inductivism, etc. For a full (recent) discussion see his *Objective Knowledge: an Evolutionary Approach*, Oxford University Press, New York, 1972.

[30] Thomas R. Blackburn, 'Sensuous–intellectual complementarity in science', *Science*, 4 June 1971, pp. 1003 ff.

[31] It is modelled on the highly successful group Justice, the British section of the International Commission of Jurists, which has done much to arouse the public and official conscience on important issues.

C. C. Hood

9

Government by other means: the grants economy and the contract State[1]

The background

Almost twenty years ago Mackenzie and Grove explored some of the features of the administrative 'peripheries' of British central government, which they found to be surrounded by a puzzling semi-public, semi-independent sector difficult both to classify and to explain in conventional terms.[2] In the following decade of the 1960s these administrative peripheries were a major 'growth sector' in the context of sharply increasing government intervention in the US and UK economies (as measured by the percentage of GNP passing through 'public' hands). Indeed, the relative position of 'central administration', in Mackenzie and Grove's sense, slightly declined in Britain in the 1960s: direct public service remuneration fell from about 31 per cent to 25 per cent of total government expenditure between 1961 and 1971, and in the United States this item remained relatively constant at 14–15 per cent, in the context of increases in government expenditure of (approximately) 161 per cent and 113 per cent respectively.[3]

The rise in government expenditure in this period was associated both with a vogue for creating 'independent public bodies' and with an overall rise in the proportion of government funds which is given to outside organisations in the form of grants and contracts. Some of these changes were of a largely book-keeping nature, such as the removal of the Post Office from the civil service establishment in both countries and the change from directly employed cleaners to contract cleaning. Nevertheless, government by such means was (deliberately?) confusing to those who were conditioned to associate government intervention in economic affairs with central 'bureaucracy' of a stereotyped 'civil service' kind.

The Americans spotted and articulated this process first, coining the phrase 'grants economy' and 'contract State'[4] in the 1960s to denote the increasing use of organisations not directly administered by government employees in the execution of federal programmes. Federal government contracts were said to have achieved in twenty years 'a scope and magnitude that now rivals simple subsidies, tariffs, taxes, direct regulation and positive action programmes in their impact upon the nature and quality of American life'.[5] Some observers even discerned 'a new kind of public sector', in which many (perhaps most) of the employees of the federal government were 'invisible'.[6]

No strictly comparable discussion took place in Britain at this time, though similar problems were appearing. If 'grants' and 'contracts' are assumed to be indistinguishable over a wide range of activities, the overall difference between the US and the UK appears to be small. It is not easy to obtain reliable figures for comparable years; but in 1968, when American discussion of the 'grants economy' and the 'contract State' was perhaps at its height, Bruce Smith estimated that grants (9 per cent) and contracts (32 per cent) together accounted for 41 per cent of the federal budget, or $71·5 billion for 'fiscal 1968' (= year ending June 1968).[7] For Britain, estimates for contracting vary; but a working figure for the same year would be that grants (33 per cent) and contracts (12 per cent) together accounted for over 45 per cent of central government expenditure, or £4856 million for 1967–68.[8] (These figures are highly approximate, and it is difficult to say how far the pattern which they depict is 'typical', because general cross-national 'profiles' of government expenditure in these terms do not yet exist.)

Components of the grant and contract sector

It is doubtful how much significance can be attributed to the preponderance of 'grants' as against 'contracts' in Britain as compared to the USA. Some writers use the terms almost interchangeably, though this is less common in Britain; and certainly the distinction between a 'grant' (theoretically, payment for work which the recipient wishes to do) and a 'contract' (theoretically, payment for work which the sponsor wishes to have done) is at best precarious. 'Grants' are seldom attruistic gifts,[9] and 'contracts' are often geared towards 'non-procurement' ends such as preserving jobs, implementing regional policy and even pursuing foreign policy (as with the various Anglo-French prestige aerospace projects which were floated during the period of Britain's first negotiations for membership of the EEC in 1961–62).

The two bulkiest parts of the grant and contract sector are defence and related science-based industries on the one hand, and welfare programmes on the other. In both countries defence is the biggest contracting area, and weapons acquisition by contract has a long history, though in the nineteenth century both governments tended to depend largely on their own arsenals for weapons and ammunition. But as war material became increasingly industrialised in the late nineteenth century (for example, with the advent of heavy rifled guns and armour-plate) there was increasing reliance on private arms manufacture; and in both countries military aircraft have always been produced entirely by private industry, with the government simply maintaining basic research establishments (the US National Advisory Committee for Aeronautics and the British Royal Aircraft Establishment).

This dependence on private industry for armaments has continued and increased, though the balance has shifted from the 'secondary' to the 'quaternary' industrial sector (that is, from manufacturing industry to research). US federal government appropriations for research and development rose from about $1·1 billion in 1950 to about $17 billion in 1970; in Britain the increase is of a broadly similar magnitude, from about £12 million in 1953 (when this item first appeared in the national income statistics) to about £130 million in 1970). The term 'contract State' was first applied to the 'R & D' field in the USA, and the British position is in some ways comparable. Federal funds seem to account for about 66 per cent of all R & D in the USA, whereas government funds seem to account for about 56 per cent of all R & D in the UK. About 80 per cent of annual R & D appropriations in the USA are spent on work performed outside government; the comparable figure for the UK is about 70 per cent.[10]

The other main component of increasing grant and contract expenditure has been increasing central funding of welfare programmes executed by lower tiers of government, which in both countries has been one of the most rapidly rising elements in government expenditure (though from different base lines: only about a quarter of state and local funds are derived from federal grants in the USA, whereas in the UK about half of local authority funds are derived from central government grants). Thus in the USA federal grants-in-aid to state and local governments rose about 12 per cent per year between 1950 and 1970;[11] in Britain the pattern is more erratic and the rate of growth is slightly slower: government grants to local authorities rose at a mean rate of about 10 per cent per year between 1951 and 1969.[12]

Problems of accountability and control

Simple-mindedly, one might think that governments resort to contracting precisely in order to avail themselves of the simplicity and spontaneous discipline of the market rather than the more ponderous process of administrative control. But this is at best a half-truth. Formal advertising for bids from 'all comers', even for simple goods, has the defect of proclaiming government's needs so clearly as to invite collusion between suppliers or speculative operations. Likewise, simple acceptance of the lowest tender is to play into the hands of the incompetent, the irresponsible or the insolvent. Accordingly, competition is almost always restricted in some way.

Thus the British government had almost abandoned 'at large' advertising of contracts by the late nineteenth century and even acted through confidential brokers in some markets to conceal its activities.[13] In the USA the formal doctrine of advertising still survives, but it is so peppered with exceptions that only about 20 per cent or less of defence procurement is now done through formal advertising.[14] In the USA about half the federal government's purchases are non-competitive, in that not more than one supplier is involved;[15] in Britain non-competitive contracts amount to about a third of the total of central government purchasing.[16]

Having thus in large part abandoned 'market discipline', governments have to return to administrative supervision of contractors' costs, even where contracts are nominally let on a 'fixed price' basis rather than on a cost-plus-profit basis (in Britain, about a third of non-competitive contracts, mostly for research, are let on a cost-plus basis). But this immediately leads into a round of problems. For example, cost control of prime contractors often turns out to depend on control of their multiple sub-contractors, who are typically much less amenable to central administrative supervision.[17] Second the 'cost' of an item is a relatively arbitrary accounting concept, particularly where there are common overheads to be allocated between 'government' and 'private' projects by contractors, or (worse) between the various national subsidiary units of international companies. The latter problem plays a large part in the perpetual rows about the prices charged by international companies selling drugs to the National Health Service, and the first can very easily generate absurdities as well. For example, cases have arisen where the British government has brought proprietary drugs priced to include R & D costs when it had already contributed to such costs in overheads connected with another contract.

Even without these problems, such monitoring operations are hampered by the shortage of specialist 'policemen' in both countries. Thus in spite of the fact that between one-third and a half of GNP in both countries passes through 'public' hands in some way, and that nearly half the sum is spent on grants and contracts, the British Exchequer and Audit Department numbers little over 500 people; and even though the General Accounting Office in the USA is over ten times as large, it too is very small in relation to the task.

In the late 1950s and early 1960s there was a build-up of anxiety over the extent to which the US federal government lacked the 'in-house' capacity adequately to supervise contracted-out operations: supervision and even policy advice were contracted out (often creating acute conflicts of interest).[18] In Britain too the government is almost permanently short of professional accountants, engineers and technical cost officers in the contracting departments, so that even the prime contractors are often inadequately supervised (this played a large part in the Ferranti and Bristol Siddeley affairs) and work is often done in arrear.[19] Not only are policing resources of this kind very limited, they are also subject to wastage to private agencies.

Even when policing resources are adequate and the issues are clear, governments have few effective weapons to deploy against unsatisfactory performers.[20] Threats to 'shop elsewhere' are scarcely credible in many cases because (particularly in Britain) the encouragement of concentration among suppliers implies that many contract relations will be recurrent. Indeed, threats not to renew contracts may be counter-productive if they lead to the 'brochuremanship' syndrome, in which contractors concentrate their talent on selling new contract proposals rather than in executing the contracts which they have already obtained.

The limitation of competition also exposes governments to the 'lame duck' syndrome, in which recurrent contracts have built up relationships of reciprocal need between governments and individual firms, so that governments may be obliged to bail out firms in trouble (such as the extrication of Yarrow's from UCS before the UCS crash of 1971). In the field of grants, too, the denial of funds is often an idle threat, especially in the case of welfare grants, where governments cannot check cost overruns or punish errant local organisations without also punishing innocent people.[21] Also, the withholding of funds is a blunt instrument, largely negative in its effects and so drastic that central officials are rarely willing to carry it out.

Indeed, the key problem for such officials is that of how to invent and adapt a suitable range of middle-range threats; and accordingly the authorities in both countries have tried to develop more 'credible' diminutives of financial punishment. Thus in the late 1950s and early 1960s 'fixed price' contracts become a popular solution, and a large number of 'hybrid' types of contract were invented as a half-way house between fixed price and cost-plus (these were known variously as incentive contracts, target prices, penalty clauses, etc., and all involved 'cost' plus a sum varying according to 'results'). But these weapons can operate only within a fairly narrow range.

First, it is not easy to persuade contractors to accept fixed-price contracts for risky, long-range projects: thus in the Anglo-French Concorde project and in the parallel US SST project (now cancelled) the great bulk of the risks had to be borne by government. Second, where (as in the case of Concorde again) there is a guaranteed minimum profit, the incentive to reduce costs diminishes as costs approach the level at which the minimum profit operates, and disappears completely when that level is reached.[22] Third, the later in the life of a contract that a fixed or 'target' price is agreed (and in practice it is common for such prices to be agreed very late), the lower the risk and the smaller the practical differences from a cost-plus-type contract.

Fourth, fixed-price contracts have drawbacks in the case of items not for sale in an open market and in which the government has no idea of contractors' actual costs (this is the logic of post-costing and of the 'truth in negotiations' laws which were introduced in both the USA and the UK in the 1960s).[23] Fifth, you can have a fixed-price contract only where work is clearly definable, but muzzi-ness of objectives and ill-defined end products are among the reasons for resorting to grants and contracts in the first place. The whole range of available 'incentives' is useful only in so far as there is some yardstick of performance, particularly in an interdependent set of contracts.

Perhaps a more fundamental influence limiting the effectiveness of changed contract procedures in reducing cost overruns is that of government agencies themselves, whose innocence in this process cannot be taken for granted. It is often expedient for them to concur with over-optimistic original estimates of project costs. Sir Robert Peel is said to have remarked that 'If you adopt the opinion of military men, we are never safe': the tendency for military authori-ties to 'gold-plate' their requirements (in the context of international technological leapfrogging and continual raising of the stakes of military equipment) and the 'conspiracy of optimism' regarding cost or technical difficulties between the military, scientists and con-tractors are hard to break by changes in contract procedure alone.[24]

Similar issues arise in the search for middle-range threats in the field of grants. In the USA 'audit exceptions' (a *post hoc* measure involving the refusal of funds for particular acts of expenditure rather than the blanket withholding of funds) are an example of this process. Martha Derthick describes the use of federal audit excep-tions in Massachusetts in the late 1940s, when the salaries of elected board members engaged in administration were disallowed as part of a campaign to secure merit appointment systems in welfare administration.[25] The relative shift towards 'project grants' (in 1970 about half of all federal grants were project grants), in which federal approval is a highly discretionary process, and away from grants obtainable 'as of right' according to clear-cut indices, may have reduced this problem to some extent, though it puts more pressure on control processes at the selection stage.

In the UK a similar process has taken place, though it began far earlier, in the early nineteenth century, when the UK 'grant system' grew up (in the USA such a system did not develop until the 1920s and 1930s). Thus the shift from specific grants to bloc grants began much earlier, particularly with the general Exchequer grant of 1929, and has gone much further. Henry Parris has described the shift away from 'all or nothing' grants to more flexible types of financial weapons, such as the power to withhold *part* of a grant (as with US 'audit exceptions') and the 'doubling up' of central and local expenditure.[26]

However, US grant administration has always been a 'diplomatic' process to a large extent. Even in Britain many of the simple nineteenth century administrative weapons have lost their cutting edge with the virtual abandonment of specific grants to local authorities (almost 80 per cent of British local authority grants are now bloc grants, compared to about 16 per cent in the early 1950s) and with the changing character of the civil service inspectorates from 'law enforcers' to 'diplomats'.[27] These changes are due in part to the development of 'internal' processes of inspection and control and to professionalism, but they mean that central government as such has few control instruments lying between draconian measures on the one hand and simple advice and exhortation on the other.[28]

Explanations

The benefits of this administrative style are certainly open to question. As a 'short cut' to programme implementation it is liberally strewn with banana skins; indeed, Altensetter (with reference to health) has discerned a 'paradox' in government by grant in that it involves more 'bureaucracy' (in the sense of clumsy 'paperwork' and checking-up procedures) than old-fashioned bureaucracy proper.[29] But it could still be argued that they are an administrative *pis-aller*, dictated by the limits of central administrative capacity in terms of information-handling—the problem of 'apoplexy at the centre'.[30] In fact the main practical relevance of cybernetics is to show that control in complex systems has to be very largely 'self-control' because of the sharp limits of information channels.[31] Thus large 'command' organizations tend to reproduce within themselves relationships analogous to 'contracts' in a market system, in an attempt to push routine activities to administrative peripheries without loss of control.

Examples of this process are the development of the 'recoup' concept,[32] target rates of return and 'public dividend capital'[33] in British public industry financing, plus the 'customer–contractor' principle in science administration. Even the large 'private' US corporations have to create simulated 'internal markets' and 'pseudo-companies' whose inputs and outputs are measured and priced; within some of these corporations there are even 'anti-trust' regulations to prevent collusion between the 'pseudo-companies'.[34] Indeed, Anthony Downs has asserted that above a certain size any large command organisation turns inevitably into a sort of market, either through corruption or through 'non-money pricing'.[35]

The other main 'administrative' defence of grants and contracts is that they constitute an advantageously flexible system of mobilising talent through self-terminating relationships. But far from being self-terminating, many grants and contracts are part of a recurrent process. In Britain contractual relationships in the fields of drugs, telephones, shipbuilding, TV, aircraft and others are typically recurrent, and the same is true for much of the grants sector. Similarly the US 'contract State' is a perpetuation of what was originally a highly irregular crash programme sparked off in the early 1950s by perceived threats of Soviet military challenge.

There is, of course, a quite different way of looking at the whole structure. Irrespective of their effectiveness or otherwise as techniques of implementing programmes, grants and contracts are political resources. They can be used to manipulate (as with the popular idea of foreign aid to poor countries as a 'Trojan horse' of 'imperialism')[36] or to generate support (as in the crudest—but by no means extinct—case where government contracts are exchanged for bribes or campaign funds).

From this point of view the whole structure takes on a different logic; and what to an 'administrator' might look like isolated 'rotten apples'[37] begin to look more like problems inherent in the system. Indeed, in a crude neo-Marxist analysis there is an obvious logic in governments becoming an increasing source of profit to private industry as economic growth expands the working class tax base from which the bulk of government revenue is drawn. Thus to the traditional 'merchants of death' (whose relative share of government expenditure is in fact declining in both Britain and the USA) are added the 'merchants of health' (perhaps the new 'villains of the piece' in 1973), telephones, computers, foreign aid and so on. (In both the UK and the USA foreign aid is very largely 'tied aid' and therefore represents guaranteed markets for domestic industry; moreover, at least half of aid-financed goods are required by US legislation to be shipped in US vessels.)

Powerful as it is, this line of analysis has three main defects. It ignores the administrative dimensions of the problem. Second, it ignores the 'ingovernmental relations' aspects of the structure, which are of major quantitative importance. Third, it ignores the large part played by much of the semi-independent public sector and by the 'non-profit' sector in the USA. Moreover, explaining government behaviour in the mixed economy by reference to the 'needs' of capitalism is a difficult and teleological process. Perhaps a more prosaic level of political analysis can be slotted in between explanations of this kind and the 'administrative' explanations which have already been discussed.

Such an analysis might begin with the most obvious effect of giving money away to outside bodies,[38] which is to neutralise the opposition to central government programmes which would otherwise come from private industry or from local authorities (this happens in the well known US tactic of spreading defence contracts around the states to gain a broad base of Congressional support). In fact, the slow growth in the productivity of public sector services relative to the private sector[39] results in these services tending to absorb a larger and larger share of social resources as economic growth proceeds, and this may imply an increasing political necessity to conceal this proportionate growth by resorting to 'indirect' administration and 'tied aid' (which draws support from both providers and receivers).[40] This may of course support the neo-Marxist argument. Indeed, one of the effects of combining high public expenditure with a relatively small number of government officials is to make the distinction between 'public' and 'private' administration hard to draw in some cases: for example, the British marriage guidance councils (voluntary bodies financed by both central and local government, plus other funds) are in a sense 'public', 'private', 'central' and 'local' at the same time.

Besides their role in mobilising support for programmes, grants and contracts may be used for the 'export' of awkward problems to local authorities or to organisations only indirectly linked with governments. First, governments may have *bona fide* reasons for not wanting to be too closely involved (as with art patronage or the administration of legal aid). Second, by avoiding a careful specification of objectives, unpopular decisions can be pushed down to local level (for example, in education or transport grants). Third, some activities are tinged with impropriety of some kind and therefore call for some form of 'unacknowledgeable means'[41] or its diminutives.

A notorious example of this was the 'Starboat Company', a

phoney Norwegian–Panamanian firm set up in 1969 to obtain for
Israel five fast French gunboats which had formally been denied
to Israel under the French arms embargo—a deal which had the
obvious complicity of the French arms bureaucracy at some level.
Similarly, in the recent Anglo-Icelandic fishing dispute the British
government's first reaction to calls for protection by harassed
trawlermen early in 1973 was to charter a Liberian-registered tug
(whose master was 'advised' by an ex-naval commander) to obstruct
the Icelandic gunboats. Only later was 'tugboat diplomacy' abandoned and a formal naval squadron dispatched.[42]

In private industry, too, it is common to hire 'outsiders' for the
performance of sensitive tasks such as auditing, management evaluation (often a means of sweetening the pill of executive dismissals),
the prevention of shop-floor pilfering, and so on. Similar tactics
can be used by governments, though this kind of thing can become
symbiotic: for example, where the costs of some service are shared
between local and central government (such as education), each can
blame the other for defects in the system, and reciprocal buck-
passing possibilities of this kind may be of mutual political benefit.[43]

Fourth, grants and contracts are a convenient means for governments to pursue incompatible policies through 'sleight of hand'
tactics. For example, over the issue of terms for entry into the EEC
in 1971, the British government unwittingly financed part of the
'anti-Market' campaign as well as the 'pro-Market' campaign,
because the anti-Marketeers' campaign focused heavily on the
alleged 'sell-out' of the inshore fishermen over fishing limits. The
self-appointed leader of the inshore fishermen in their fight against
the government's terms was the Fisheries Organisation Society—a
body almost wholly financed by government grant. Another example
is the offer of grants for hotels, tourism, coastal improvements and
the like in the same places where other grants are available for
developing mining or fishmeal factories, and leaving the resultant
conflicts to blow up at local level. At best, this is a means of holding
options in a world of uncertainty; at worst, it is the 'tunnel vision'
so often associated with programme-oriented administration.

Fifth, there is the use of grants and contracts in administrative
'outflanking operations' between levels and branches of government
and even of outside institutions (as with the use of grants and contracts as a means of circumventing the rigidities of the academic
tenure system). This can work in a variety of ways. For example, the

supersession of the old royal patent system by a centralised system of stationery purchasing was one of the means used by the British Treasury to secure its central financial control over other government departments.[44]

More often, of course, grants and contracts (like 'independent' public corporations) are used as a means of evading orthodox financial control and of by-passing established constitutional structures. For example, the avoidance of Congressional scrutiny, the by-passing of civil service laws over salaries, perquisites, etc., and to some extent the avoidance of judicial review, were among the reasons for the increasing use of contracts with 'non-profit corporations' by executive agencies in the USA.

For example, the Office of Economic Opportunity in its early years used contracts with so-called private agencies to by-pass the state welfare bureacracies and to build up the political strength of racial minorities.[45] In Britain such tactics are much less overt, and the corresponding urban programmes (such as the educational priority areas and the community development projects) have been channelled through local authorities, though funded by central departments. But in Britain, too, a dominant motive in many 'quasi-government' arrangements fed by grants has traditionally been the avoidance of direct local authority control. For example, organisations like the Scottish Special Housing Association and the Northern Ireland Housing Trust have rather obvious 'outflanking' motives; and similarly organisations like the passenger transport authorities, water authorities, and the new area health boards which put local authority representatives in a minority *vis-à-vis* Ministerial appointees.

Conclusion

It may be that much more subtle political tunes can be played with these instruments than those indicated here; but certainly grants and contracts as a method of *administration* can quickly be pushed to the point of diminishing returns, and it is easy to find innumerable examples of gigantic waste and inefficiency, not to mention straight corruption, in the 'contract State'. An analogy might be drawn with the old system of tax farming in England, which ended in the seventeenth century at a point when the collection of taxes by contract had become so vexatious (partly because tendering was being rigged by collusive syndicates) that direct administration was re-adopted.[46] This is the argument put forward by J. K. Galbraith and others for nationalising the main US defence contractors.[47]

It is true that some of the more irregular incarnations of government by contract are on the wane (for example, the dismemberment of the OEO and a general disposition to create public corporations rather than non-profit 'private' contractors). But it is unlikely that central administration will wholly replace the grant and contract sector, because (if the analysis above is correct) the political logic of grants and contracts still seems very strong, in spite of the administrative problems involved.

Notes

[1] This is an adaptation of a paper relating to the Anglo-American Carnegie Corporation Project on Accountability and Independence, 1970–1972, originally presented at the ninth IPSA conference, Montreal, August 1973.

[2] W. J. M. Mackenzie and J. W. Grove, *Central Administration in Britain*, Longmans, London, 1957.

[3] Sources: *Annual Abstracts of Statistics* (UK and USA) and annual memoranda by the Financial Secretary to the Treasury on the Estimates.

[4] So far as I know, the phrase 'contract State' was invented by H. L. Nieburg (*In the Name of Science*, Quadrangle Books, Chicago, 1966) and the 'grants economy' by K. Boulding (*Economics as a Science*, McGraw-Hill, New York, 1970 and (with M. and A. Pfaff) *Transfers in an Urbanized Economy*, Wadsworth, Belmont, Cal., 1973).

[5] Nieburg, *op. cit.*, p. 185.

[6] V. K. Heyman, 'Government by contract', *Public Administration Review*, XXI, 1961, p. 59.

[7] B. L. Smith, 'Accountability and independence in the contract State', in B. L. Smith and D. C. Hague (eds.), *The Dilemma of Accountability in Modern Government*, Macmillan, London, 1971, pp. 19–21.

[8] These figures have been taken from the *Memorandum by the Financial Secretary to the Treasury on the Estimates, 1969–70*, Cmnd. 3971, and from correspondence with the Treasury and other purchasing departments. C. Turpin offers figures in *Government Contracts*, Penguin Books, Harmondsworth, 1972, p. 16, but these are not complete.

[9] The classic analysis of 'gifts' is M. Mauss, *The Gift Relationship*, Cohen & West, London, 1969.

[10] Figures for the USA taken from M. Reagan, *Science and the Federal Patron*, Oxford University Press, New York, 1969, and *Statistical Abstracts of the USA*; figures for the UK taken from *Statistics of Science and Technology*, HMSO, London, 1970.

[11] E. B. Staats, 'New problems of accountability for federal programs'

160   C. C. HOOD

address to the American Society of Public Administration, April 1971, p. 7.

¹² Source: *Annual Abstracts of Statistics*, HMSO, London, 1952–72.

¹³ B. Pool, *Navy Board Contracts, 1660–1832*, Longmans, London, 1966; *Report of the Select Committee on Contracts*, H.C. 93, 1857.

¹⁴ D. F. Page, *Negotiation and Management of Defence Contracts*, Wiley, New York, 1970.

¹⁵ Staats, 'New problems of accountability for federal programs', *op. cit.*

¹⁶ Public Accounts Committee, *First, Second and Third Reports*, H.C. 166–1, 265–1, 297, 1969–70.

¹⁷ For example, see Public Accounts Committee, *Third Report*, 1961–62.

¹⁸ C. Danhof, *Government Contracting and Technological Change*, Brookings Institution, Washington, 1968, pp. 100 ff.

¹⁹ *Epitome of the Reports of the Committee of Public Accounts, 1938 to 1969*, H.C. 187, 1970, pp. 497–9 and 409–10.

²⁰ *Cf.* D. O. Porter and D. C. Warner, 'How effective are grantor controls? The case of federal aid to education', in Boulding, Pfaff and Pfaff, *op. cit.*, pp. 276–302.

²¹ M. Derthick, *The Influence of Federal Grants*, Harvard University Press, Cambridge, Mass., 1970.

²² H.C. 166–1, 265–1, 297, 1969–70, p. xxxvi, para. 93(c).

²³ M. Edmonds, 'Government contracting and renegotiation', *Public Administration*, L, spring 1972, pp. 45–54.

²⁴ *Government Organization for Defence Procurement and Civil Aerospace*, Cmnd. 4641, 1971; G. Williams, F. Gregory and J. Simpson, *Crisis in Procurement: a Case Study of the TSR-2*, United Services Institution, London, 1969.

²⁵ Derthick, *op. cit.*

²⁶ H. Parris, *Constitutional Bureaucracy*, Allen & Unwin, London, 1969, pp. 203–9.

²⁷ O. Hartley, 'Inspectorates in British central government', *Public Administration*, L, winter 1972.

²⁸ J. A. G. Griffith, *Central Departments and Local Authorities*, Allen & Unwin, London, 1966.

²⁹ C. Altensetter, 'Determinants of health service delivery in the USA and West Germany', paper presented to the ninth IPSA conference, Montreal, August 1973, p. 15.

³⁰ L. A. Gunn, 'Functional decentralization in British central government', *New Atlantis*, 1972.

³¹ *Cf.* S. Beer, *Brain of the Firm*, Allen Lane, London, 1972.

³² R. Wettenhall, 'The recoup concept in public enterprise', *Public Administration*, XLIV, 1966, pp. 391–413.

³³ M. Howe, 'Financing State steel: the irrelevance of public dividend capital', *Public Administration*, XLIX, 1971, pp. 309–20.

³⁴ P. Bonini, R. Jaedicke and H. Wagner, *Management Controls: New Dimensions in Basic Research*, McGraw-Hill, New York, 1964.

³⁵ A. Downs, *Inside Bureaucracy*, Wiley, New York, 1967.

[36] T. Hayter, *Aid as Imperialism*, Penguin Books, Harmondsworth, 1971.

[37] *Cf.* J. Q. Wilson, 'The police and their problems: a theory', *Public Policy*, XII, 1963, pp. 190–1.

[38] C. C. Hood, 'The rise and rise of the British quango', *New Society*, 16 August 1973.

[39] A. Martin and W. A. Lewis, 'Patterns of public revenue and expenditure', *Manchester School*, September 1956, pp. 203–44.

[40] *Cf.* H. M. Hochman and J. R. Rodgers, 'Pareto-optimal redistribution', *American Economic Review*, LIX, September 1969.

[41] W. J. M. Mackenzie, 'Unacknowledgeable means', unpublished lecture, 1950.

[42] C. C. Hood, 'British fishing and the Iceland saga', *Political Quarterly*, XLVI, July–September 1973, p. 351.

[43] R. A. Chapman (ed.), *The Role of Commissions in Policy Making*, Allen & Unwin, London, 1973.

[44] F. R. Cowell, 'Central Purchasing', *Public Administration*, X, 1932, No. 1.

[45] D. Moynihan, *Maximum Feasible Misunderstanding*, Free Press, New York, 1970.

[46] *Cf.* E. E. Hughes, *Studies in Administration and Finance, 1558–1825*, Manchester University Press, 1934.

[47] J. K. Galbraith, 'The big defence firms are really public firms and should be nationalised', *New York Times Magazine*, 16 November 1969, p. 50.

J. M. Lee

10

'Central capability' and established practice: the changing character of the 'centre of the machine' in British Cabinet government

Established practices at the 'centre of the machine' have had a strong influence on the manner in which management theories have been absorbed in British government. Cabinet business still follows recognisable patterns. Recent changes in the machinery of government have not been an attempt to destroy one game and replace it by another with a different set of rules. They represent an expression by the principal participants of what they can do within the tradition they understand. The actual disposition of responsibilities in the Cabinet arena at any given moment may well be much less important than the changing character of tone and tempo in the channels of communication between the centre and major departments. It is an illusion to suggest that the decision-making system can be improved through a single centre of expertise, unless there is to be a drastic shift in constitutional doctrine. The present structure of Cabinet government still permits several dialogues to take place simultaneously.

The White Paper of October 1970, *The Reorganisation of Central Government*, proposed that 'there should be *a capability at the centre* for the assessment of policies and projects in relation to strategic objectives'.[1] This proposal was accompanied by an explicit statement that 'the structure of inter-departmental committees ... needs to be reinforced by a clear and comprehensive definition of government strategy which can ... provide a framework within which the Government's policies as a whole may be more effectively formulated'.[2] It was argued that the Cabinet requires something more in reaching decisions than the briefing provided to individual Ministers by their separate departments or recommendations based on a compromise worked out in an official committee. It needs a staff which can contribute a fresh and critical slant to the analysis of policies submitted for its consideration.

The central policy review staff (CPRS) under Lord Rothschild was appointed to constitute this 'central capability'. It consists of fifteen to twenty-five people in a small multi-disciplinary unit attached to the Cabinet Office. The same White Paper declared a moratorium on further major disturbances: '... A period of stability is of the highest importance if the machinery and staff who constitute it are to work efficiently and well.'[3] Emphasis for the future was to be on improving 'the methods by which collective policy decisions are currently taken'.[4] The whole machinery of government required a period during which it could adjust to the consequences of major reforms.

'Central capability' was announced with the final set of amalgamations between government departments as a supplement to the whole exercise in reform. Its position and style were a reflection of the debate on Cabinet government during the preceding decade. Between 1963 and 1970 a series of reorganisations brought into being the 'large departments'—Ministry of Defence, Foreign and Commonwealth Office, Department of Trade and Industry, Department of Health and Social Security—and introduced important modifications to the ways in which they interrelate at Cabinet level. The work undertaken by eighteen departments in 1963 is now performed by five.[5] The reduction in the number of departments has created a cadre of senior staff at Under-Secretary and above which carries the real burden of co-ordination. During the past five years almost 200 new senior posts have been created (about 140 under-secretaries and fifty-odd deputy secretaries) to manage both the 'large departments' and the centre itself. The overall statistics in Table I are deceptive because the 'open structure' at Under-Secretary and above, which was created in response to the recommendations of the Fulton committee, has brought a large number of technical and professional staff into ranks previously largely reserved for the administrative grade. But there has been a real growth in the disposition of senior staff.

The reorganisation of central government during the 1960s was part of a much broader set of adjustments in British political life. It bears little relation to the mandate claimed by the major political parties or changes in the personal ascendancy of individual ministers. Administrative problems themselves encouraged a movement in favour of amalgamating allied functions within the same policy area. The civil service acquired a greater interest in 'scientific

management' during the years which preceded the deliberations of
the Fulton committee (1966–68). Ministers became interested in
reducing the size of the Cabinet, while civil servants saw advantages
in grouping the major policy areas within broad expenditure programmes. The principal precedents were set in 1962 through the

Table 1　Senior staff: Under-Secretary and above

	1967–68	*1970–71*	*1973–74*
Cabinet	9	19	25
Treasury (and DEA before 1969)	46	32	32
Civil Service Department	—	31	24
Total at the 'centre'	55	82	81
Ministry of Agriculture, Fisheries and Food	19	32	34
Department of Education and Science	18	20	23
Department of Employment	13	21	62
Home Office	16	25	28
Total in 'small departments'	66	98	147
'Large departments' (and con-stituent parts before 1970)			
Health and Social Security	28	52	68
Environment	45	84	68
Trade and Industry	62	91	102
Defence	38	91	126
Total in 'large departments' and constituent parts before 1970	173	318	364
Foreign and Commonwealth Office (equivalent)	*n.a.*	192	*n.a.*

Source　These figures are taken from the estimates.

functional model for a Ministry of Defence recommended by the
Chief of Defence Staff, Lord Mountbatten, after he had completed
the unification of the command of forces in the field.[6] The present
Prime Minister[39] experienced something of a debate on functional
organisation for technology during the year he spent as President of
the Board of Trade (1963–64), a period marked by a rather painful
deterioration in Conservative party experience of Cabinet manage-

ment. Those who lived through the organisational difficulties of 1958–63 were sympathetic to some measure of reconstruction.

The White Paper of October 1970 spoke in terms of 'the functional principle', which was interpreted as providing an organisation according to 'the task to be done or the objective to be attained . . . rather than, for example, dividing responsibility between departments so that each one deals with a client group'.[7] A functional allocation of responsibilities between large departments was thought to be an appropriate method for reducing the weight of interdepartmental negotiation and sharpening the focus of work at the centre.

Conventions at the 'centre of the machine'

But the only major changes at the centre took place before a 'central capability' was conceived. The Department of Economic Affairs was created in 1964 from the National Economy Group in the Treasury, and abolished in 1969. The Treasury was split into two in 1968 in order to create the Civil Service Department from its pay and management divisions, and at the same time the Cabinet Office was made responsible for its own establishments. The centre had now three major parts—Cabinet Office, Treasury, Civil Service Department (CSD)—instead of the 'seamless web' of Treasury/ Cabinet Office. The public expenditure control functions of the Treasury are now physically separate from the manpower control functions of the CSD. There has been little formal change of structure in the private offices of non-departmental Ministers, including that of the Prime Minister, which form the core of central activity.

This contrast between the fairly familiar shape at the centre and the new pattern of departments underlines the character of established practice, and its adaptability to new demands. Since the 1920s the day-to-day workings of Cabinet government in Britain have rested on a shifting balance between the influence of the Treasury/ Cabinet Office, which identifies the interests to be co-ordinated, and the action of non-departmental Ministers—including the Prime Minister—who manage the Cabinet and who relate the work of the administration as a whole to Parliament and the party in power. The attitude of the government at any given moment emerges from the internal debate within this balance, which may not always be apparent from any formally recorded decisions. Some decisions are quickly overtaken; others are never followed through.

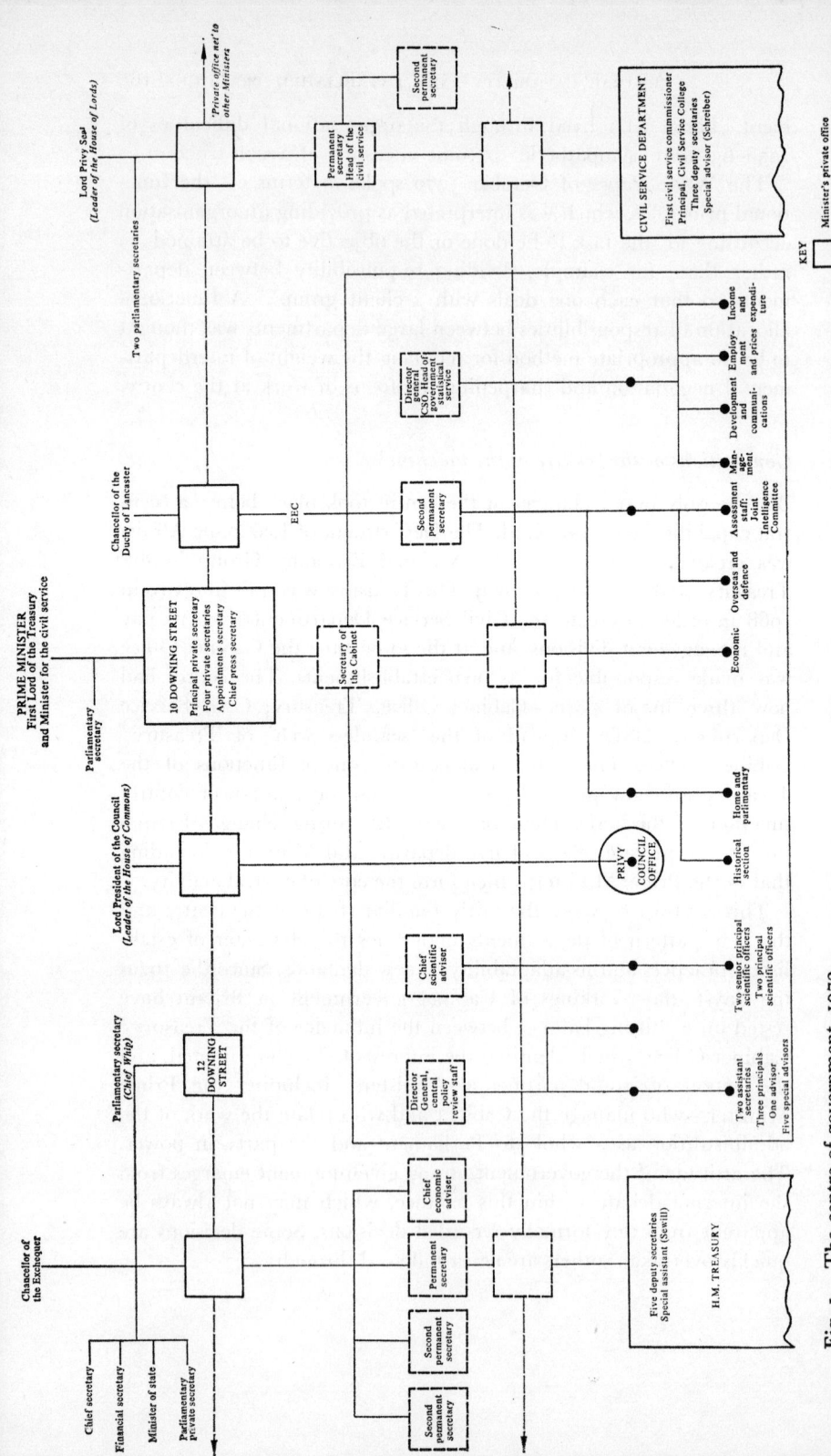

Fig. 1. The centre of government, 1973.

The organisational expression of this system is the basic division between the 'private office network' and the central departments. There is always a number of non-departmental Minsters who combine the roles of Cabinet committee chairmen and parliamentary managers. (At the moment these are the Lord President of the Council and the Lord Privy Seal.) See fig 1. The Chief Whip's office (Parliamentary Secretary to the Treasury) nestles within the central department structure, but is physically reparate in No. 12 Downing Street, and acts as the major link with the other private offices. All Ministers are in touch with the private office system, all Ministries with the central departments. Any attempt to introduce a 'central capability' seems to present a choice between developing the staff of non-departmental Ministers and elaborating the forms of central departmental control. Non-departmental Ministers are normally only supported either by giving them an extended private office or by appointing a small staff inside the Cabinet Office to service the group which they are leading.

Co-ordination and discipline are effected through different groupings of Ministers and civil servants, often acting in committee. These groupings cut across the two separate but closely linked systems of intelligence. First, Ministers keep in touch with each other through their private offices, which concentrate on the 'daily problem'[8] of maintaining the day-to-day business of government against the background of party discipline in Parliament. Second, the Treasury and its 'offspring', the Civil Service Department, as well as the Cabinet Office, secure their own information from what other departments volunteer, what they can be asked to submit, and what interdepartmental correspondence and committee minutes reveal. One of the dangers of using the decision-making idiom is that it tends to exaggerate the monolithic quality of the information system. The 'centre' is much more like a stock exchange for the brokerage of vital information, without the discipline of a market price. The skills developed by Ministers and civil servants in these two contexts are a constant influence on daily practice. They are naturally reluctant to cross the 'fatal Rubicon'[9] of revealing their differences in public. It is not surprising that the government admitted in the White Paper of October 1970 that 'the task of producing a strategic definition of objectives . . . can only be approached gradually'.[10]

There is an element of ambiguity in the idea of 'central capability'.

It should not be regarded with too many 'managerial' preconceptions. Those who advocate improvements in the decision-
making system tend to over-emphasise the degree to which there
is any value in regarding the 'centre of the machine' as primarily
a place for 'decisions'. If it were such a place, then 'central capability' would take the shape of a central department designed to
assess all the available information. Those who regard the centre
as a forum in which various kinds of discipline can be imposed upon
the reluctant agencies of government tend to stress the function of
the centre as an instrument of compromise. If Cabinet or non-
departmental Ministers had no more than a disciplinary function,
then 'central capability' could be little more than a system of
'private intelligence' to report on individual agency action. In
practice, the centre of the machine combines both functions by
associating long-term assessment with the central departments and
intelligence reporting with the 'private office net' or an *ad hoc*
Cabinet Office unit.

A reconciliation between the conception of the CPRS and traditional Cabinet practices, after the Treasury had been split in two,
constitutes a major element in the current internal debate at the
centre. This debate is, of course, hardly public knowledge. The
principal participants try to impose their own conceptions of what
they would like to see on others, and new practices are in fact the
product of such mutual role definition. Those who regret the
separation of the CSD from the Treasury consider possible forms of
reunion. Sir Richard Clarke, the official who was chiefly responsible
for the first steps in public expenditure planning, gave some
lectures in March 1971 in which he prophesied that the threefold
division at the centre (Cabinet, Treasury and CSD) would not hold
in its present form.

The CPRS appears to cut across the traditional balance between
the influence of the Treasury and that of non-departmental Ministers, and to be associated with both long-term assessment and
private office reporting. It seems to add a third set of crucial relationships between the centre and departments to those two so
recently separated—the public expenditure control functions of the
Treasury and the manpower control functions of the CSD. Sir
Richard Clarke has also argued that 'there can be only one sense
of expertise at the centre',[11] and expressed his fear about 'different
ground rules at different parts of the centre'.[12]

But it looks as if the sequence of the major reorganisations in government has reinforced this threefold pattern. The main interest in studying 'central capability' lies in understanding the impact on the character of the centre made by the combination of a new 'central policy review' and a new structure in the major departments of state. All the available evidence suggests that there has been a considerable modification in the style of operations at the centre, without changing the fundamental features of a Cabinet system.

The White Paper of October 1970 issued a warning that the reorganisation had 'placed an additional responsibility ... to ensure that the collective responsibility of Ministers is not eroded'.[13] In outlining a general philosophy—'the desirability of the comprehensive approach in government organisation'—the White Paper argued that the large department will be:

less open to the risk of being parochial and will therefore be more answerable to Parliament and the community at large. Equally it will have less need to fear for and defend its interests against other interests so that in the formative stages of policy it must and will be ready to discuss issues with other departments. In this way, the full range of facts and issues will be presented to Ministers for their collective decision.[14]

This statement was an expression of hope rather than an effective provision for action. There can be no adequate guarantee that 'additional responsibility' will be respected, except through the tone and tempo of current practice.

The problems which the government now faces require much more positive action at the centre, and, paradoxically, it looks as if this is performed with the least degree of awkwardness if the accepted forms of central machinery are retained. The more positive orientation can be enshrined with established practice because the items appearing on the agenda at the centre can be handled only with the flexibility which it provides. The centre has to be aware of policies within the component parts which make up the 'allied functions' of each of the large departments in order to judge their wider implications. The choice between different policy instruments—spending, taxation, regulation—affects more than a single large department can control. Similarly, the centre under the new arrangements becomes increasingly the point at which issues are debated which involve the client rather than the service.

A new vigilance can be introduced within the 'centre of the machine' without any further departure from the conventions of

Cabinet government than the creation of the CPRS. The latter, as
an administrative device, may not be retained by a future government.[40] Its presence symbolises the changing character of the setting
in which it works rather than an essential instrument of the more
positive style. The challenge of new problems is already being met
through the accepted combination of private offices and central
departments.

The Prime Minister's standing

First and foremost, the incorporation of a 'central capability' for
the assessment of policies in relation to 'strategic objectives' has not
changed the technical standing of the Prime Minister in the
machinery of government. No. 10 Downing Street remains the
centre of the 'private office net' and is not directly linked to
ministerial responsibilities. The Prime Minister's personal staff at
No. 10 continues to be listed in the *Imperial Calendar* under his
formal departmental attachments at the Treasury and CSD, just as
the Whip's office at No. 12 Downing Street is to be found under
the Parliamentary Secretary to the Treasury.

A small symbol of this stability in formal structure is the range of
Downing Street buildings themselves, which were reopened after
restoration in the last days of Macmillan's premiership.[15] No. 10
was designed to incorporate the Prime Minister's private rooms, the
official residence with accommodation for guests, and 'offices for a
staff of about fifty'.[16]

Lord Rothschild, the head of the CPRS, is in touch with the
Prime Minister through his own person—'I suppose I see the Prime
Minister, on average, every five to seven weeks'[17]—and not
through any executive office or Prime Minister's department, in
spite of the fact that many arguments which preceded the establishment of this 'central capability' rested on the assumption that
only the Prime Minister's close personal involvement would carry the
necessary weight to counteract the strength of the major departments. Harold Wilson has said that he now would like to see a strong
Prime Minister's department,[18] but has not indicated the detailed
changes he would himself introduce. There are few grounds for
believing that any continuation of the CPRS under a Labour
administration would necessarily require a shift in the Prime
Minister's technical responsibilities.

The major political difficulty which stands in the way of giving an executive department to the Prime Minister is a constitutional, not a technical, one. It is not just that he is already in charge of a non-executive department, the Cabinet Office, but rather that he could never himself take full responsibility for all the activities performed in his name without appointing a junior or deputy Minister, who would then be in an awkward position in relation to the Cabinet as a whole. Very few administrations carry the necessary pair of Ministers who might run a Prime Minister's department endowed with real possibility above that carried by an enlarged private office. Similarly, almost all the suggestions which have been made for bringing the Prime Minister into a department concerned with 'strategic objectives' raise questions of status for the Permanent Secretary in charge. Like Ministers, Permanent Secretaries must relate to each other in ways appropriate to their experience and influence. Any change at the 'centre of the machine' is a matter of some importance to senior civil servants.

This difficulty was faced squarely in 1968, when the Civil Service Department was created from the pay and management divisions of the Treasury. The Prime Minister was designated Minister for the Civil Service but his day-to-day duties were performed by one of the non-department Ministers, the Lord Privy Seal, who was also the leader of the House of Lords. The head of the civil service was permanent secretary of the new department.

Alternative models of central organisation

It is theoretically possible to convert the whole of the 'centre of the machine' into one single large department under the Prime Minister and the head of the civil service. It would, of course, depress the status of the Chancellor of the Exchequer and raise sufficiently awkward questions about his relationship with the Premier to rule it out. Such an arrangement would have the appearance of a return to the traditional preponderance of the Treasury. Between the wars Sir Warren Fisher as Permanent Secretary of the Treasury and 'head of the civil Service' had tried to ensure that the growth of the Cabinet Office—itself the most successful extension of the Prime Minister's private office—should not threaten the basic pattern of one single department to which a number of non-departmental Ministers are attached, each with his own private office.

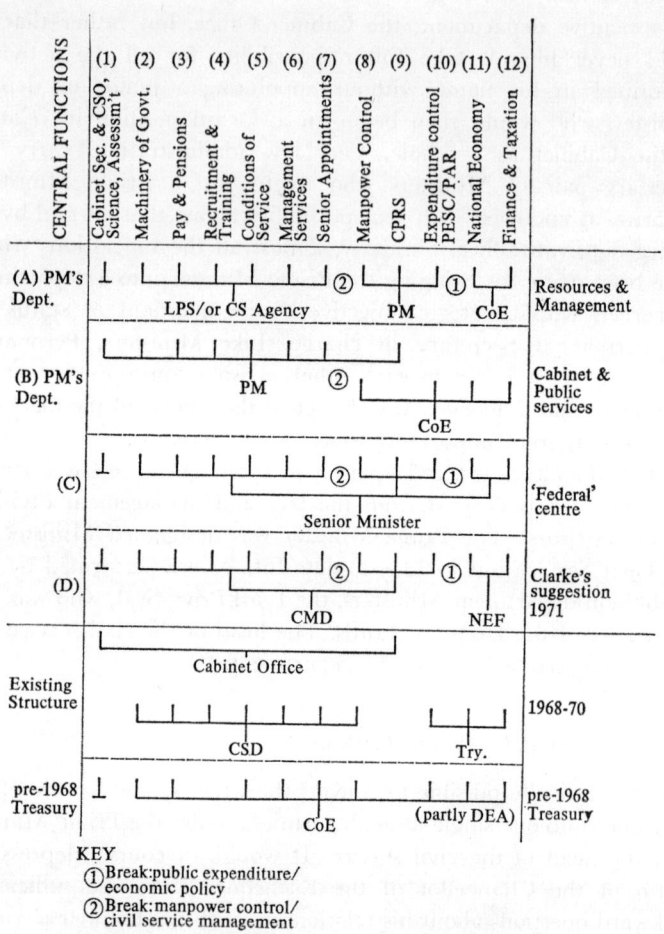

Fig. 2.   Models of central organisation:
suggested spans of control.

But the thrust of the argument in favour of providing an office concerned with the whole administration's 'strategic objectives' has always been to select important functions from the general mass of central responsibility and give to them a special significance by placing them under the Prime Minister's control. The idea of a Prime Minister's department carries several meanings, but they are all designed to further a sharper sense of corporate thinking at the centre.

There are two principal alternatives, each of which suggests its own minor variations. (See fig. 2.) Both share the same constitutional difficulty. The first is a 'resources and management' model which joins together the public expenditure divisions of the Treasury and the manpower control and perhaps the pay divisions of the Civil Service Department, and places under the Prime Minister these two sets of functions which before 1968 were under the Chancellor of the Exchequer. Now that the Civil Service Department has been created, this alternative could be pursued only at the expense of separating out yet another junior Minister's department within the centre of the machine or some sort of agency to manage the civil service. It might be argued that this particular combination would provide a more suitable place for the CPRS than the Cabinet secretariat, but it would deprive the Treasury of the links between the national economy group and public expenditure, and leave the Civil Service Department bereft of its most influential section.

The second alternative is a 'Cabinet and Public Services' model which leaves the CPRS in conjunction with the Cabinet secretariat but adds to them the bulk of the Civil Service Department functions. With this particular combination it would be possible to return the manpower control functions to the Treasury and reunite them with the public expenditure divisions. There could be some reallocation of functions between Cabinet and Public Service sides. For example, the machinery of government division, now in CSD, might be transferred to join CPRS functions. But this method of bringing the CPRS closer to the Prime Minister would do little more than demote the Secretary to the Cabinet to a slightly lower status under a 'Super Permanent Secretary' to the Prime Minister who encompassed Cabinet, Civil Service Department and CPRS functions.

Any permutations based on these two major alternatives pose the problem of finding an appropriate set of constitutional relationships between the non-departmental Ministers at the centre and their departmental colleagues, and between senior staff. It is hard to break with the convention that the Prime Minister is supported by an extended private office as well as the only other kind of office which fits into these arrangements, the Cabinet Office.

The alternative to bringing important functions under his direct supervision is to make No. 10 Downing Street into another kind of 'central capability'—a special kind of strengthened private office.[41] This would be difficult to effect without transforming the character of the civil service which staffs it. There is no precedent for any Prime Minister's private secretariat. A few trusted 'partisans' may be added to his staff, but he is expected to take over what he finds.

Between 1964 and 1970 discussions on the machinery of government initiated within the Conservative opposition by Edward Heath were a counterpoint to the actions of the Labour administration under Harold Wilson. The principal melody was experiments in organising the large departments—the three different versions of the Ministry of Technology were perhaps the most notorious— while the accompaniment was primarily taken up with variations on the theme of a 'central' capability'. Wilson did not convert No. 10 into a 'power house' as some had expected, but on taking office in 1964 set up the Department of Economic Affairs—'. . . instead of regarding economics as just a question of money, whether internal or external money, we were trying to change industry'.[19] This meant taking functions away from the Treasury and Board of Trade in order to create an economic planning department concerned with regional development. After the Cabinet reshuffle of August 1967 the Prime Minister himself took charge of the management. The ministerial arrangements for the CSD were very similar to those followed for the DEA.[20] Many of the alternatives considered by the Conservative opposition which became associated with the term 'Prime Minister's department' were in some manner that party's reply to the DEA arrangements.

The 1970 compromise: a reflection of debate

The White Paper of October 1970 marked something more than the implementation of Conservative Party planning. The situation in which the government set up the CPRS arose in a compromise between official thinking in the civil service and the recommendations of a Conservative Party study group. The latter, which had prepared a 'black book' to present to the Prime Minister on his election, was in favour of taking the public expenditure divisions away from the Treasury and erecting some kind of Prime Minister's office on the 'resources and management' model. The civil service had been prepared for such a proposal by the publicity given to the study group's work in David Howell's articles and Conservative Political Centre pamphlets,[21] and was itself in a position to consider the best way of incorporating a 'strategic policy unit' into a Cabinet system dominated by the new large departments. Harold Wilson was shown the first fruits of this thinking, which gave a little more scope for initiative than the CPRS formula, but at a time when he was preoccupied with the run-up to the general election. The White Paper after the election was the product of a great deal of planning before it, and the expression of a general agreement on the Prime Minister's part not to introduce any further departmental forms into the centre of the machine. David Howell did not become the junior Minister in a Prime Minister's department but a parliamentary secretary at the CSD. The CPRS was firmly attached to the Cabinet Office, and not, as the 'black book' had requested, to the Prime Minister himself.

The Conservative Party in opposition was initially concerned with what it called the problem of 'scaling down government' or reducing the size and importance of the bureaucracy. Its first study group on the machinery of government (1965–66), which worked out a case against the DEA, did not recommend the setting up of a Prime Minister's department,[22] but came out in favour of a 'central cost effectiveness unit'. This proposal was embodied into the party election manifesto of 1966, *Action, not Words*. Although they had originally intended to make their tour of the United States and Japan into an opportunity to study technology, Ernest Marples and Mark Schreiber in the autumn of 1966 found that they were increasingly faced with organisational and budgeting questions. In April 1967 the party supported the setting up of a Public Sector Research Unit at Ernest Marples' parliamentary offices in Bridge Street, with Mark Schreiber working full-time. This unit, of which David Howell's pamphlets were the most visible sign, was largely devoted to cost effectiveness questions, an area of interest which brought it into contact with private sector discussions of 'corporate planning'. The businessmen invited to attend the seminar which it organised at Sundridge Park in September 1969 added a new dimension to the party's 'preparation for government'.

The Labour Party in office was troubled by the relationship between party advisers and full-time civil servants. Before the general election of 1964 Harold Wilson discussed his plans for building up the Cabinet secretariat and No. 10,[23] and on winning the election had brought with him not only Thomas Balogh as economic adviser but also his own private office secretary, Marcia Williams. The latter has written an account of her period of office.[24] She found it extremely hard to work with Derek Mitchell, the Prime Minister's principal private secretary, who had been appointed partly with a view to preparing for a Labour administration. The tensions between the 'party faithfuls' and senior officials were particularly marked during the government's debate on the important issues, the devaluation of sterling and the British application to join the European Economic Community. But even after February 1966, when Derek Mitchell had been replaced by Michael Halls, the Prime Minister's former private secretary at the Board of Trade in 1951, there was still considerable irritation on both sides. The 'irregular' advisers felt obstructed; the civil servants unjustly pilloried. The hostile tone of the first chapter of the report of the Fulton Committee on the Civil Service (1968) captures something of the atmosphere generated by the extension of No. 10 to include personal advisers. Thomas Balogh had, after all, written an essay against the higher civil service, called the 'apotheosis of the dilettante'.[25]

It is not surprising that some senior civil servants have expressed their own private concern about the state of 'strategic planning' within the major parties, whether in opposition or in office. There seemed to be too great a discrepancy between the opportunity in the large departments for devoting resources to long-term policy studies and the rather quirkish directions of political party investigations which were extremely vulnerable to personal rivalries or conspiracy theories. Some saw a need not only for a 'think tank' inside government to monitor and investigate the major long-term questions which large departments might neglect, but also for independent research institutes outside government. The situation called for a more synoptic approach than that which traditional disciplines were capable of giving.

The CPRS device, a multi-disciplinary unit of mixed membership (civil servants and 'outsiders') was acceptable to both ministerial and civil service interests. It provided an embodiment of 'corporate planning' on which businessmen recruited by the party in opposition had laid such stress, and at the same time seemed to avoid something of the embarrassment associated with the Labour government's attempts to employ 'outsiders'. The Cabinet Office was the most appropriate place to house the CPRS. The 'businessmen's team', another product of the Conservative Party Sector Research Unit, was attached to the CSD.

The CPRS from the very beginning had to define its own role, and differentiate itself in the eyes of the major departments from the normal pattern of relationships between centre and periphery. It has a sense of choice in determining its own position and influence by striking its own balance. It must not appear to be a mere extension of the Cabinet Office, nor a remote and ineffectual centre for research. It must avoid preparing an instant reaction to an immediate crisis on the one hand, and devoting too much of its limited resources to a long-term study on the other.[26] The result is that a unit of this kind can evolve its own characteristic dialogue within the framework of established authority and, equally important, provide a new point of access for departments to reach the centre.

Information systems: central department style

The development of a central 'information system' has also followed traditional lines. Innovation is primarily to be seen within the framework of a single central department—the Treasury. The CSD follows in the same mould. The White Paper of October 1970 declared that 'the necessary basis for good government is a radical improvement in the information system available to Ministers'.[27] 'A system for regular reviews which would provide more and better information ... would be designed to provide Ministers with an opportunity to identify and discuss alternative policy options which can then be explored in greater depth before final decisions are taken on the expenditure programmes.'[28] The system prescribed by a team of businessmen was called 'programme analysis and review' (PAR) in their report of October 1970, and grafted on to the Treasury's 'Public Expenditure Survey Committee' (PESC). The parallel is so deliberate that the supervising committee for PAR (PARC) is chaired by the same Treasury official who runs PESC. After the PAR report had been implemented, Mr East, who had pioneered this particular approach, was transferred from the CSD team to the Treasury, where it could be married with the PESC machinery.

Similarly, the two other innovations which were announced in the White Paper—a review of department tasks and an examination of the location of government offices—were attached to existing work in the Civil Service Department. Although the White Paper stressed that the CPRS 'will work for Ministers collectively',[29] it did not make quite so explicit the fact that the existing central departments would undertake all the other improvements in 'the methods by which collective decisions are taken'.

The reorganisation of central government itself, by reducing the number of departments, was in many respects a reflection of the developing system in public expenditure management and control. The Treasury had seen the relationships between different policy areas in its attempts to refine its methods of analysing public expenditure headings. The groupings which were chosen between 1964 and 1970 were partly based on Treasury interests.

The major argument in favour of separating the pay and management divisions from the Treasury to form the Civil Service Department was that management services and career management questions would be neglected unless they were made the specific responsibility of a new central department. The CSD was charged with developing an information system which would have a completely different emphasis from that of the Treasury. There seemed to be a danger in associating public expenditure control in the minds of other departments with the need to concentrate on the improved management of staff. The CSD was required to promote a new dialogue with departments, but it still carried the old Treasury weapon of control over departmental establishments.

There was an ambivalence inherent to the evolution of an 'information system' through a central department. Both the Treasury and the Civil Service Department retained an instrument for disciplining the other departments—public expenditure and manpower control—and yet they were called upon to secure departmental co-operation in supplying 'advance information' when departments seemed increasingly self-sufficient. The large departments all designed their own systems for the analysis of information. One of the great advantages of the large department is that it employs its own specialists and creates its own style of long-term planning. Most departments have devised some form of policy planning unit.[30] The balance in the 'brokerage' of information has shifted. The Treasury and the Civil Service Department, if they are to be able to anticipate calls on future resources, need to be fairly close to the policy advice of the major departments, and yet none of the latter is going to reveal the precise hierarchy of its priorities while it can be penalised from the centre. A new code of inter-departmental talk becomes necessary.

The basic difficulty arises from the ambiguity of 'collective responsibility' itself. It means that the government as a whole can be held to account by outsiders, but it also means that individual parts of the administration may be required to stand by actions in which they were not directly involved. Individual departmental Ministers are technically and statutorily responsible for the services provided, and expect to be given some margin of play in their relationships with the centre. Any information system based on the central department has to reflect the wide variety of different bodies which perform the basic administrative operations. The new large departments are coming to recognise the legitimate interests of the centre, and vice versa. The function of the CPRS in presenting information to Ministers collectively 'on a basis free from purely departmental considerations'[31] is obviously vulnerable to depart-mental criticism.

The 'new style' has been grafted in to longer-term developments in the evolution of what constitutes central department activity. The 1970 arrangements added Conservative Party thinking to the existing endeavours of the Treasury and CSD. The businessmen recruited by the party acknowledged this in their concentration on supplementing the PESC machinery.

New methods of analysis

PESC examines the returns made by departments showing what they expect to spend (at constant prices) on each of their programmes over the next five years, on the assumption that there are no re-sources or suggest switches from one heading to another if they envisage changes in priorities. All spending programmes are approved within this broad general framework. PAR provides a method of evaluating individual parts of a particular programme. But a PAR report is prepared by the responsible department for submission to an appropriate Cabinet committee, and not by the Treasury. It is comparable to the 'programme memoranda' which used to be prepared by a number of small interdepartmental committees set up between the Treasury and a few selected departments. Although the CPRS can now be involved informally with a PAR report and brief the Cabinet on its final shape, the choice of PAR subjects lies largely with departments which undertake the work.

The new PAR dialogue between the centre and the departments is a good example of the necessary ambiguities of the Cabinet system. Not everything can be 'PAR-ed' at the same time. These arrangements did not meet the obstacles experienced when President Johnson introduced PPBS into American federal government in 1965. Each department can place slightly different nuances of meaning on its communication with the major authorities at the centre—the Treasury, the CSD and the CPRS—can use PAR as a vehicle for justifying a shift of resources which it has already determined on other grounds, such as the development of nursery education by the DES. PAR is less frightening to departmental susceptibilities than a Treasury expenditure directive or a staff inspection. There is nothing mechanical in PAR reports; they are expressions of political choice.

The addition of PAR to Treasury activity emphasises the peculiar qualities of the public sector which the 'businessmen's team' had to acknowledge. The team took its origin from the Sundridge Park seminar of September 1969, arranged by the Conservative Party Public Sector Research Unit. Its ideas were based on the application of 'corporate planning' methods to government. The CPRS was conceived originally in these terms. The seminar benefited from the businessmen's experience in the setting up of planning units in private industry which could act as the 'guardian of the company conscience'.

But the main impact of the businessman's contribution was to accelerate the process by which those parts of the public sector which had commercial characteristics could be reorganised. They fitted much more successfully into the CSD's consideration of 'units of accountable management', and threw themselves enthusiastically into the design of new departmental agencies.

The growth of the CSD did not rest on its contribution to collective decision-making, which was minimal. The department was designed to 'rationalise' the structure of the periphery, not to meddle with the centre. Except for the machinery of government divisions, which could always be located at some other part of the 'centre of the machine', the CSD was directed towards an 'information system' which would help to standardise the staff regimes in each agency throughout the public sector, and encourage the use of more sophisticated management systems.

Table 2 Administrative staff at the centre: ten years' growth

	1963–64		1973–74	Increase
Cabinet				
Secretariat	43		123	
CPRS	—		26	
CSO	71		193	
Historians	37		10	
Total	151		352	201
Treasury				
Public Sector	97		156	
National Economy	29		122	
Finance	105		76	
Others	5		47	
Total	236		401	165
Civil Service Department				
Pay and Superannuation	149		160	
Manpower, etc.	129		92	
Personnel Management			154	
Machinery of Government			33	
Management Services			105	
Planning			38	
Total	278		582	304
Information	14		15	1
Civil Service Commission	544	Recruitment	388	
	—	College	354	
Office services				
Cabinet	220		257	
Treasury	807		588	
CSD	—		559	
Total	1,027		1,404	377

Source Taken from the annual estimates.

It is doubtful whether this massive operation could have been mounted after the Fulton report in 1968 without a new department carrying the prestige of the head of the civil service. The contrast between the Treasury and CSD in the growth of administrative staff is very striking. The 'centre of the machine' has changed the balance of its structure since the mid-1960s. In spite of the abolition of the DEA and the reallocation of many of its staff to the Treasury, the major growth areas have lain in the Civil Service Department and the Cabinet Office itself.

The CSD remains the most vulnerable of the central 'information system'. It would be particularly weakened if its manpower control functions were shifted back to the Treasury or to some kind of Prime Minister's department. The 'information' it requires always carries less urgency than the more clamant consideration of resources. From the beginning it was in danger of becoming a department of elderly principals and executive officers supervising 'unfashionable' establishment work. The presence of the head of the civil service cannot totally remove this threat, as he has the influence to contribute to much more than his strictly departmental duties.

The CPRS's position in the Cabinet Office is a much more stable arrangement than the attachment of the businessmen's team to CSD. It is much more concerned with the PAR/PESC dialogue of the Treasury and departments than with the centralisation of management information with the CSD. But it has to continue to argue for its separate right to an existence which is independent of the Treasury. Sir Richard Clarke said in March 1971 that he hoped the Treasury and CPRS would work together and 'will not indulge in separate dialogues with the Departments'.[32] He believed that if they were not brought together, they could create 'a dangerous rift at the centre' which should be avoided, because 'a clash at the centre on public expenditure engages the discipline and viability of the relation between the centre and the Departments'. But he was speaking before the CPRS had established its own style of operations.

The growth of the Cabinet Office

Finally and obviously, the pressures of Cabinet business push anything which is not a Treasury or 'private office' matter in the direction of an extension of the Cabinet Office. Ministers without portfolio and civil servants with cross-departmental interests find their natural home in the units which revolve around the Cabinet secretariat. The CPRS is not the only unit to develop new strength within this environment. The most visible expansion has been in the Central Statistical Office. The office of the Chief Scientific Adviser and the assessment staff for joint intelligence in overseas and defence matters have also grown. The problems which led to the creation of large departments have also encouraged the growth of the Cabinet secretariat itself. Those who sat down to the fiftieth anniversary dinner in October 1966 could hardly have envisaged that the number of senior administrative staff was going to increase almost threefold in the course of the next five years.

This expansion corresponds to a development in Cabinet government which Patrick Gordon Walker endowed with the term 'partial Cabinet'. By this he meant 'a number of Ministers who constitute part only of the Cabinet but act for a time as if they were the Cabinet'. In explaining that a 'partial Cabinet' is an organised part of the system he made an analogy with the distribution lists used by the Foreign Office in the circulation of telegrams among Ministers. The lists vary according to the type of telegram, just as the 'partial Cabinet' varies according to the issue concerned.[33] The Cabinet committee is the most generally accepted form of a 'partial Cabinet', but other *ad hoc* groups come within the same classification. It may often be necessary to 'mix' Ministers and officials in a more informal manner than the committee system allows. The more a Cabinet relies on different kinds of 'partiality', the more staff work is required to service the meetings and prepare specific material.

The growth in the number of administrators seems to be part of a long-term trend in which the strictly secretarial work—the minute-writing—becomes the task of those in the higher ranks of the service, while their juniors organise material and compose the necessary background papers. In 1963 below the Permanent Secretary there were ten senior staff to seven principals; by 1973 this proportion had become thirty-four senior staff to twenty-eight principals, almost a fourfold increase. The size of the secretariat began to grow in the late 1960s and was accelerated after the appointment of the CPRS in 1971. When he brought Michael Halls into No. 10 in February 1966, Harold Wilson also approved the appointment of two new Deputy Secretaries in the Cabinet Office.

Their work has been increased by the large number and variety of informal groupings. This phenomenon can be seen in the course of the discussions on Britain's entry into the European Economic Community. For example, although not a strictly Cabinet Office affair, the regular meetings which were designed to see how the government and the European movement in Britain could co-operate, held between late 1970 and November 1971, show the degree of flexibility in arrangements at the centre.[34] Similarly, Christopher Soames in conducting secret talks with the French government through Michael Jobert during March–April 1971 reported not to the Foreign Office but to a small group of Ministers and officials.[35]

Table 3   Cabinet Office secretariat

Rank	1963	1968	1973
Deputy Secretary	1	3	7
Under-Secretary	2	5	13
Assistant Secretary	7	6	14
Principal	7	8	28
Total	17	22	62

Some people have suggested that the shift away from formal Cabinet committees as the principal form of 'partial Cabinet' stems from the acute difficulties and embarrassment which accompanied the linked issues of the devaluation of sterling, the reduction of the defence commitment, and the application to join Europe which dominated Cabinet affairs after 1965. Devaluation is certainly the issue on which the most information of 'partial Cabinet' activity has been 'leaked' in recent years.[36] The withdrawal of defence investment from east of Suez, a decision taken over the period February 1966 to January 1968, was also a subject on which the Cabinet system itself was to some commentators an inadequate instrument for resolving the issue.[37] The main thrust of such comments is that the 'centre of the machine' is now obliged to organise a more positive style in co-ordination.

Problems themselves suggest new functions which can be handled only at the centre. There are, for example, an increasing number of issues which can be identified through the development of 'social indicators'. Part of the increased size and importance of the Central Statistical Office lies in its position to standardise the presentation of appropriate data, exemplified in its production of the regular review *Social Trends*. The more material is collated in a standard manner, the greater the opportunity to comment and insist on further refinements. The Chief Scientific Adviser is also in a position to insist that matters are referred to him. It is sometimes possible for a unit attached to the Cabinet Office to explore possible contingencies before they are themselves presented on the main political stage. For example, the Chief Scientific Adviser was able to consider 'population policy' before the subject was debatable at large.

The entry of Britain into the European Economic Community has formally and publicly extended the size of the Cabinet secretariat through the appointment of a second Permanent Secretary for European Affairs in October 1969. This side of the office was particularly strengthened by the 1970–71 discussions, and now takes the major role in relating British policies to those of the EEC.

The strengthening of the Cabinet Office can perhaps best be understood in terms of the pressure of events which can stimulate its traditional functions. Cabinet is the natural point at which to set up organisations which override normal departmental concerns—the contingencies which can be anticipated, civil emergencies, subversion and war. The Cabinet Office business which is outside the normal secretariat work takes its style from security and war book questions. The changes which took place during the late 1960s were in the nature of a political 'war'. Some of the principal participants could, of course, follow second world war precedents from their own direct experience.

'Safeguarding the collective responsibility of Ministers' becomes a subtle exercise in war-time. The tendency is to concentrate on 'the war effort' rather than attempt too heavy a centralisation of all matters. There must be some kind of balance between 'corporate thinking' and 'partial Cabinet' solutions. The CPRS, by organising regular seminars at Chequers, keeps the whole administration together in spirit, although it cannot hope to cover more than a section of the hierarchy of values. The CPRS could not counteract 'Cabinet disintegration' if it were placed elsewhere.

Conclusion

Cabinet government now means more than one Minister's reaction to its claims: 'the only definition of what goes to a Cabinet committee is what a Minister thinks he can't safely get away with ...'[38] There is a more complex set of claims for reference to the centre. But each issue is likely to raise its own peculiar set of requirements and therefore its own 'partial' arrangements. The large department may have removed some business from the centre, and may still cause the Cabinet Secretary some anxiety, and yet there has been such a gradual transformation in the range and scope of government business that the 'centre of the machine' is still extremely hard pressed. There seems to be little likelihood of a revival of the 'policy Cabinet' idea—the supreme instrument of Cabinet on a war-time footing. Harold Wilson's 'parliamentary committee' was an aberration designed to exclude James Callaghan, and an expression of internal Cabinet divisions rather than a new instrument of decision. 'Partial Cabinets' in different forms are the order of the day.

The reorganisation of the centre between 1968 and 1971, as well as the final stages in the organisation of the large departments, has differentiated three forms of dialogue between the centre and departments outside the normal range of interdepartmental consultation under the aegis of the Cabinet secretariat. The CPRS from under the wing of the Cabinet Office has contacts with departments in specific areas of enquiry and in the PAR studies which it was designed to monitor. The Treasury continues various exercises in improving the methods around PESC. The CSD collates and analyses civil service and management information. As well as these three points of contact, departments may find other Cabinet Office units such as the CSO requiring their attention.

These forms of central leverage—separate and slightly differentiated channels of communication—followed established practice. The Prime Minister has not decided to give himself the unusual position of a departmental chief for special 'strategic planning' purposes. The application of the concept of 'a Prime Minister's department' has not gone further than the DEA in its final stage or the CSD at present, in which his involvement is very slight. The split of the Treasury between pay and management on one side (CSD) and finance, national economy, and public expenditure on the other (post-1968 Treasury) continues the dialogue of manpower and public expenditure control, but in separate compartments. Any other kind of split might have weakened the idea of CSD from the beginning. There is an historical and constitutional logic about keeping the premiership out of the departmental responsibilities at the centre, and about splitting the Treasury. The siting of the CPRS in the Cabinet Office avoided any quarrel with these arrangements.

All the suggestions which have been made before and since in order to create a different 'balance of power' at the centre begin with the presupposition that the separate and distinct parts of this new style in policy analysis—PESC/PAR, the CSD and the CPRS briefing or Cabinet Office requirements—should be brought under the same control, regardless of the subject being considered. The established practice seems to be that each subject determines its own type of co-operation, and this tendency has been reinforced by the manner in which the existing institutions are managed. Sir Richard Clarke's prophecy that the threefold division at the centre would not be sustained has yet to be fulfilled.

There are two principal connections which the Treasury and CSD now embody and which any change in the balance might damage (see fig. 2). First, the Treasury has the satisfaction of close links between the national economy and finance groups and the public expenditure divisions. Public expenditure is an important element in economic and fiscal planning ((1) in fig. 2). Second, the CSD retains the important levers of manpower control alongside its responsibilities for the management of the civil service. This combination gives to the department a strength in negotiation with others ((2) in fig. 2). These two connections might be retained in some larger 'federal' centre, but they would be destroyed if the present threefold dialogue were deliberately converted into a more unified system of control.

The evidence that the 1970 arrangements continue effectively to the improvement of collective decision-making is not available. The 'additional responsibility' to which the White Paper referred cannot be examined in public. But while the doctrines of collective responsibility are retained, the present constitutional position seems to rest on a simple paradox. Only a strong Prime Minister is able to put into effect the reforms which a weaker one might think desirable. A Prime Minister who has the necessary standing to make a fundamental shift in the structure of the centre of the machine has no need to bring it about. He usually prefers to follow the conventions of established practice, which recognise the Cabinet as an arena in which independent and responsible Ministers can reach agreement, and in which the discipline required for the administration as a whole can be identified and enforced. The most far-reaching changes which might be introduced do not depend on the Prime Minister's personality; they imply a redefinition of his responsibilities which would have to be made both explicit and public. 'Different ground rules at different parts of the centre' are the price of 'safeguarding the collective responsibility'.

Notes

This paper was written in July 1973 for delivery at the UK–Canada symposium on the machinery of government in September 1973, Montreal Canadian Political Science Association meeting.

1 Cmnd. 4506, para. 16.

2 *Ibid.*, para. 45.

3 *Ibid.*, para. 17.

4 *Ibid.*, para. 43.

5 See the Civil Service Department's 'genesis' chart.

6 Michael Howard, *The Central Organisation of Defence*, Royal United Services Institution, London, 1970, especially pp. 14–15.

7 Cmnd. 4506, para. 8.

8 Richard Crossman, *Inside View*, Cape, London, 1972, p. 115; since 1971 private secretaries have had opportunity of meeting 'in the flesh' instead of always on the telephone through the annual end-of-session party held in No. 10.

9 Sir Anthony Part, quoted by Anthony Sampson in the *Observer*, 28 February 1971, p. 19.

10 Cmnd. 4506, para. 46.

11 Sir Richard Clarke, *New Trends in Government*, HMSO, London, 1971, fourth lecture, para. 85.

12 *Ibid.*, para. 82.

13 Cmnd. 4506, para. 13.

14 *Ibid.*

15 *Keesing's Contemporary Archives*, London, 1963; *The Times*, 29 October 1963, p. 5.

16 Cmnd. 457, 1958, p. 4.

17 The *Listener*, 28 December 1972, p. 880.

18 *Ibid.*, 15 February 1973, p. 206.

19 The *Listener*, 15 February, 1973, p. 206.

20 *The Times* used to print at regular intervals 'The corridors of economic power', a ministerial diagram.

21 *The Times*, 14 March 1967, p. 13, an article preceding the announcement of Mr Marples' terms of reference, *ibid.*, 16 March 1967, p. 1; *Whose Government Works?*, 1968; *A New Style of Government*, 1970.

22 *The Times*, 31 August 1972, letter from Humphrey Berkeley, a member of the committee.

23 The *Listener*, 5 March 1964, pp. 379–81, 396.

24 *Inside No. 10*, Weidenfeld & Nicolson, London, 1972.

25 In Hugh Thomas (ed.), *The Establishment*, 1959.

26 W. J. L. Plowden, 'The CPRS: the first two years', Political Studies Association conference paper, 1973.

27 Cmnd. 4506, para. 15.

28 *Ibid.*, para. 51.

29 *Ibid.*, para. 47.

30 Geoffrey K. Fry, 'Policy-planning units in British central government departments', *Public Administration*, L, summer 1972, pp. 139–55.

31 Cmnd. 4506, para. 16.

32 Clarke, *op. cit.*, fourth lecture, para. 76.

33 P. Gordon Walker, *The Cabinet* (second edition, Fontana, London, 1972, p. 88).

34 Uwe Kitzinger, *Diplomacy and Persuasion*, Thames & Hudson, London, 1973, p. 199.

35 *Ibid.*, p. 114.

36 E.g. Colin Seymour-Ure's review of the evidence in *Parliamentary Affairs*, XXIV, 3, summer 1971, pp. 196–207.

37 Phillip Darby, *British Defence Policy East of Suez: 1947–68*, Oxford University Press, London, 1973, p. 331.

38 Crossman, *Inside View*, p. 58.

39 I.e. Mr Heath.

40 Retained in 1974 by Mr Wilson, who also created a 'policy unit' in No. 10.

41 Mr Wilson in 1974 invited Dr Bernard Donoughe to create a 'policy unit'.

Geraint Parry

11

Participation and political styles

'Government of the people, by the people, for the people' has become one of the most popularly accepted definitions of good government, and rightly so. It embraces in succinct terms those who are to govern, those who are to be governed and the purposes of government. But this very same phrase has also aroused widespread doubts among professional students of politics, and again, rightly so. Does this celebrated piece of rhetoric, they ask, really specify who are the people who govern, and what is meant by governing 'for' the people? At best, they may say that in the modern world all that may properly be expected is government 'of' the people and 'for' the people but that one may never realistically look for government 'by' the people. What is basically at issue here is the nature of participation in the politics of large modern States in a world of technology and organisation. But political participation is a complex, heterogenous phenomenon. It is not one undifferentiated activity. Participation in politics means simply to 'take part' in politics. Once that is said, it becomes very obvious that there is a host of ways in which an individual or group can take part in political activity. The word 'participation' tends to conceal this variety under a single heading and to give the misleading impression that 'participation' can be aggregated and maximised in some simple manner.

Political participation must be differentiated both as to the forms or modes of activity and as to the purposes of participation. On the other hand, mode of participation and purpose of participation must be understood together. It is the aim of this essay to suggest in tentative and outline form how the varied purposes of participation may profoundly affect the mode of participation which is appropriate. Certain 'styles' of political activity and of institutional structure may then appear to follow from the purposes of participation. Participatory theory may then issue into participatory practice.

Recent studies have done much to refine our understanding of the variety of modes that participation can take. In the past, studies of participation tended to concentrate on voting and on involvement in political groups—activities relatively amenable to investigation.[1] But it is clear that these by no means exhaust the avenues open to the citizen to participate in politics and it is no less clear that in certain countries voting and group involvement are either not available or are irrelevant as modes of influencing political outcomes. For these reasons scholars have attempted to broaden the field of study to embrace any activity which attempts to influence the formulation, passage or implementation of public policy—a definition drawn deliberately wide enough to cover political mobilisation in developing territories, community action in modern cities, policy application in China, as well as electoral activity in 'Western democracies'.[2] In the context of specifically democratic politics, too, the analysis of participation has become much more subtle. Sidney Verba and Norman H. Nie in their significant study of participation in America (itself part of a cross-national study)[3] have distinguished four basic modes of democratic participation in the USA—voting, campaigning, communal acts, which include contacting officials on social issues, and 'personalised contacts', in which actors attempt to secure some purely private benefit. Each mode of participation requires different degrees and types of information, each varies in its difficulty and in the degree of conflict it involves. And there is a significant tendency for each mode to attract a different sort of participant. There are voting specialists and campaigners and communalists.[4] One might say that each mode of participation demands a different political 'style'.

But even these refinements, important as they are, are insufficient to encompass the complex character of political participation. Verba and Nie deliberately limit themselves to what one may broadly term citizen participation. The call for extended political participation, however, often goes further than the demand for greater use of the standard channels of citizen involvement and proceeds to ask for the opening up of official decision-making, so as to involve the participation of more than the established elites and pressure groups. It is here that Professor Mackenzie's thought-provoking article on collective decision-making has so much to offer in the understanding both of the actualities of decision-making and of the potentialities for extended participation.[5] Mackenzie has suggested that whilst 'the decision' in any organisation might be best understood in a highly formal manner—a 'performative utterance' by authorised persons identified by an appropriate 'rule of recognition'—the process leading up to this formal stage may best be viewed as a series of moves and counter-moves, each of which affects the probability of the formal outcome. And there are many games that people can play in attempting to prevent or anticipate, pre-empt or circumvent that final outcome.[6]

What this stresses is that there are many stages—if that does not already imply too much of a regular process—to any decision. Each stage requires different skills, and though one man may play many parts in certain decisions, in most instances decisions in complex organisations are now the work of a large number of individuals. It is not easy for the political historian, nor often for those involved, to tell precisely who played the crucial role in making the decisional utterance almost inevitable or how this role was played. It might have been the mere performance of a routine administrative act rather than any 'world-historical' decision that tipped the balance. The significance for present purposes is that this analysis of the decisional process displays the variety of decisional activities and, indirectly, the variety of potentialities for participation. To raise a demand for more 'participation' or to reject it on the grounds that decisions must be taken by experts can be seen to involve incomplete appreciations of decisional activities. The capacity or incapacity to take part in any decision is not related to that decision 'in itself' but to the activities which go to make up that decisional 'utterance'. A person's capacity to participate effectively in the building of a hospital is to be estimated by his capacity to contribute to the thousands of lesser 'decisions'— from choosing a local hospital in preference to a large teaching hospital down to the selection of colour schemes—which together make up 'the decision' to build.

The capacity to participate and the nature of effective participation are also related to the purpose of participation, and this in turn will influence the sorts of decisional activity it is worth the participant involving himself in. Elsewhere I have suggested that participation has broadly three purposes, each of which has its associated political theory.[7] These purposes are 'instrumental' where the individual participates in politics to promote or defend his own interests; 'developmental' where participation is part of a process of self-education; and 'altruistic' or 'communitarian' where the participant is less concerned with self and more with promoting the good of his community. The lines between these three types of participation must not be too sharply drawn. A person may have more than one objective in mind when he takes part in political activity. He may alter purposes in mid-stream. He may find participation educative as a by-product of instrumental participation. Nevertheless, these categories do seem to correspond to the main theoretical approaches that have been taken to political participation.

Corresponding in turn to these purposes of participation there arise logically three 'styles' of political activity and institutional structure. The notion of a 'political style' has been variously pursued. For some it is a matter of leadership psychology—a steady pattern of decision-making whose origins can be traced to early experiences in the future leader's pre-political life or his earliest encounters with politics.[8] For other scholars the study of political style is, quite strictly, an outgrowth of stylistics. They analyse the politicians' use of rhetoric, of metaphor or of pronouns. One such study of French presidential candidates attempts to distinguish a style of the left from a style of the right by such methods as the quantitative analysis of 'communal' words such as *nous* and personal words such as *je*. Intriguingly, de Gaulle was one of those to employ *nous* more frequently than the anticipated *je*—and this was not a 'royal we'.[9] Political style may quite simply refer to the prevailing concern of the political apparatus in a country—with stability or flexibility.[10] Most convincingly, as A. F. Davies has suggested, it refers to a characteristic disposition of a politician to centralise or devolve decisions, to defer them or to face them.[11] With due caution such a disposition might be ascribed to a political culture and not merely to particular politicians. In all cases 'style' refers to a habitual pattern of actions or of verbal utterances which the politician employs in his attempt to reach his objectives or perform his expected role. It is part of the politician's art rather than his objectives—even though art and meaning may be closely intertwined.[12] In the present instance, participatory 'style' refers to the characteristic kinds of political action and political institutions appropriate to the realisation of the three kinds of participating objective.

Instrumental participation presupposes an economistic attitude to the need for political involvement. One participates for the benefit it brings one, and the benefit must be such as to outweigh the costs of participating. Associated with such instrumental beliefs has often been a long-standing assumption that each individual is the best judge of his own interests and that no other individual can be trusted to protect one's interests without his being given some incentive to do so. But even these assumptions would not be sufficient to stimulate the rational man's participation unless it were likely that this participation would materially contribute to the achievement of his interests. If this is not so and if these interests will be satisfied whether or not the particular individual participates, then the rational potential participant will receive the benefit without incurring the costs of participating. This, Mancur Olson has argued,[13] will be the appropriate response in any large group where one individual's involvement will make no noticeable difference to the achievement of a public good which is indivisible and which is thus obtained by all, regardless of whether they contributed their energies and money in striving for it. It will only make sense to participate where the group is so small that the individual's participation will count, or where only those who participate gain certain extra selective benefits aside from the main indivisible public good or where failure to participate is punishable.

Where the appropriate conditions obtain, what kinds of instrumental practice should one expect? Traditionally, such instrumentalism has been associated with techniques to enforce a close dependence of the ruler upon the ruled. In some cases this was to be achieved by the separation of powers which would prevent the government from exercising absolute power over its subjects. With the radical Utilitarians the government would be held on a tight rein by being subject to annual elections which would threaten the office-holders (who were by definition self-interested and power-seeking) with defeat if they deviated from the pursuit of the interests of the electors. Such devices as strict delegation and recall have also been part of the armoury of instrumental participation. Popular control combined with distrust of governmental authority are reflected in this manner of conducting politics. At the same time this very instrumentalism must be committed to a level of participation which does not impede the attainment of the very objectives of participating. Participation is necessary to efficiency, but the instrumentalist will not seek to participate past the point of diminishing return.[14] In this respect representative government will generally be preferred by the democratic instrumentalist to most forms of direct democracy, since in large units some kind of political division of labour will assuredly appear most economical of political energy.

It might seem that Olson's economic analysis is highly restrictive of rational political participation. But this is not necessarily so. Public policy decisions are at first glance prime examples of indivisible public goods—they are embodied in laws applicable to all members of the polity. But as Verba and Nie have argued in this very connection,[15] not all governmental decisions are of this nature. The amount of discretion permitted in modern legislation to the administrator means that there can be a great deal of variance in the implementation of decisions in matters of zoning, issue of licences and the like. Here individual participation can be quite effective and there is a manner of participating appropriate to this end. This is not voting or campaigning but what Verba and Nie term 'particularised contacting'. It is a 'rational' form of participation because the issue is, by definition, important to the participant. To an extent he chooses the issue in that, although he may be attempting to resist or redirect a policy which he himself has not shaped, he does select from amongst a host of problems which face him. He knows what he wishes to achieve, and the American experience indicates that if he can find his way around he has a fair chance of getting at least some of what he wants. Again, those who know the system do better.

Once the range and variety and the ebb and flow of political decision-making begin to be understood, on the lines which Professor Mackenzie has indicated, then also the variety of forms of participation will also begin to be comprehended. Participation can then appear far more rational an enterprise than when one narrows the definition to either voting or mere group membership. Such greater sensitivity to the nuances of political influence enables one to recognise that participation does not merely involve a decision to vote or not, or to join or not. It requires a range of skills which the rational and subtle participator can employ as he shifts from one course of action to another with the changing political situation.

This is recognised by Albert Hirschman in his brilliantly perceptive book, *Exit, Voice and Loyalty*.[16] He is concerned primarily to understand the rational conduct for a person faced with some failure by a firm, an organisation or a State to 'deliver the goods'. He subsumes this rational conduct under his three headings of exit, voice and loyalty, which are all forms of participation. As he points out, the economists' response to economic (and by extension political) failure is to 'exit'—to move to another source of supply, to leave the organisation, to vote for someone else or even not to vote. The politician's response is to speak in an attempt to remedy the decline. Hirschman's essay attempts to trace the likely consequences of exiting and speaking in various circumstances. He shows that the exclusive employment of either technique can sometimes bring about the ruin of one's very objectives and that the intelligent, instrumentally minded participant must know how to strike the balance between leaving and speaking and staying loyal to the enterprise—the modern version of knowing when to be a 'lion' and when a 'fox'. The logic of resignation, the perception of when to speak and when to be silent, the assessment of whether loyalty will pay in the long run are all now seen as part of what it is to take part in politics. This is what one might call a situational logic. It is worth giving voice only if someone is lending an ear, and it is only worth exiting or being loyal if there is someone paying attention.

To encourage the use of vocal participation at the expense of other forms such as voting could, however, raise difficulties of a different order. The evidence of current societies indicates that those most capable of using voice to good effect are those with the highest socio-economic status. They are also those who most readily use their feet to exit from the public to the private sector in transport, health services and education. If private education were abolished in order to concentrate resources on the monopoly State school system, then it might well happen that wealthier and better educated classes would be stimulated to use their voices to press for changes in State education. This might also correspondingly reduce the effectiveness of other classes in obtaining improvements. Whether this is a good thing or not is more of a matter for dispute than Hirschman seems willing to acknowledge. He is excessively neutral in simply describing the better-off parents as more 'quality-conscious' in educational matters. They may instead be seeking a different type of education directed towards different values. Indeed, the use of voice seems far more likely to produce such selective benefits than to bring about a major improvement in public goods. Nevertheless, what Hirschman's book does emphasise is that in different situations different participatory responses are rational. As political science labours to comprehend what the political insider already 'knows', one realises how much analysis of participation has been limited by restricting itself only to the most obvious of political inputs.

But even when operating within Olson's picture of rational participation there is one further way in which the instrumentalist may extend the range of effective political activity. Participation is illogical only if the group is so large that individual efforts will make no difference to the outcome. Individual participation will, however, count in smaller groups. Moreover, not only may an organisation or a governmental jurisdiction be too small to embrace all those who could benefit from its services but it could also be too large. This could mean that a service which it could provide will not be undertaken (or only inefficiently) because the beneficiaries are not large enough to form a majority or an effective voting bloc. They may, for instance, be a physically concentrated, deprived group in the society but yet not a majority. Reduce the size of the jurisdiction so that it coincides with the boundaries of the deprived group and then that group may effectively demand and use the service.[17] Traditionally, decentralisation and devolution have been more characteristic of the developmental style of participation. But here Olson argues, on instrumental, economistic lines, for the possibility of a separate jurisdiction for every collective good with a unique catchment area. The potentialities of this argument for, say, the reform of urban institutions have not been taken up as yet by political scientists. Clearly, the complexities of such arrangements would defeat any strict attempts at their institution. As with other instrumentalist projects, one feels that the very generality of 'the political' is in danger of disappearing amidst the settlement of narrower, almost privatised demands.[18] Yet these issues are central to the vaguely expressed demands for a community-oriented politics. What is a community in modern society? Is there a community corresponding to every governmental service? How does the demand for community politics relate to the demand for the optimum provision of governmental facilities? At least, as Olson says, the arguments 'show that both the ideology that calls for thoroughgoing centralization of government and the ideology that calls for maximum possible decentralisation of government are unsatisfactory'.[19]

Developmental theories of participation have looked for ways to minimise involvement in the political process rather than seek the maximum return in terms of goods and services for the minimum outlay in terms of participation. This indicates a contrasting political style. Politics is seen as part of a learning process in which participants will develop their own character. Politics is a co-operative activity, and the acts of co-operation will, so the argument goes, sensitise each individual to the aspirations, beliefs and feelings of the others in his community. In this way the individual is moralised.[20] The importance of political activity to such schooling lies in the generality of politics—the characteristic quality apt to disappear in a purely instrumental particularised attitude to the distribution of government services. If political activity is, as Professor Mackenzie has suggested, concerned with generality in claims to allegiance— a view which without too much stretching might accommodate the contrasting accounts of Easton and Oakeshott, then such activity can be seen as offering the widest scope for personal moral development.

But does it also offer the most intense form of education? Despite the apparent contrast with instrumentalism, a cost–benefit analysis is not inappropriate to the developmentalist. What political structures will most effectively promote human development? Olson's problem does not arise in this context, since it is basically the taking part which counts, and not winning the game. Only those who participate can gain the relevant benefit. Even so, the potential participant must seek some reasonable assurance that the activity will in fact provide the looked-for stimulation, that it will stretch his human capacities.

Is it, then, to be expected that the representative institutions of modern technocratic society will afford these opportunities for self-development? In general, the developmentalists' reply has been firmly in the negative. Modern institutions do not encourage participation. They provide openings for only limited elite action. The participation input open to most citizens is so remote from the point of governmental output that the citizen cannot feel that his efforts have been worthwhile. Modern participation is so reduced in intensity that, apart from the very few at the centre of things, the citizens receive no pleasure from political activity. This has been the burden of the developmentalists' complaint. They would agree with the assertion, in an influential textbook, that modern civic man is not a political animal[21]—but they would deplore the situation.

At their boldest the developmentalists seek to reconstruct political institutions so that they will match more closely the developmental style.[22] The aim has been to find the size and scope of jurisdiction which most effectively conduces to political and moral education. The traditional response has been to argue that the most intense learning environment is the small community—perhaps the political equivalent of the tutorial. The image of the Greek *polis* as the most heightened political experience has, of course, made a major impact on European thought. It is reflected both in attempts to imbue the nation State with the communal qualities of the *polis* and in suggestions that the nation should be displaced by revived city States. J. S. Mill reaches not dissimilar decentralising conclusions from individualist premises. Self-development is something which comes with practice—the practice of exercising responsibility for the circumstances which most affect one's life. This exercise of responsibility is best promoted by bringing self-government within the reach of the individual through devolution and decentralisation. The public should reinforce all arrangements, such as jury service or local self-government, which involve the individual in public decision-making. The central government in turn should not arrogate to itself any powers which could just as effectively and equitably be handled by those intimately affected by its exercise.

Developmentalism thus leans towards forms of direct democracy and related devices such as referenda, elective administrative offices and filling offices by rota. But the notion of self-development is imprecise and certainly difficult to measure. Rarely does it seem to imply the development of the character of the particular individual, warts and all. Rather it implies the development of some particular combination of desirable qualities—which are not for Rousseau what they are for John Stuart Mill. Does it, however, follow that the size of jurisdiction appropriate to the cultivation of certain of these qualities—say fraternity or the awareness of alternative aspirations—is identical with that which will most satisfy other developmental objectives such as offering opportunities for taking part in significant decisions? And will either jurisdiction coincide with that which will ensure the just distribution of communal resources? There are sound reasons for thinking that there will be no such coincidence,[23] just as there is no single optimum size for every form of education in the ordinary sense. In this case the grounds for compromise between jurisdictions needs to be examined.

Moreover, there is an inevitable problem of balancing the claims of developmentalism and instrumentalism. Developmental theory often appears as a complete alternative to instrumentalism and even appears to regard development as an end in itself. But there is something odd about such participation as an end in itself, about participation in participation. One participates *in something* and there is, consequently, always an end product in terms of governmental action even though the priority may still be the satisfaction gained from involvement. Thus the concern for the end product may come to affect the kind of political pattern which might be expected to emerge from developmentalist attitudes. In a strict sense a purely developmentalist political style may be impossible. The tension between these considerations is not mere abstract possibility but very real in, for example, development programmes where the objectives are both to educate the recipients of assistance to look after themselves by taking part in the running of the programme and to ensure that the assistance is fairly and efficiently distributed. As in the case of instrumentalism, the ideologies of maximal decentralisation or maximal participation are too simplistic as they stand, and the obvious need is for a close, detailed examination on the one hand of the aspirations of the theory of development and on the other of the kinds of decisional structures which can satisfy these aspirations.

Altruistic or communitarian theories of participation seem to fall somewhere in between instrumentalism and developmentalism in their demands on the participants' time and resources. Because those who have stressed self-development as a reason for political participation have believed that this will in turn contribute to the communal good there is a strong family resemblance between developmental and altruistic notions of participation. Nevertheless, it seems worth keeping them distinct, since the political styles attendant upon them can be expected to differ. The altruist may or may not feel that his political activity conduces to his own moral awareness. He may act out of a sense of duty or out of patriotism. What concerns him is that he should so act as to maximise what he perceives to be the good of the community or even what he believes that the community wants—either the general will or the will of all.

The level of participation this will require of the individual depends on an estimate of what he can contribute to the general good in comparison with others. Where each citizen's diverse skills and knowledge are considered to carry equal weight with any others in fostering the public good, then widespread participation can be the prevailing style. It makes sense to 'rule and be ruled in turn' after the manner of the Greek *polis*. It is probable, as Weber long ago suggested, that such assumptions will be found largely in less complex societies where specialised skills are less in demand in government. Where these assumptions are absent the level of participation will depend on a number of factors, notably the demand for, and supply of, persons with the relevant political skills.

The altruist, it is being suggested, will not assume that his own services are universally in demand. He will certainly act so as to ensure the more active involvement of those he considers best fitted to make decisions. But these may or may not include himself. A due *considered* deference to those with the appropriate abilities would be fully consistent with communally minded politics.

But by contrast with the distrustful, instrumental view of political leaders as delegates, subject to recall and strict mandate, the communitarian is liable to take a more Burkean view. He looks to the participation of 'the man of good will' who should be allowed the necessary political time and freedom to formulate and carry through policies which will effect the general good. In turn, the office-holder will not, by definition, be a power-seeker except in so far as he sees himself specially fitted to tackle the problems at hand. Rather, he will see himself as performing a duty to the public—a duty he will gladly lay down once it is fully performed or once he feels that another could do it as well. Nor is this a remote, idealistic picture of political conduct. Prewitt's study of local government representatives in non-partisan elections shows that such attitudes are very widespread.[24] They see their task as doing what they believe right for the community. They consider it demeaning to suit policy to the electorate's views. They often do not seek re-election since they have done their turn or finished the tasks they had set themselves. Even many of those who seek re-election declare that they are unconcerned whether they succeed or not. Like the instrumentalists, they may well consider the rival advantages of exit, voice and loyalty, but their concern will be with the consequences of these participatory techniques for the success of the policies they are promoting for the common good.

From other standpoints such attitudes are not even idealistic. Those who stress the need for accountability and for control of political leaders through electoral sanctions may be nonplussed by leaders who neither seek power for themselves nor fear political defeat. For such leaders a sense of responsibility is to be preferred to responsibility in terms of accountability. Some such 'men of good will' may even not participate if required to face competition in order to be elected. To those more concerned with accountability the risk of such a 'sense of responsibility' is that it may encourage an elitist paternalism which may further descend into a total disregard for the wishes of the ordinary citizen. Whilst the citizen still retains his electoral remedy, a deferential attitude to expertise, particularly in complex, technological societies, might result in a reluctance, on altruistic yet misinformed grounds, to remove the leadership. In this way technology might mentally disfranchise the inexpert. At the same time the elites may comfortably adjust to one another to produce a consensus on substantive or on procedural matters, secure in their own estimation of their ethic of responsibility.[25] Indeed, on communalist grounds such disfranchisement might be perfectly rational over a wide range of governmental decisions on matters of science, technology and economics. Paradoxically, the altruistic participant may think that his best contribution to the public good is to let others get on with the job of ruling. But if he is more confident of the need for his particular skills he may instead believe that he should be permitted to take part in decision-making with little interference from the less enlightened whose guarantee lies in his own sense of communal responsibility.

I have here tried to suggest a threefold typology of political styles associated with a threefold categorisation of theories of participation. As with most typologies, pure forms of the type are rare if not impossible. The typology is intended as a contribution to understanding the logic of the arguments for and against the extension or restriction of political participation. Such arguments amount, too often, to mere assertion and counter-assertion because it is unclear both as to what purposes greater participation would serve and as to what would logically follow for political conduct and institutions once these purposes were clarified. Just as in the case of other political ideals, such as liberty or equality, it matters what liberty or what equality is being urged upon us, so too with participation. It is always best to ask who is to participate, how and why, and to realise that such questions and their answers are intimately connected with one another.

Notes

[1] The data are usefully collected in Lester Milbrath, *Political Participation*, Rand McNally, Chicago, 1965.

[2] See, for example, the essays in G. Parry, (ed.), *Participation in Politics*, Manchester University Press, 1972.

[3] S. Verba and N. H. Nie, *Participation in America*, Harper & Row, New York, 1972. See also S. Verba, N. H. Nie and Jae-on Kim, *The Modes of Democratic Participation: a Cross-National Analysis*, Sage Professional Papers in Comparative Politics, 1971.

[4] See Verba and Nie, *Participation in America*, ch. 4 and *passim*.

[5] W. J. M. Mackenzie, 'Models of Collective Decision-Making', *Social Sciences: Problems and Orientations*, Mouton for UNESCO, The Hague, 1968, pp. 356–70.

[6] There are few better guides, as Professor. Mackenzie has often pointed out, than Cornford's *Microcosmographia Academica*, Bowes & Bowes, London, 1953.

[7] 'The idea of political participation', in Parry (ed.), *Participation in Politics*, where, however, the 'altruistic' theory is not fully developed.

[8] See the work of James D. Barber, *The Lawmakers: Recruitment and Adaptation to Legislative Life*, Yale University Press, New Haven, 1965; 'Classifying and predicting presidential styles: two weak presidents', *Journal of Social Issues*, XXIV, 3, 1968, pp. 51–80.

[9] J. Roche, *Le Style des candidates à la présidence de la République 1965–69, Étude quantitative de stylistique*, Privat, Toulouse, 1971.

[10] As in the work of Herbert Spiro, *Politics as the Master Science*, Harper & Row, New York, 1970, pp. 49–54.

[11] A. F. Davies, 'The concept of administrative style', *Australian Journal of Politics and History*, XII, 1, 1966.

[12] For a summary discussion of style and content in literature see Graham Hough, *Style and Stylistics*, Routledge & Kegan Paul, London, 1969, ch. 1 and *passim*.

[13] *The Logic of Collective Action*, Schocken, New York, revised edition, 1971. For a critique of aspects of Olson's argument see Brian Barry, *Sociologists, Economists and Democracy*, Collier–Macmillan, London, 1970, pp. 24–46.

[14] See L. J. Sharpe, 'American democracy reconsidered', part II, *British Journal of Political Science*, III, 2, 1973, pp. 129–67, for a perceptive critique of American democratic theory somewhat along these lines.

[15] *Participation in America*, pp. 48–50.

[16] Harvard University Press, Cambridge, Mass., 1970.

[17] See Mancur Olson, Jr., 'The principle of "fiscal equivalence": the division of responsibilities among different levels of government', *American Economic Review: Papers and Proceedings*, LIX, May 1969, pp. 479–87.

[18] See also Verba and Nie for doubts about the 'political' quality of 'privatised contracting'. *Participation in America*, p. 49. Some of the consequences of such privatising of politics are shown in Theodore Lowi's

important critique of interest-group politics, *The End of Liberalism*, Norton, New York, 1969. What is probably the first such analysis of English politics was presented by Professor Mackenzie as the 'ungovernable interests' model. 'Models of English politics', in Richard Rose (ed.), *Studies in British Politics*, second edition, Macmillan, London, 1969, pp. 52–62.

[19] *The Logic of Collective Action*, appendix to 1971 edition, p. 170.

[20] *Loci classici* of such views are the works of J. S. Mill and of de Tocqueville.

[21] Robert A. Dahl, *Modern Political Analysis*, Prentice-Hall, Englewood Cliffs, N.J., first edition, 1963, pp. 55–6.

[22] See David Thompson, *The Democratic Citizen*, Cambridge University Press, 1970, for the handy distinction between constructive and reconstructive theories.

[23] See the comments of Dahl in *After the Revolution?* Yale University Press, New Haven, 1970, ch. 3.

[24] K. Prewitt, *The Recruitment of Political Leaders: a Study of Citizen–Politicians*, Bobbs–Merrill, Indianapolis, 1970.

[25] On elite consensus see the work of Arend Lijphart, 'Consociational democracy', *World Politics*, January 1969, pp. 207–25, and *The Politics of Accommodation*, University of California Press, Berkeley, 1969. For an impressive and detailed application and extension of Lijphart's theories see Robert Presthus, *Elite Accommodation in Canadian Politics*, Macmillan of Canada, Toronto; Cambridge University Press, London, 1973.

Richard Rose

12

Why build houses?

The literature of information systems often presupposes that we know what it is that we want information about. But before we invest time, trouble and technique in devising new methods for analysing statistical information, we should consider how government has existed for generations without the promised benefits of new methods of urban analysis. To introduce a new information system into government we must first have an accurate idea of what information busy policy-makers do and will consume. It may be that the advancement of knowledge about housing policy is less a technical problem of social science than it is a political problem, arising from conditions endemic to government by complex bureaucracies.

The discussion that follows reports findings from a series of interviews with housing policy-makers in Scotland. The situation is described in the first section. The next two sections describe the housing objectives cited by policy-makers, and the indicators cited as useful in evaluating activities related to their objectives. Collectively, these objectives and indicators are the stuff of any 'steering' or cybernetic model of politics. They describe where policy-makers think they are going, and how they know where they are today. The fourth section considers the source of the policy-makers' objectives, and the concluding section describes the implications for any effort to develop *and* apply a housing information system.

1. *Housing in Scotland*

Western governments have moved well beyond a minimalist concern with the regulation of building standards and public health to a Welfare State concern with the provision of a 'tolerable' house for every family. This is true whether the government of the day expects houses to be provided primarily by private contractors reacting to market mechanisms or by public corporations building and renting subsidised housing. By positively intervening in the housing market the State can reinforce decisions made about land-use planning by actively ensuring that land in specified places is promptly put to housing use.

Housing is important because, like education, health and hospital services, it affects everyone in society. It is not specialised, like services for the blind, or privileged, like university education. The State's role in housing is limited, in so far as publicly built and State-owned housing is usually awarded to persons judged in relative need. The fact that housing is a private good rather than a collective good (like water, or land-use planning), makes it less certain that tenants of public housing and those responsible for the houses will necessarily engage in a continuing dialogue or feedback of information. Dissatisfied tenants may exit from a council house, rather than voice protest.[1]

Scotland is a particularly rich site for research in housing, and Glasgow outstanding in Scotland, because of the great political concern about the state of Scotland's housing. The great and rapid growth of Glasgow in the nineteenth century has left behind a legacy of slum houses. Scotland has always built a disproportionately large number of council houses, and Glasgow is the major builder of council houses within Scotland, erecting upwards of 5,000 units a year. At present the city of Glasgow owns more than 150,000 council houses—and the number and proportion increases annually. Notwithstanding this programme, there still remains a backlog of tens of thousands of 'sub-tolerable' slum houses in Glasgow.

Confronted with a major housing problem, there are three broad strategies that a social scientist might adopt. He might develop a model of the stocks and flows of houses, and household formation. This would be an appropriate task for an economist concerned with questions of supply and demand. Or he might study what tenants think of houses that are built for them.[2] Research in Whitehall and in Washington made me sensitive to the fact that economic data and social evaluation, while undoubtedly important and interesting, are not necessarily sufficient. In a paper entitled 'The market for policy indicators'[3] hypotheses were advanced to explain the conditions under which new types of information would be consumed or ignored by busy policy-makers. The study reported here was designed to examine empirically what kinds of objectives policy-makers articulated, and what indicators they had for their policy objectives. In short, description of the existing information system (or lack thereof) should precede prescription.

The discussion that follows is based upon the replies given by a variety of housing policy-makers to a lengthy questionnaire about housing information The questionnaire focused upon matters of considerable concern to those interviewed, for the average discussion lasted more than two hours. The open-ended nature of the questionnaire, and the fact that the author conducted nearly all the interviews himself, made it possible to record information in the respondent's own words, and to adapt and probe for additional information as circumstances suggested appropriate.

Defining policy-makers presents considerable theoretical problems. There are many people who are, *ex officio*, important in implementing high-level decisions, even if they are not necessarily makers of decisions. Because of the amount of detail involved in the design, siting, construction and letting of houses, it can be argued that implementation is as important as or more important than deciding housing parameters at the national level. Of the twenty-eight people interviewed for this study, fourteen were senior public officials (that is, career local government civil servants) in Glasgow corporation, four were elected councillors with major housing concerns, eight were senior civil servants in the Scottish Office, the central government department concerned with housing in Glasgow, and two were concerned with housing work in Glasgow, though not public officials. Statistically speaking, one cannot make any statements about the generalisability of these findings. Hence findings are not presented in tabular form, and the data can at most provide only indications of magnitudes or of the variety of outlooks. Practically speaking, the problems of these men are those likely to crop up everywhere in Britain.

The selection of individuals for interview was made by the author. The intention was to choose in each institution charged with housing responsibilities the senior person concerned, as a civil servant or elected politician. The persons interviewed are the managers of housing policy. Most of them are men with many years' residence in Glasgow and long involvement in the problems of Glasgow housing. Nearly all the local officials are professional men, whether architect, sanitary inspector or accountant. By contrast, Scottish

Office officials tend to be 'generalist' administrators, and councillors even more generalist in outlook. Nearly everyone showed
a strong concern with improving housing in Glasgow. If experience
made people wary of new ideas, it did not make them complacent
about existing conditions. The men interviewed reflect the 'voice of
experience' and 'professional knowledge'. They are not expert
designers of information systems, but potential consumers for new
information.

2. Why build houses?

The potential objectives of policy-makers are numerous. Policy-
makers may be concerned with social conditions, or they may be
concerned with economic goals. Alternatively, policy-makers may
have physical objectives, e.g. building schools, highways or hospitals.
Some are specially sensitive to the electoral consequences of decisions
in government. Civil servants can worry about job security, administrative convenience or power.[4]

The significance of multiple objectives becomes clear when one
asks the seemingly naïve question 'Why build houses?' A building
contractor or the spokesman for a union in the building trade may
see housing as a means to economic gains. An architect may have an
economic objective or be responding to an aesthetic impulse. A social
worker is likely to see new housing as a means to improving social
conditions. An administrator with long experience in government
may argue that the inertia of past legislation and past political
commitments make it impossible for government to stop doing anything once it has made a major commitment in social policy. What
is particularly noteworthy about the foregoing catalogue of motivations is that most treat houses as *means* to an end, rather than
regarding housing as an end in itself. It is thus possible to conceive
of other means being substituted for housing. For example, building
workers might dig and fill holes in the ground as a form of 'make
work' employment less expensive than constructing thirty-storey
flats, and social workers might give money to poor people living in
slums rather than give them new council flats where improved
amenities carry the burden of higher rents

The first thing one learns when interviewing public officials is
that some do not have objectives. Instead they have functions. To
define one's role in terms of objectives is to have an active and pur-

poseful outlook. A city planner will think in terms well suited to models of long-term social planning, preparing a strategy, co-ordinating public and private sector activities, or implementing proposals for the redevelopment of the environment. By contrast, some officials may have functions instead of objectives, passively reacting to stimuli from outside. For example, a public safety official may have as one of his functions responding to reports that a building is unsafe. In such circumstances officials do not require information to fit into dynamic planning models of the sort conventionally described by information systems. Instead, they require highly specific stimuli related to statutory duties. Politicians may have active objectives, e.g. to build more houses, or passive functions, e.g. to criticise proposals that civil servants put before them. Both activities were cited by the same councillor in one interview. Many officials have clearly specified functions that affect housing policy—but are not stated in housing terms. For example, the city assessor has the statutory function of valuing housing and apportioning the burden of the rate by technical criteria.

The objectives cited by housing policy-makers differ greatly in type. The following grouping was arrived at inductively, in an attempt to summarise how the objectives of policy-makers fit into more general models of society.

Social (of or pertaining to individuals or groups of people).

'To provide houses for those who cannot provide their own.'
'Housing homeless people.'
'Providing homes for the elderly.'

Economic (concerned with money expenditures or economic efficiency in the broadest sense, e.g. supply/demand or cost effectiveness criteria).

'Maintaining a high level of occupancy and rent revenue in local authority owned housing.'
'Buying and selling land on behalf of the city.'
'Supervising the central government subsidy scheme for local authority housing.'

Physical (of or pertaining to tangible material resources in the built environment, e.g. houses, or natural environment, e.g. land use).

'Building houses for the corporation.'
'Inspecting property for condemnation as unfit.'

Political objectives (concerned with generalised goals disputed publicly as between parties and/or pressure groups).

'To rehouse Labour voters within the city's boundaries.'
'To improve upon the house-building record of the previous administration.'
'To give advice to the Secretary of State to argue the case for Scotland with the Treasury.'

Bureaucratic (concerned with administrative regulations or procedures, or with the management of policy within government).

'To act as clerk to two committees.'
'To conduct correspondence with central government and lawyers about housing matters.'

Residual (not covered otherwise by the above categories).

'To revise the accounting system for the housing programme.'
'To do good architecture.'

Among the persons interviewed, the frequently cited objectives are, in order of importance, physical, economic and bureaucratic. Those infrequently cited are social and political objectives. Local government officials most frequently give bureaucratic or economic responses. Elected officials and policy-makers in the Scottish Office are about as much concerned with day-to-day routine as are those who are *ex officio* appointed to handle non-political and non-social tasks. One must wonder whether, in the city of Adam Smith, a hidden hand is expected to provide the political and social values required to make housing activities consistent with the wishes of members of the community.

Another way to characterise the outlook of policy-makers is to see how many objectives they cite when asked to name their chief functions. Does a policy-maker have a single goal to maximise, or is he concerned with keeping three or four potentially conflicting objects in equilibrium? The average respondent mentioned three or four housing functions. They are thus in a position to co-ordinate or trade off choices within a *limited* sphere of competence. Most policy-makers are concerned with objectives of two (or more) types, e.g. with physical and economic functions, or with economic and bureaucratic activities or, occasionally, with social and bureaucratic, or political and physical objectives.

One other feature of housing objectives is the time span involved. The well known prescription of disjointed incrementalism advocated by Braybrooke and Lindblom may describe how housing policy-makers work—but it cannot, in economic terms at least, justify such behaviour, for public housing in Britain requires sixty years to amortise its cost even at subsidised rates.[5] Moreover, the communities built by the corporation are likely to be inhabited for a century or even more. Hence short-sighted decisions cannot be 'written off' and abandoned; instead, they must be endured through successive generations.

Three questions were asked, designed to identify immediate functions, objectives for the next five years, and those for a twenty-year period. Everyone interviewed was ready to speak of objectives in a five-year period, and a majority could also identify twenty-year objectives, though sometimes simply by extrapolating short-term goals, e.g. 'the same as for the next five years'. In the case of city planners it is possible (on paper, at least) to integrate current, five-year and twenty-year plans, identifying immediate tasks (some responding to past problems), then altering objectives in a five-year plan, and achieving 'solutions' to present problems a generation hence. But some senior officials were overtly sceptical about twenty-year plans. One noted, 'So much depends upon what happens to the population, and economic conditions elsewhere.' Long-term objectives are less likely to concern bureaucratic or economic matters than short-term objectives. Instead, they will stress physical objectives, e.g. 'getting rid of all the slum houses'. Politicians did not paint pictures of a 'bright tomorrow'; they were among the most cautious when asked to look ahead. It is uncertain whether the greater emphasis given to 'extra-bureaucratic' objectives or to physical achievements in longer-term views augurs well for future-oriented information systems. It may mean that information systems are useful in the elaboration of long-term strategies, or that information systems are not related to the immediate objectives of policy-makers.

3. *Are housing objectives measurable?*

In their concern with devising optimum means of allocating resources, economists have forgotten one precondition for the application of their techniques. Before goods can be economised (i.e. allocated rationally) they must be empiricised, that is, identified by relating general concepts to material phenomena through reliable methods. In political terms, the absence of any method for empirically verifying objectives may be an advantage. In default of reliable measures no one can ever say that a policy has failed to reach its objective. If groups are in conflict it may be possible to make a decision which is politically rational, if it is an ambiguous symbol capable of being considered consistent with both of two inconsistent objectives. Alternatively, symbolic objectives may be invoked to satisfy one group, while substantive achievements satisfy another.

The less reliable and valid the indicators of success or failure defined in relation to a policy-maker's own objectives, then the less certain he is whether his activities are successful. To have objectives without means of evaluating progress through the feedback of information is to be constantly moving in unknown directions. Moreover, if a public official in a large organisation defines his objectives in vague or ambiguous terms, he will confuse or mislead not only his supporters but also those administrators who are expected to be carrying out his wishes.

In order to explore to what extent policy-makers had means of recognising feedback of information, after each question concerning objectives they were asked what would be regarded as an indication that things were going well or not going well. The question gains in value in that the colloquial term 'indication' is the same as the concept 'indicator'. The policy-makers showed no difficulty in citing what they regarded as indicators of success, or what they regarded as signs of trouble, or failure to achieve their objectives. The indicators that housing policy-makers cited could be classified under four headings:

1. *Completely reliable* (probability approaches 1·00 that two independent observers would make the same observation), e.g. 'Every house in Glasgow has its own toilet'; 'The ratio of publicly owned to privately owned or rented housing.'
2. *Reasonably reliable* (the probability is high but less than 1·00

that two independent observers would make the same observation), e.g. 'Every house has adequate plumbing'; 'The number of
appeals against rents is low.'

3. *Low reliability* (the probability is non-random, but closer to randomness than complete reliability, that independent observers
would agree in judgements), e.g. 'Complaints to councillors
decline.'

4. *Unreliable* (the probability of inter-personal agreement
approaches randomness), e.g. 'The level of vitality in the city';
'The feeling of a sense of community.'

Different types of policy objectives vary in the ease with which
they can be empiricised. Economic objectives stated in money terms
can be readily measured. So too can physical objectives, such as
building 5,000 houses a year. *If* a reliable definition can be agreed
for a slum house, then slum clearance objectives are also readily
measured. But policy-makers may wish to avoid a reliable definition
of a slum in order to minimise the problem. Bureaucratic objectives
may have easily empiricised indicators e.g. the amount of time it
takes to process a land condemnation action, or tend toward
vagueness, e.g. 'co-operation' between Scottish Office and local
government. Political indicators may be reliable, for electoral
success is easily measured. But they may not be valid—that is, one
cannot infer from the fact of electoral success that this specifically
endorses the housing policy of the winning party. The broadest of
social objectives can be among the least reliable objectives to
measure.

Because of the author's interest in the use of social indicators,
each policy-maker was also questioned about his awareness of social
objectives. The subject was first broached in a semi-directive manner,
asking, 'Who is supposed to benefit most from the housing policies
that you are concerned with?' The replies of local government
officials differed notably from those of central government officials.
Within local government, two types of answer were given: about
half those interviewed gave bureaucratically oriented answers,
naming other local government officials or institutions as the beneficiaries of their activities. 'The people who benefit most are those
for whom I act as an administrative co-ordinator.' The replies were
made in a matter-of-fact rather than cynical manner. By contrast,
the other half were client-oriented, referring to people in slums, in

council houses, or to everyone in Glasgow, whether home-owner or tenant. By contrast, every councillor and every central government official gave a client-oriented reply. They differed in that some thought in terms of individual families as clients, whereas others thought in collective terms, that is, in terms of 'the community' or 'the region'. The indicators cited as evidence of needs vary greatly in reliability. In some cases reliability is assured even if validity is uncertain: 'The size of the waiting list for local authority houses.' In others reliability is less but the political significance may be greater: 'Public opinion does not accept that it is right for a family to be without a water closet today.' Local authority officials have one measure of need denied officials in central government departments. One official said that he measured popular need by 'walking around on foot'.

In a second effort to elucidate social indicators, each person was asked for signs that housing needs are changing. All but two persons saw signs of changing needs. There was virtual unanimity that the change reflected a desire for better housing. In the words of one respondent, 'People no longer want *any* roof over their heads, but the right roof.' There was also a high level of agreement among policy-makers about the indicators of changing preferences: market activity—specifically, council houses standing empty because tenants will not live in them, or potential tenants not necessarily accepting the first house offered them by the corporation. A few persons also mention physical evidence of changing needs or political evidence, e.g. comments by councillors or officials of tenants' associations.

The replies emphasise two basic points. The first is that most housing policy-makers have relatively 'hard' measures of their objectives, that is, they can specify readily quantified or empiricised data that will tell them how well they are doing or flash danger signals. The second point is that the indicators are 'hard' because they are not social indicators but physical or economic. To note this is to imply not that their objectives are anti-social but, rather, asocial. Other things are more important. People begin to count when they can show by market mechanisms what they think of publicly provided housing services.

4. *Where do the objectives come from?*

To demonstrate the ultimate origin of the objectives of policy-makers would be a forbidding task, involving problems of individual motivation and institutional history. Within the scope of this paper one can only consider possible sources of objectives, and suggest which seem most important in the light of the evidence at hand.

1. *Politicians' definitions of goals.* In one sense, public officials and politicians must be in harmony, in so far as the politicians are meant to defend or be responsible for what is done in their name. But this coincidence of statements need not mean that politicians define precise objectives. Local politicians and public officials influence each other. Politicians reflect both partisan values and ideas acquired in their daily political routines. Public officials—especially in a city where only one party has long dominated—will not be unaware of party political views. When political objectives are stated explicitly— e.g. 'Build 5,000 council houses in a year'—this becomes a major objective. The architecture department issues monthly to councillors a pocket-size card reporting house-building progress on a monthly and annual basis. But it does not have equally specific guidance about how this objective fits with others.

The views of councillors (and of the governing party of the moment) are only one among many influences that officials must assimilate; it is up to them to make the specific proposals as to what shall be done in the name of housing policy. Moreover, among the limited number of councillors interviewed there was a readiness to define objectives in terms of immediate management concerns rather than more general political values. In the symbolic relationship of politicians and officials, immediate organisational demands tend to drive out less immediate and tangible ideological objectives.

2. *Statutory specification of objectives.* The mind of the Minister achieves permanence and binding force when it is enshrined in legislation or directives authorised by statute. A long-dead Minister or the proponent of a now discredited idea can still constrain present day decisions if his Act of Parliament has not been repealed or substantially amended. Housing policy-makers cannot ignore the many parameters determined by legislation, because they provide positive authority to act, as well as negative inhibitions. Moreover, statutes and the instruments based upon them also affect financial subsidies. What is called housing policy is not so much a single strategy, developed at one point in time, as the accumulation of a

series of statutory powers, enacted by Parliament with reference to all Scottish local authorities in the course of more than half a century.

In addition to interviews, a thorough analysis was made of the chief Acts of Parliament concerning housing in Scotland since 1919. There are several points to note of special relevance. The first is the multiplicity of justifications that have been adduced as reasons for legislation. Some demands are physical: insanitary slum dwellings. Others are social: the ills and evils that result from overcrowding. Others are economic: the employment of building workers. And some are political, with social control overtones: arrest trouble among a potentially alienable working class. A second point is that the *outputs* of legislation are not improved social conditions but intermediate goods, which are *inputs* into the social system. Legislation does not improve the lives of people who live in slum houses; it simply provides a possible means to alter these conditions for better or worse. Typically, a central government statute confers enabling powers upon local authorities. To encourage action, central government offers financial incentives to local authorities, usually associated with some form of standard-setting, or monitoring of local implementation. In other words, the immediate objective of housing legislation is to get local authorities to do something about housing. The social objectives are second- (or third- or fourth-) order consequences.

To test the importance of legislation in determining the objectives of policy-makers, a series of questions was asked about the major Acts and administrative rulings affecting individuals, their intent, and indicators of their consequences. In one extreme case the respondent described the intention of the Act by taking the text from his desk and reading it aloud. In a few cases, such as the 1969 Housing (Scotland) Act, explicit and reliable indicators are established by law. This Act provides a statutory definition of an intolerable house. The absence of statutorily defined physical conditions makes a house intolerable; previously public health inspectors were able to use their discretion, and classify the number of unfit houses by any one of a number of criteria. In a relatively small number of cases legislation and implementation seem to fit together in the view of those writing a law and those carrying it out. For example, Factory Acts are intended to make places of work safer, their consequence is perceived as raising the minimum standard of safety, and the indicator of success is the number of accidents. But often public officials take their definition of intent from the political climate in which the Act is passed, rather than from precise statutory statements. The cause-and-effect relationship between an Act and its consequences is seen as uncertain and contingent in political life, as in social science models. While social scientists try to be statistically precise, few public officials suggested quantified measures to evaluate the consequences of the major acts governing their work.

3. *Quantified data.* To explore the attitude towards existing statistical data as a source of goals, each person was asked to describe the statistics considered most useful and those considered useless or even misleading. Every policy-maker could cite some statistics useful to him in his everyday work. Typically, the data came from within his own department and, inevitably, within his sphere of responsibility and competence. The information more often than not was process-produced, that is, generated by record-keeping activities in complex organisations, and required for financial or auditing purposes.

Most policy-makers could also cite statistics that they considered useless or misleading. The objections were varied and not necessarily mutually exclusive:

All statistics can be misapplied—and politicians will.

A lot of documents which go to committee have lots of numbers which are not summarised. The standard of oral reporting is better.

Many of the *other* departments' statistics are a load of rubbish.

In view of the comments often made about the literary bias in British public service, it is noteworthy that no one poured scorn on statistics *per se.* The general attitude appeared to be moderate and realistic. Policy-makers trust most those statistics that are generated in proximity to their own work, with interpretations supplied by themselves. They distrust statistics compiled by external bodies and, even more, the inferences that others may draw from them. This implies that a generalised system of housing information produced by a centralised research unit would not likely be given much attention by policy-makers, because of its institutional remoteness from the departments immediately concerned with housing.

4. *Outside sources.* The extent to which new information will be

consumed by policy-makers is a function not only of the content of the information but also of the receptiveness of the intended consumers. The demand for additional information was tested both positively and negatively. First, each policy-maker was asked whether there was any information or research that he would like which was not presently available, and then whether he thought that there was too much information available, given the time available to think about it. The second question was intended to see whether people wished to cut down on the flow of information.

Almost every official interviewed was in favour of additional information being collected. Usually the policy-maker described a specific piece of research that he would like done about an immediate problem. In the case of local authorities, the definition of a problem was often narrow and non-political, e.g. 'We need a study of rain penetration through windows.' By contrast, central government officials tended to mention very general goals requiring basic research, e.g. 'The problem is no longer a need to know how many houses to build. We need to know the size of the housing problem, its specific characteristics, and solutions.' The contrast between local and central officials is further emphasised by the fact that half the local authority personnel said that they did not have any research requirements, whereas only one central government official thought himself without a need for further information. In other words, people more remote from day-to-day administration and/or more concerned with general questions of strategy are more open to new sources of information.

The contrast between local and central government is also illustrated by the contrasting responses given to a question about having time to digest existing information. Nearly every central government official commented upon the shortage of time to think about information and/or the thoughtless way in which housing information is presented. The following quote epitomises such views:

There is not enough time to think. This is caused by the sheer amount of paper we have to deal with and the way in which housing information is dished up. A lot of it is jumbled, and the subject lends itself to meaningless jargon.

Local councillors also felt the pressure of time, and considered there was more information about than they could digest. One added shrewdly that the problem was not knowledge but power. 'We know

what the problem is. What we want is the wherewithal to solve it.'
Most local government officials, by contrast with central government
administrators, did not feel that there is too much information to
digest. This is not to suggest that they have ample leisure, but that
they are readier to ignore information. For example, one official
commented, 'Using housing as a vehicle of research in mathematical
models produces irrelevant statistics. I don't waste any time on it.'
Other officials concentrate attention upon a few data sources. As
one man said, 'We know what we want. We have our minds
made up.'

5. *New techniques.* The assimilation of new techniques of analysis
inside public authorities provides an alternative mechanism for
the introduction of new information. In the period of the study,
cost–benefit analysis and output budgeting (PBBS in American
terminology, or PAR in British) were the chief new techniques under
discussion in government. Explicit questions were asked about knowledge of each technique, and whether the respondent could give
a quantifiable statement of benefits, or a precise measure of outputs.

(a) *Cost–benefit analysis.* Nearly all the central government officials
had heard of cost–benefit analysis, and about half the local officials
and councillors. However, most of those who had heard of the
technique (and all those uninformed of it) could not give a constructive answer to the question 'If forced to give a reply by an
economist, what would you say are the chief benefits of your policy?'
The most articulate gave the following sorts of answers:

It is difficult to judge the benefits of a policy. Unless social benefits are
included, the calculation is meaningless. But the price that is put on
these benefits is often arbitrary. Beside, the rate of discounting future
benefits is also important, and interest rates can be arbitrary or change
rapidly.

It all depends upon how many variables can be costed. When there are
environmental considerations this is very difficult.

Your guess is as good as mine. It is playing at games!

The only official prepared to recommend a cost–benefit analysis of
his own task was, appropriately enough, a professional engaged in a
task which was often undertaken by private consulting agencies. He
suggested that the cost of providing his service within the corporation could be compared with that of having the same work contracted
to outsiders.

(b) *Output budgeting.* This technique was virtually unknown among local government officials at this time, but familiar to about half the central government officials. In part, this arose from the introduction of PAR (Programme Analysis and Review) to central government. PAR exercises are meant to occur annually, one per department; hence they do not usually impinge upon individuals, nor was interest expressed in it. The comments by those who had knowledge of output budgeting were consistently negative. For example:

It is bloody difficult to say what our output is. New Towns? The environment?

It is very hard to measure outputs, except in ultimate terms: the conditions in which people live their lives. It is also hard to know what the intermediate steps are between the ultimate end, and where we are at present.

On the basis of the replies obtained in these interviews, it seems unlikely that the existing repertoire of new techniques will lead to a large or prompt alteration in the definition or measurement of housing objectives. Many criticisms of the new techniques are based upon an informed awareness of limitations rather than on an obscurantist fear of the unknown or the bureaucratic desire to be sheltered from external evaluation.

6. *Professional training.* A marked feature of local government officials in Britain is the importance and thoroughness of their professional training. Respondents often had several qualifications, each highly specific. Each official is a specialist in his work. The qualification is established in two ways: by formal instruction (often part-time education while serving an apprenticeship), and by long service in a single line of work. Local authority officials are often not graduates but boy entrants to a career which is advanced by night school education, further qualifications and seniority. Their approach to their job is thus much conditioned by experience, which intensifies commitment to specialised concerns without compensating concern with broader objectives. An architect will be concerned with how many houses he builds, and how they look; an accountant with how much they cost, and whether the costs attract subsidy under existing statutes. These indicators are usually physical or economic, and reliable within their profession. They are usually insensitive to

social or political considerations. Bureaucratic procedures force officials to attend to organisational responsibilities—but not to think outside their departmental framework.

By comparison with local government officials, both central government personnel *and* local councillors are generalists lacking any formal qualifications concerned with housing policy in any of its specialised forms. Central government civil servants are almost without exception arts graduates. Local councillors are often non-graduates. In both instances, individuals come to housing without any formal commitment to evaluating policy in accounting or legal or architectural terms. This very amateurism may give them a greater openness to fresh ideas. On the other hand, it makes their evaluations less reliable and provides no certainty of consistency in action. Moreover, because central government civil servants and local councillors are in non-executive positions, advising or directing corporation officials, they lack knowledge of specific detail, and the ability to put their ideas immediately into effect.

7. *The environment of policy.* Individuals without specific prior training are likely to learn through personal interaction in their political environment. Even for those with professional training, their immediate environment is likely to lead them to emphasise some points and discard others. What, then, is the environment in which housing policy-makers find themselves? When asked the best way of keeping informed, nearly every local government official referred to bureaucratic procedures, e.g. 'By just going to meetings and getting the papers I keep informed.' Only two officials referred to professional contacts as a major source of information, and only two referred to evidence obtained from members of the local community, whether citizens or clients of their department. Two also referred to explicitly political resources: 'I look at what the central government circulars say, and I look at the party majority.' Councillors, by contrast have a wider range of information resources: political, bureaucratic and, for the more involved, professional channels of information. Central government officials are like local authority officials, relying upon bureaucratic mechanisms for information about housing policy. They are less likely to have first-hand contacts with clients, and often lack professional channels of information.

When policy-makers scan information they do so selectively.

Information will be useful if it is perceived as relevant to how others evaluate them—or to the standards they believe should be used to evaluate their work. Separate questions were asked on each point. The great majority of policy-makers believed that their work was evaluated differently from the way it should be evaluated. The exceptions tended to be persons with narrowly circumscribed technical tasks, like ensuring completion of houses on time, or conducting 'housekeeping tasks' with promptness and efficiency. A small but noteworthy group did not have any idea of what criteria should be used by others to evaluate their work. These findings are general, without regard to political role.

The majority of policy-makers saw some difference (not necessarily a contradiction) between standards they expected others to use, and the standards they wished themselves to apply. The discrepancies arise in a number of different ways:

They are always asking, 'When am I getting a house?' People should be more concerned with how the whole city's housing programme is going. (Councillor)

They look at the houses, or they live in one. We should be judged by whether our houses produce 'satisfaction'. But that is something that's not quantifiable. (New Town official)

By houses classed as unfit. They should evaluate us by houses actually cleared away. (Construction/demolition official)

People judge by short-term things, by the number of disasters. They have an instant reaction. They should judge us in the long term. By looking ahead, or looking back to see what's been accomplished. (Scottish Office official)

The kinds of external evaluations perceived were often 'political', i.e. troublesome occasions of criticism and conflict, or social but self-interested. The recommended criteria for evaluation were not longer-term questions of social change or political achievement, but rather economic, physical or bureaucratic criteria for which a reasoned case could be made on the basis of specialised knowledge. In other words, housing policy-makers do not hold long-term goals derived from some picture of a desired social state. Instead, they wish to be evaluated in terms of criteria specific to their professional bureaucratic roles. One official even rejected the idea that a senior housing policy-maker should be judged by those outside his department: 'Each official and each committee is allowed to get on with his own job. There is not much concern with cross-evaluation.'

In summary, it would appear that the objectives of housing policy-makers studied herein are derived primarily from three sources: bureaucratic structure, legislative statutes and professional training. Awareness of at least two of these concerns is virtually mandatory for anyone concerned with housing. If one asks what can be ignored, the answer is: 'Almost everything else'.

5. *Conclusions*

The problem of improving housing information is not so much a problem of housing research as it is a problem of applying knowledge. In governmental terms, the value of knowledge is to be judged not by scientific criteria of precision but by the criterion of utility. It may be better to concentrate less effort upon the development of more sophisticated information systems, and more effort upon the application of knowledge that already exists. Transference does not depend upon inventing new statistical techniques, but in finding out how to transform existing indicators of housing policy into forms capable of incorporation in existing legislative statutes, administrative procedures and professional norms. The following propositions describe the situation.

1. There is no such thing as a housing policy, if by this one means a set of decisions consciosuly related to each other. Individual policy-makers usually operate with objectives restricted to a limited number of problems, and a limited number of concerns within each problem.
2. There is no central decision-making mechanism for housing policy. Powers are divided between central and local government, within local government and between public and private sectors.
3. It follows from the above that there is no client for an integrated information system that monitors housing supply and demand, because there is no public agency which has terms of reference and objectives as broad as those encompassed by theorists of public choice and social indicators.
4. Because those most open to information have the least time to digest it, and those who feel freest of time pressures have least inclination to digest additional information, the market for policy indicators in housing will most nearly resemble a cartel, with a low exchange of information occurring in circumstances in which this is beneficial for both sides of an exchange.[6]

Positive conclusions are best listed separately:

1. The more specialised the information system (i.e. the more closely it is fitted to a single department or task), the more likely it is to be utilised. Policy-makers are not opposed to quantification or analysis in principle. Data on paper, including quantification data, are accepted as a desirable part of a manager's routine. A housing manager can see the value of a computerised system for collecting weekly rents, or an assessor can see the value of collecting rates by computerising information. But neither may see the point of an integrated housing information system. Data relevant to housing can be so formated on magnetic tape that it is impossible to integrate data sets collected by separate local authority departments and by central government—if anyone were motivated to try.

2. Policy indicators contained in statutes or statutory directives will be attended to. Time and again subjects made reference to statutory powers and obligations. Sometimes this was done critically, sometimes to imply approval, and sometimes neutrally. But at all times policy-makers showed a positive feature of bureaucracy: regard for rules. Hence measures of housing based upon statutory authority will become incorporated in the policy-maker's frame of reference. This is true not only of regulations concerning physical objectives, such as minimum housing standards, but also those concerning financial subsidies for housing.

3. Policy indicators registered by market influences will be attended to. In this study, market information was registered by policy-makers when prospective council tenants began to refuse certain types of council houses; rent revenue dropped, and the occupancy of council houses dropped. In a society where housing is relatively scarce, market indicators must be specially devised, for the market is not free, and preferences cannot necessarily be registered by classical economic activities.

The alternative to the above conclusions is easily stated but difficult to secure. It is to change the structure of government to create a central point for review of housing policy. As and when this might happen, an information system could be provided to assist such a body in exercising public choice. If this were to occur in the field of housing, it would be a major innovation. It would achieve a degree of centralisation of policy-making that even the Prime Minister himself has yet to achieve in what is nominally but not always accurately described as 'central' government.[7]

Acknowledgement

This chapter is reprinted from *The Management of Urban Change in Britain and Germany*, ed. Richard Rose (1974), by permission of Sage Publications Ltd, London.

Notes

[1] See John M. Orbell and Toru Uno, 'A theory of neighborhood problem solving: political action vs. residential mobility', *American Political Science Review*, LXVI, 2, 1972.

[2] Bruce W. Headey, *Indicators of Housing Satisfaction*, Survey Research Centre, University of Strathclyde, occasional paper No. 10, Glasgow, 1972.

[3] Richard Rose, 'The market for policy indicators', in Andrew Shonfield and Stella Shaw (eds.), *Social Indicators and Social Policy*, Heinemann, London, 1972.

[4] See Richard Rose, 'Models of governing', *Comparative Politics*, 1973.

[5] *Cf.* David Braybrooke and C. E. Lindblom, *A Strategy of Decision*, Free Press, New York, 1963, and Rose, 'Models of governing'.

[6] See Rose, 'The market for policy indicators', p. 138.

[7] More generally, see ch. 10 of the revised edition of Richard Rose, *Politics in England Today*, Faber, London, 1974.

John Sanderson

13

Reflections upon Marxist historiography: the case of the English Civil War

To someone concerned with making sense of the events in Britain between the accession of James I and the flight of his grandson in 1688, the Marxist account of the period offers a sort of intelligibility, and therefore a sort of excitement, which almost all other accounts conspicuously fail to match. An encounter with some of the most relevant literature (mainly the works of A. L. Morton, David Petegorsky, Maurice Dobb and Christopher Hill, as well as the pronouncements of Marx and Engels themselves) suggests that there is a recognisable Marxist account of seventeenth century British (or at least *English*) history with discernible features, which I shall endeavour first to set down, and then to reflect upon with the object of forming some judgement as to their historical authenticity.

As with any other period, the Marxists have insisted that we think in terms of what Dr Hill calls 'total history';[1] that is to say, we must observe a social whole, being aware of the interrelatedness of the social phenomena which the academic division of labour currently prevalent ('blind-alley specialisation')[2] may mislead us into regarding as mutually isolated. 'The advantage,' Hill tells us, 'that Marxist-influenced historians have is that they think of history as one, taking for granted that there are likely to be connections between the culture and the economics of a society, however difficult it may be to analyse them.'[3] Dr Hill's own work has constantly exemplified this manner of proceeding, and a sympathetic reviewer of his book *The Century of Revolution* was thus moved to remark that few would read it 'without gaining ... a stronger feeling of the wholeness of life, of the fact that politics, painting and potatoes all belong to one world ... Marxists will hail the book as a vindication of their method.'[4]

The Marxist's study of human society which has led him to recognise the interrelatedness of the various areas of human activity has convinced him also that the way in which men provide the material necessities of life for themselves constitutes (as Marx puts it in a famous passage) 'the real foundation, on which rises a legal and political superstructure and to which correspond definite forms of social consciousness'.[5] To understand a society it is thus necessary to examine its economic processes, and with societies other than the most primitive this leads to a consideration of the way in which the most prominent of a society's classes periodically struggle for overall control. Given these premises, what does the Marxist historian find when his attention is devoted to the middle period of what Dr Hill has called 'the century of revolution'? His findings can, perhaps, be arranged under four main headings.

1. The Marxist sees the English Civil War as a genuine revolution, as a crucial stage in the development of modern European society. The English revolution thus indicates the rise of a class to political power which has hitherto been in a subordinate position in the body politic. Therefore what one is in effect witnessing in reconstructing sets of events like the French and English revolutions is the dramatic confrontation of two different forms of society, characterised by two different 'modes of production'. Thus Marx wrote that the Great Rebellion in England and the events of 1789 in France were not merely English and French revolutions: they were 'revolutions of European pattern . . . they were the proclamation of political order for the new European society. The bourgeoisie was victorious in these revolutions; but the victory of the bourgeoisie was at that time the victory of a new order of society, the victory of bourgeois property over feudal property, of nationality over provincialism, of competition over the guild, of partition over primogeniture . . . of enlightenment over superstition . . . of industry over heroic laziness, of civil law over medieval privilege.'[6]

In addition the Marxist asserts that the rising class should be designated 'progressive', in that the future, involving *inter alia* an increased human control over nature, lies with its members. Their antagonists, on the other hand, representing a fundamentally obsolescent form of society, may properly be called 'reactionary', for they seek in effect to fetter man's advance towards a materialistic plenitude which is one of the defining characteristics of communist society as envisaged by Marx and Engels. 'It cannot be too strongly insisted upon [A. L. Morton has told us] that the Civil War *was* a class struggle, *was* revolutionary and *was* progressive. A royalist victory would have meant a dead hand imposed upon the development of the country, feudal forms devoid of real content ossified into a monarchical tyranny, the persistence of a less advanced form of social and political organisation.'[7]

2. As the Marxist historian sees the matter, what happens in a genuinely revolutionary set of events is that a society's institutions of social control are overthrown, or at least drastically remodelled, so as to accommodate the needs of the new incumbents. The new class thus succeeds in a significant sense in imposing its social and political imperatives upon the body politic: in this particular instance 'the divine right of kings was squarely opposed to, and finally broken upon, the divine right of private property'.[8] And this destruction and remodelling take place because the old institutions oppressed the rising class, in particular acting in such a way as to inhibit the progressive economic developments of which it is capable. Early modern English history thus saw a situation in which 'the political order remained feudal, while society became more and more bourgeois', and what Engels regarded as 'historical necessity' required the suppression of this disjunction between the State institutions and civil society, and this was accomplished by the Civil War and the Revolution of 1688.[9]

From this interpretation of English history it follows that the French historian Guizot was profoundly mistaken in supposing that 'the only issues involved in the whole struggle between Charles I and Parliament were purely political prerogatives'. For Marx, Guizot's account was defective in that it contained 'not a word about the reason why Parliament and the class represented in it needed these prerogatives'. Also absent from Guizot's work was a consideration of 'Charles I's direct interference in free competition, which made England's trade and industry more and more impossible', and of the way in which Charles's 'dependence on Parliament . . . became the greater the more he sought to defy Parliament'.[10]

3. At the same time, however, fear of the lower orders (who are recruited by both sides) tends to be constantly present in the minds of those who might be called the primary contestants in the revolutionary situation. The fact that substantial plebian participation is necessary to the success of the bourgeois revolution is the cause of what A. L. Morton calls 'the double and ambiguous character' of revolutions of this nature. Such revolutions, he explains, are 'always

the work of a combination of class forces, the bourgeoisie drawing into the struggle, under the banner of freedom from privilege, big sections of the lower classes. As a result, when once the first stage has been passed, a further struggle tends to develop between those sections which want to limit the revolution ... and those determined to proceed to destroy or limit the power of the men of property.'[11]

4. Finally, because political ideas tend to reflect economic interests, the erstwhile ruling class (which in this instance gathers itself around the monarchy to make its last stand) will be found to have what might be called a *status quo* ideology, reflective in some way of the interests of the people concerned; while the insurgent (and would-be ruling) class will have a revolutionary ideology which reflects the interests of the *whole* society, and which can therefore form the basis of a potent appeal to other sections of society whose support the insurgents need. Furthermore, in the social disruption which is caused by these revolutionary social developments other ideologies make their appearance, and these are to be interpreted as reflecting the aspirations and interests of classes other than those effectively competing for sovereign power. Thus Engels writes in *Anti-Dühring* of how, in asserting itself, the bourgeoisie 'was always and inevitably accompanied by its shadow, the proletariat ... [Thus] bourgeois demands for equality were accompanied by proletarian demands for equality. From the moment when the bourgeois demand for the abolition of class privileges was put forward, alongside it appeared the proletarian demand for the abolition of classes themselves ...'[12] These lower class ideologies represent what Dr Hill has recently called 'the revolt within the Revolution'[13] but they also represent the 'premature' appearance of demands incapable of being met until society has gone through a further prolonged period of evolution.

We begin with the assertion that the events in question constitute a genuine revolution, the essence (so to speak) of which being the replacement of a fundamentally 'reactionary' feudal ruling class by a bourgeois 'progressive' one.[14] That startling innovations (often giving rise, indeed, to millenarian expectations) are to be found in the Civil War period is, of course, manifest. It was in this period that the monarchy and the House of Lords were abolished, that an acknowledged king was in effect driven from his capital to return only to be publicly done to death for the crime of making aggressive war upon his people. Subsequently the nation underwent a period of military rule before embracing the late king's son as a restored monarch. Now the impact of the Great Rebellion emerges clearly in the political literature of the Restoration, and perhaps nowhere more strikingly than in the contemporary writings of John Locke, who welcomed the return of the Stuarts in a manner which gave little hint of his subsequent view of them: 'I no sooner perceived myself in the world but I found myself in a storm, which hath lasted almost hitherto, and therefore cannot but entertain the approaches of a calm with the greatest joy and satisfaction.' Consequently he would endeavour to dispose men's minds 'to obedience to that government which hath brought with it that quiet and settlement which our own giddy folly had put beyond the reach, not only of our contrivance, but hopes'.[15]

We have, then, in this period, dramatic events aplenty; but do they represent the movement of one class against another? If we assume that the 'reactionary' class was sustained by, and found expression in, the interlocking institutions of Church and monarchy, there seems little reason to doubt that these institutions had become exceedingly unsatisfactory in the eyes of (amongst others) important commoners and allied members of the nobility, whose hopes for reform were centred upon the Parliament which met in 1640. Economic grievances featured significantly among those expressed by the Long Parliamentarians. Apart from feudal survivals or revivals (such as wardship and knighthood fines), unparliamentary taxation, and the sporadic governmental attempts to prevent the enclosures upon which 'progressive' landowners were intent, I take it that it was the matter of monopolies, which in this context aroused the most heated controversy, and predictably Dr Hill had a striking passage on them in *The Century of Revolution*.[16] 'Our ancestors [complained a contemporary in a document of special significance for the Marxist] drank the juice of their own wines, reaped and eat the fruit of their own harvest ... we [on the contrary] labour not for ourselves, but to feed excrescences of Nature, things grown up out of the ruin of Natural Members, Monopolists.'[17] Monopolies, it would appear, bore hard upon all those unable to get a hand into the till, probably hurting the consumer most, but frustrating the would-be producer and unquestionably placing a fetter upon his economic activity, a fetter which (along with most of the other economic grievances) was to some extent removed by the actions of the Long Parliament.

At the same time, constitutional and religious issues jostled with economic ones in the minds of parliamentarians and in the minds of those whom they represented, and a reading of such relevant documents as *The Grand Remonstrance* does not suggest that economic grievances occupied any sort of hegemonic position. Of course, those who were upset by monopolies almost invariably wanted Parliament to have a larger share in the government of both Church and State, and the historian shares with contemporaries the difficulty in distinguishing the types of issue involved. How great this difficulty is has been shown by Dr Brian Manning. He has described how, because of the constitutional crisis of 1640–42, a paralysis of trade spread rapidly outwards from the capital, alarming merchants and gentry and provoking to violence the poorer sort, driven to desperation. In turn this tumult and disaffection in both capital and counties was used by the opposition leaders to put pressure upon reluctant peers and the king to submit to their demands. If the constitutional crisis remained unresolved, Pym and his supporters predicted that popular rage would overwhelm the commonwealth, producing what Pym called 'an equality of misery and distress'. Although Parliament was able to make use of this widespread popular rage, its leaders did not create it and (one has the impression) were glad enough to channel it, with what must have been considerable misgiving, against the 'popish lords' and 'evil advisers' held to be responsible for the current *impasse*.[18]

As the populace was becoming angry with the persons said to be responsible for the current predicament, John Milton was writing that the tyranny with which his Englishmen had to contend was 'an ambiguous monster', having both a civil and a religious guise, which guises were represented by the Earl of Strafford and Archbishop William Laud respectively. The *ambiguity* of the monster reflects the difficulty of the historical problem involved here: that of distinguishing the relative importance of the various types of complaint made against the policies and regime of Charles I.[19]

Whatever the solution of this problem may be, it is clear that the economic activities of an important section of the population were molested by government-inspired or -sustained regulations; and this is precisely the situation (the Marxist tells us) which produces revolution. But what of the 'sides' who made, or sought to suppress, the revolution? Here it may be suggested that the data available are less than conclusively favourable to the interpretation in question.

Messrs Brunton and Pennington, in their book *Members of the Long Parliament*, did not find that MPs who eventually sided with their king were strikingly different in social origin or occupation from those who worked for a Parliamentary victory, and these authors were thus sceptical of any split between a 'progressive' bourgeois party and a 'reactionary' feudal party in the Long Parliament. In particular, I imagine that the Marxist would have been pleased to find the merchants cutting a more impressive figure in Parliament than they apparently did.[20] But Brunton and Pennington deal only with MPs, and such data may be less than decisive to the contention, advanced principally by Dr Hill, that the Civil War was in essence a conflict in which the economically advanced south and east confronted the backward north and west, with the ports being 'all for Parliament'.[21] In *The Century of Revolution* Hill produces maps of England and Wales illustrating this thesis. The great importance of the south-east (and particularly of London, which far outranked any other city in size of population) to the Parliamentary cause must be unquestioned, but some ports served the king,[22] and one cannot help thinking that Hill's maps would have had a rather different effect if Scotland had been included in them.[23]

The conclusion would appear to be, then, that the various ways in which economic enterprise was hampered by the early Stuart governments *did* constitute a considerable grievance for economically active persons and that this grievance was substantially remedied by the actions of the Long Parliament, in which these persons were represented. We must observe, however, that this type of grievance was only one among others, and that grievances tended to merge and to be mutually supporting. Moreover, on the matter of the composition of the sides contesting the Civil War the evidence is suggestive rather than conclusive.

What, however, of that other 'revolution' commonly recognised by students of the period, the revolution whereby the army which Parliament had created first purged and then disbanded its creator, while in between these events the king was tried and executed? A. L. Morton tells his readers that the initiative taken by the army when the fighting in England was substantially over was a 'second revolution' which heralded the rule of the 'revolutionary petty bourgeoisie', who were apparently more radical and more determined than the conservative 'big bourgeoisie' who had been responsible for the original revolution of the Long Parliament.[24]

This analysis finds striking confirmation (when allowance has been made for a certain exaggeration) in such documents as the *Memoirs* of Denzil Holles, a leading oppositionist of 1642 and one of the five MPs whom Charles had sought to arrest. Holles describes the rise of 'the violent party' both in the House of Commons and in the Parliamentary army, which first manoeuvred, then bludgeoned, the moderate men into defeat. The salient characteristics of the violent party, according to Holles, were the comparatively low social standing of its adherents and its intention to rule despotically. He writes that 'the meanest of men, the basest and vilest of the nation, the lowest of the people, have got the power into their hands; trampled upon the Crown, baffled and misused Parliament; violated the laws ... suppressed the Nobility and Gentry of the Kingdom ... and now lord it over the persons and estates of all sorts and ranks of men, from the King on his throne to the beggar in his cottage'. Earlier, Holles and other moderate men had protested against various Stuart malpractices, but these malpractices were 'but flea-bitings' when compared with the onslaught of the new tyrants: 'in grievances ... their little finger has been heavier than the loins of Monarchy ... we were then chastised with Whips, but now with Scorpions'.[25] Not surprisingly, Morton tells us that the 1648 intervention of the army came at 'a moment of peculiarly delicate class relations',[26] and from a Marxian standpoint, developments of this kind clearly call for an especially careful analysis.

The recent researches of Professor David Underdown, described in his book *Pride's Purge*, indicate that there *were* significant (albeit not dramatic) social differences between the purgers and the purged:[27] to this extent Morton's analysis is borne out. Thus a 'class analysis' of this particular set of events turns out to be helpful and suggestive. But is it a specifically *Marxian* analysis? Marx maintains that, *in general*, political power is a reflection of the distribution of economic power within society, and that the State power is used by the economically dominant class to guarantee the integrity of the exploitative socio-economic system within which it operates. With respect to *particular* periods, however, Marx holds that this analysis needs modification. Thus when the economic position of a ruling class has been eroded by the development of the mode of production, there will be a period wherein this class *still* exercises political power although the economic basis of that power has disintegrated; in this situation we find 'base' and 'superstructure'

temporarily out of alignment as a doomed class clings anachronistic-
ally to political power.[28] This misalignment of the State and civil
society can be only temporary, however, and in due course the
latter asserts itself and the State becomes once more the instrument
of the ruling class. The question remains, can it become the instrument of a section of society (in this case the petty bourgeoisie) which
has not been, and cannot now be described as, the 'ruling class'?

Regarding the success of the revolutionaries in destroying or
drastically remodelling society's controlling institutions, at least a
prima facie Marxian case again presents itself. Charles I had dis-
pensed with Parliament altogether during the fourth decade of the
century, having told MPs that 'parliaments are altogether in my
power for their calling, sitting and dissolution' and that 'as I find
the fruits of them good or evil, they are to continue or not to be'.[29]
His opponents suspected that what was in train in the 1630s was the
onset of a Continental-style absolutist regime in which the king and
his Ministers ruled through an appointed bureaucracy without the
encumbrance of having periodically to confront the peerage or the
nation's elected representatives. Henry Parker, a leading Parliamentary theorist, thus regarded Charles's refusal to summon Parliament during the 1630s as 'the grievance of all grievances',[30] while
Mrs Lucy Hutchinson, recalling the period subsequently, claimed
that, having observed the operation of the monarchy in France,
Charles 'thought himself no monarch so long as his will was confined
to the bounds of any law'. The king, she believed, 'was the most
obstinate person in his self-will that ever was, and so bent upon being
an absolute uncontrollable sovereign that he was resolved either to
be such a king or none'.[31] This view contains an element of partisan
exaggeration but there can be no doubt that only the direst necessity
obliged Charles again to summon Parliament, and one has the
distinct impression that he would have been glad enough to bid a
permanent goodbye to the institution which his Archbishop of
Canterbury called 'that noise'.[32]

The Long Parliament having assembled, Charles was obliged to
acquiesce in the attainder of his right-hand man, the Earl of
Strafford, in the dismantling of the machinery of conciliar government and in the abolition of many of the hated monopolies. Here-
after, by the terms of the Triennial Act, Parliament was supposed
to meet regularly whether Charles found its fruits good or not, and
the current Parliament was not to be dissolved without the consent of

its own members. These measures are, of course, part of the story of the development of parliamentary government in Britain, and it is clear that the 'constitutional revolution' of 1641 was by no means completely reversed at or after the Restoration: the monarchy as restored in 1660 or as instituted in 1689 was thus *not* the monarchy that had been under attack in 1640. As Charles signed both the Act of attainder against Strafford and the so-called Perpetual Parliament Act he is reported to have said that 'My Lord of Strafford's condition is happier than mine', and we may safely agree with him that his position at this juncture was indeed parlous. For a God-appointed sovereign the events of 1641 constituted no ordinary political defeat, and he was in particular to recall the ignominy of his abandonment of Strafford when in 1649 his own turn came to face the axe. Before the commission of that 'crime *Leviathan*' (as Bishop King called it),[33] however, Charles and his supporters had fought two civil wars of fluctuating fortune, and for the king the almost total political defeat of 1641 was followed by a total military defeat which put him at the mercy of his opponents.

May we conclude, however, from all this that the divine right of kings was 'broken upon the divine right of private property'? The monarchy of the 1630s was assuredly broken in some sense by the 'constitutional revolution' of 1641, and it was broken by a Parliament concerned, among other things, with preserving and enlarging the property rights of 'the political nation' as therein represented. But it must be added that many of the men of 1641, and many of the MPs who led in battle the opposition to the Cavaliers, had several surprises in store for them before they were destined to welcome back the monarchy in 1660. In particular, if they were strong enough to defy Charles and to assert 'the divine right of private property' against him, they were not strong enough to prevent either the drastic mutilation of the legislature or the onset of Cromwellian military rule. It was during Cromwell's period of dominance that, according to David Petegorsky, the bourgeoisie was obliged to accept 'a system of regulation more rigorous than that which it had fought to overthrow';[34] and it was Cromwell, as Thomas Hobbes gleefully pointed out, who taxed anybody and everybody without consent. 'When their New Republic returned into Monarchy by Oliver, who durst deny him Money upon any pretence of Magna Charta, or of these other Acts of Parliament which you have cited?' Hobbes demands of his Cokean opponent in his *Dialogue of the Common Laws of England.*[35] Cromwell's army, in Dr Hill's words, 'had as little respect for the sovereignty of Parliament as Charles I, and far more strength',[36] and it was he who dismissed with contempt what remained of the 'perpetual' Parliament, and though we may consider that his shortcomings as a political leader were made clear in the 1650s, while he lived he was immovable.

Nevertheless, the substantial return in 1660 to the position of 1641 indicates that in the broadly constitutional sense the Parliamentarians of 1642 *had* succeeded, though when they and their like were being purged by Colonel Pride or languishing under Cromwell many of them must have wondered whether the whole business had been worth while. This, of course, was the point of those stinging remarks made by Hobbes in the *Behemoth* about the short-sightedness of London businessmen: they had been forced to submit when the army invaded the capital in 1648, and if they had been thinking clearly they would have realised much earlier that obedience to their lawful sovereign was the best way to protect their property.[37]

Again, from the standpoint of the Marxist looking for a successful bourgeois revolution, it is hard to see how further paradoxes can escape recognition in considering the Restoration settlement. What, for instance, of the repeal of the Triennial Act in 1664 (Charles II's 'fine rebuff to the old Parliamentary gang', as it has been called by a student of the period[38])? The king had indicated that he would not countenance the meeting of a Parliament against his will (an eventuality provided for in the 1641 Act); the Cavalier Parliament, while decreeing that Parliament should meet at least once every three years, repealed the 1641 Act, with its offending provisions (which were, it was said, 'in derogation of His Majesty's just rights and prerogative'[39]), and the attendant discussions revealed some disillusionment with the institution once held infallible by its protagonists. Thus Sir John Holland told his colleagues that 'I had rather never live to see a Parliament called than to see a Parliament to be called and sit contrary to the good will of the King, for Sir, it is not now as when this Act passed, for now Sir, we have the sad and dear experience of that which was then incredible I think to most Englishmen (I am sure it was so to me) that through the long sitting of a Parliament contrary to the Good Will of the King greater and more desperate mischiefs have arisen both to the King and People than ever have or possibly can arise through the long intermission of Parliament, though those inconveniences be very great'.[40]

Of even greater significance in this context is the fact that with respect to the precipitant of the violence in 1642 (i.e. the struggle for control of the militia) the Parliamentarians were destined to be unsuccessful, for this control was placed unequivocally in the hands of Charles II, the relevant Act declaring that 'the houses of parliament cannot, nor ought, to pretend to the same'.[41] Now this matter had become critical in 1642 with the king's attempt to arrest the five Members and with the outbreak of the rebellion in Ireland. Parliamentarians feared that if Charles were allowed to retain his traditional control over the armed forces, the army which would have been raised to suppress the rebels in Ireland would be used to suppress Parliament itself, thereby effectively reversing the constitutional reforms of 1641. In a sense, then, it was the totality of the constitutional gains made by the Long Parliament that was thought to be in question when the Militia Ordinance brought the sides to blows in the autumn of 1642, and it is significant to note that royalist political writings of the period had as one of its main concerns the establishment of the king's *trustworthiness*: thus it was often conceded that his pre-1640 policies had been to some extent misconceived, but it was asserted that a monarch chastened by his subsequent experiences could be relied upon to accept the reforms of 1641 and to refrain from any vengeful pursuit of those who had ventured to criticise and oppose him. After the drawn battle of Edgehill (an encounter which temporarily knocked a good deal of the stuffing out of both sides) we thus find Charles declaring that 'We have often said, and we still say, that we believe that many inconveniences have grown upon this Kingdom by the too long intermission of Parliaments; that Parliaments are the only necessary sovereign remedies for the growing mischiefs which time and accidents have and will always beget in this Kingdom.'[42] This chastened, moderate attitude adopted by the king and by many of his literary supporters was intended to contrast with the ruthless determination of his opponents to establish themselves in absolute power over the commonwealth.

Now the events of 1642–60 probably chastened *everyone*, and while Parliament did not wrest control of the armed forces from the king, it had shown that it could cause a deal of trouble in the event of an attempt to reverse the pre-war constitutional reforms.

The historian, unlike the contemporary, knows that these reforms were destined to become a permanent part of the constitutional landscape; but if we discard the deceptive illumination of hindsight, if we read our history *forwards*, instead of *backwards* (reading it backwards must, one supposes, be a constant tendency of the Marxist, convinced as he is of the determined character of much of his story), our understanding of the events of the Restoration period may undergo some degree of revision. We may thus come to take more seriously the impression of impending despotism which so disturbed contemporaries. Let us pursue, for instance, the matter of the control of the armed forces. In *God's Englishman* Dr Hill tells us that the Interregnum 'left behind ... in the memory of the ruling class a fixed hatred of standing armies',[43] but it was James's standing army which, notwithstanding this 'hatred', crushed the Monmouth rebellion on Sedgemoor. In the broader context, A. L. Morton writes that while his father had claimed the throne by divine right, Charles II 'knew that he was King by permission of the landlords and merchants ... and could be dismissed as easily as he had been summoned'.[44] However, Morton is subsequently constrained to conclude that after surmounting the Exclusion crisis Charles ruled 'with a more absolute power' than any previous Stuart ruler; indeed, that he had 'a force too formidable to be directly challenged'.[45] Little wonder, then, that Dr Hill tells us that 'the compromise of 1660 [had] swung too far to the right',[46] and with James firmly in the saddle after the defeat of Monmouth, it would have been only the most perceptive of Englishmen who could have predicted his ignominious departure from the English scene so soon afterwards. A close student of James's career has written that 'had he been able to remould England nearer to his heart's desire, he would have achieved a polity on the French model and have been in England in all things what Louis was in France: James never said, "L'état, c'est moi," but it was his aim to be able to say it.'[47] That such a king was deposed is, perhaps, not surprising; but given the context of an (at least) partially successful bourgeois revolution, it is somewhat surprising that he succeeded to the throne in the first place. The steps in the direction of absolutism taken by the royal brothers tend, it seems to me, to disfigure the picture of the Revolution of 1688 as a 'decorous epilogue',[48] 'a comparatively puny event',[49] a 'readjustment',[50] 'an easy ... operation',[51] little more than a tidying up after the more dramatic events of the fifth and sixth decades of the century. Indeed, one is struck by the contrast between the Revolution of 1688 and the events of 1637–42: in the early period first the Scots and then the English successfully defied their king; in the later period the king's downfall was secured by a foreign invader supported by twelve thousand armed men. Some Englishmen corresponded with the Saviour Prince, and many others whose duty it was to spring to the assistance of their sovereign notably failed to do so. But it was William who put James away. And one may be permitted to doubt whether he should be regarded (as he is by A. L. Morton) as the 'nominee' of the Whigs, or whether he undertook the hazardous operation of 1688 merely to become a tool of the bourgeoisie.[52]

The impression of impending absolutism already referred to is somewhat strengthened by the apparent popularity of Filmer's ideas during the 1680s, as contrasted with their relative insignificance during the Civil War, which was their actual point of origin. Such matters are hard to assess, but there seems to be little reason to doubt Locke's contention that Filmerism was 'the Currant Divinity of the Times',[53] and another prominent Whig, Algernon Sidney, held Filmer to be so important as to merit what might be called a 'scaffold refutation'. At Sidney's execution for treason in 1683 an attendant sheriff received from the prisoner a paper vindicating constitutional government and demanding to know why *he* stood condemned when Filmer's 'wicked principles' were so widely proclaimed: 'If he might publish unto the world his opinion, that all men are born under a necessity derived from the Laws of God and Nature, to submit unto an Absolute Kingly Government, which could be restrained by no Law, or Oath; and that he that hath the power ... had the right; and none must oppose his Will, but the persons and estates of his subjects must be indispensably subject unto it; I know not why I might not have published my opinion to the contrary, without the breach of any law I have yet known.'[54] Sidney's summary of Filmer, it will be observed, is accurate enough: this is what many Tories *said* they believed in. The contrast with what is to be found in *Eikon Basilike* (that most popular of Civil War publications) or what was said by almost any royalist writer of the Civil War period, is considerable.

My third point concerns the tendency of the original contestants in a non-proletarian revolution to draw back from their original stances in the face of the possibility or the actuality of lower-class intervention in politics. 'Propertied circles', Maurice Dobb tells us in *Studies in the Development of Capitalism*, recoiled in alarm when they heard the voices of the Levellers and the Diggers: 'Thus we have displayed with remarkable clearness that contradictory feature that we find in every bourgeois revolution: while this revolution requires the impetus of its most radical elements to carry through its emancipating mission to the end, the movement is destined to shed large sections of the bourgeoisie as soon as these radical elements appear, precisely because the latter represent the small man or the dispossessed whose very claims call in question the rights of large-scale property.'[55]

Milton's *The Tenure of Kings and Magistrates* castigated those whom the author called the 'Malignant backsliders'[56] who had once opposed the king but who now (i.e. in 1649) drew back from what Milton regarded as the logical outcome of a civil war between a people and its miscreant monarch. But it is clear enough, as Dr Hill emphasises in *The Century of Revolution*, that the backsliding began before the outbreak of hostilities, and that it continued more or less unabated until that event which a despairing Milton regarded as the absolute catastrophe, the Restoration of 1660.

The king's isolation in the early period of the Long Parliament made possible the dismantling of the machinery of conciliar government as it had evolved down to 1640, along with the destruction of its principal agents. Charles at this stage appears to have had nothing but enemies; but defections from the opposition helped him build a party with which he sustained hostilities until 1648, and so powerful was the royalist challenge that Parliament (despite talk of its 'vastly superior resources')[57] in desperation tipped the balance of the war by summoning to their aid the Scots who had seemed so formidable during the Bishops' Wars. Further defections (such as that of Denzil Holles, already referred to) accompanied the rise of Cromwell and the 'violent party', and the establishment of first the republic and then the protectorate. Subsequently, according to the Marxist account, the propertied classes came together in the face of almost continuous intrusions from the lower orders to establish what is invariably referred to by historians of this persuasion as 'the compromise of 1660'. Men of property are thus understood to have frightened themselves half to death during the Rebellion, and to have seen the need for a return to monarchical government as a guarantee of their security against those who would overthrow society—Diggers, Levellers, Fifth Monarchy Men and the rest. It was safe in 1660 to embrace the monarchy, for counter-revolution was no longer a danger: 'Ten years ... of the rule of industrial capital sufficed to lay the spectre of feudalism. But the spectre of communism could only grow.'[58]

Now while a reference to a more generalised disillusionment and weariness would seem to be necessary in explaining the Restoration (and why is Dr Hill so reluctant to accept the genuineness of the popular rejoicing: the Marxist interpretation surely requires that, to an extent, it should be genuine?),[59] much of this analysis plainly has the ring of truth. Thus the Marxists have put us on familiar ground when we read of the defection to the king of Sir John Hotham, the man who locked the king out of Hull: his son (who also defected) feared that 'the necessitous people of the whole kingdom will presently rise in mighty numbers ... If this unruly sort have once cast the rider it will run like wildfire in the example through all the counties of England',[60] and many of the MPs who did not wait (as the Hothams did) for the actual commencement of hostilities to go over to the king doubtless found distasteful the activities of the London mob, whose menaces had contributed so much to the coercion of both king and peers in 1641, and whose activities found echoes in the localities. Thus Sir Edward Dering (who had once been a distinguished supporter of the Root and Branch Bill) complained of 'such a leud licentiousness ... as never way in any age, in any Nation, until this Parliament was met to-gether':[61] clearly, the implications of stirring up the populace were beginning to sink in. In this context Dr Hill has also pointed out that many defecting MPs held estates in royalist-controlled areas, and thus had very pressing material reasons for being loyal to the king.

While fear for their estates and fear for lower-class initiatives in politics must go a long way in explaining the king's ability to build a party wherewith to contest the war, it might be suggested that another relevant motive much less frequently emphasised by the Marxists is fear of the tyranny of a Parliamentary faction. The most celebrated of the early defectors, Edward Hyde, was deeply influenced by this motive, and royalist propaganda throughout the period (some of it, of course, composed by Hyde himself) returned again and again to this theme. In due time Charles was able plausibly to cast himself in the role of the defender of our 'fundamental laws' and traditional political framework against the dictatorial endeavours of a Parliamentary clique. Consequently, in his *Answer to the Nineteen Propositions* of June 1642, Charles took himself to be the protagonist of what he called our 'regulated monarchy'; and, to the chagrin of Thomas Hobbes, described English government as a judicious mixture of monarchy, aristocracy and democracy. Because the House of Commons *already* had (in Charles's view) quite sufficient power to prevent tyranny, he felt justified in rejecting the peremptory demands contained in the *Nineteen Propositions*, warning against the dictatorship of 'some close committee' of the House of Commons, and prophetically drawing attention to the threat to the House of Lords implicit in current political developments.[62] And some months later (in reply to Henry Parker, who had written a *critique* of the king's *Answer*), Bishop John Bramhall is to be found reiterating this line of argument. For Bramhall, Parker's talk of the 'arbitrary' power inherent in Parliament had finally revealed the full extent of Parliamentary ambitions: 'Now the mask is off [Bramhall protested] . . . We chose you to be our proctors, not to be our lords. We challenge the laws of England as our birthright and inheritance, and dislike arbitrary government much in one, but twenty times worse in more.'[63]

Bishop Bramhall, attempting to provide 'a ready remedy for the biting of an asp', brings me to my final point, which concerns the ideologies of the Great Rebellion. Space permits little more than the baldest assertion that, predictably enough, there were rival ideologies, and that the original revolutionary ideology (which justified the taking up of arms against the king) was amenable to exploitation by groups wanting more from the war than the suppression of his despotical ambitions. The royalist *status quo* ideology featured order, hierarchy and the 'descending'[64] character of political power, and dwelled upon the preposterous, ungodly and illegal nature of the Parliamentary enterprise. The royalists argued that God had forbidden resistance explicitly in the scriptures (in the fifth commandment and in such passages as Romans xiii) and implicitly in His Creation, wherein all His creatures had an allotted place. Furthermore, He had indicated His preference for monarchy as a governmental form explicitly in the scriptures (for instance, in His appointment of Saul), and implicitly in His creation: 'There is one God in the world, a monarchy; one soul in the body, a monarchy; one sun in the heavens, a monarchy; one master in each family, and one monarch in each society.'[65] This type of theory, it should be noted, was usually expressed with considerable restraint:[66] it was not generally held that monarchy was the only conceivable form of government, that Parliament was unimportant or that its activities reflected no genuine grievances.[67] But it *was* held that in our 'well-tempered monarchy'[68] sovereign power belonged to the king-in-Parliament, and that for a majority at Westminster to seize control of the militia against the express wishes of the king was a blasphemous, illegal and unnatural act against which any king of England would have stood his ground.

The Parliamentarians subjected this theory of order to two main sorts of attack. They attacked the idea that political authority should be understood as 'descending' from God to his earthly vicegerents (and thence to lesser magistrates) in such a way as to preclude the propriety of armed resistance. Parliamentarians agreed that *in the most general and abstract sense*, God (in His desire to provide for the governance of His creatures) was the originator of political authority, but saw no reason to conclude from this that princes were invariably the direct recipients of that authority. On the contrary, Parliamentarians tended to see the community as the *effective* source of political power, and they upheld the right of Parliament, in defence of liberties and property rights, to act on behalf of the community, even to the extent of armed resistance to a tyrannical king and his evil counsellors. This 'ascending' theory of politics finds expression in such pamphlets as Henry Parker's *Observations upon some of His Majesty's Late Answers and Expresses* (1642). Here we read that 'all rule is but fudiciarie', and that the people are 'the fountain and efficient cause'[69] of the power of princes; and in pursuit of that overriding political maxim *salus populi suprema lex*, Parliament (which represented the people) was justified in taking coercive action to suppress the commonwealth's enemies.

This 'ascending' theory of politics enabled Parker and his colleagues to answer the question of what happened when, because of disagreements between king and Parliament, the constitution became deadlocked, and the commonwealth put at risk. Parker argued that Parliament, because of its representative character, was justified in taking over the State, exercising the same sort of power over the body politic as the individual exercised over his natural body. Similarly, Charles Herle saw English government (in normal times) as the co-ordinate responsibility of the three Estates, but maintained that the original constitution contained a provision (consented to both by the people and by successive monarchs) whereby in times of crisis two Estates could 'supply' the deficiency of the third in the event of any dereliction of duty. Parliament's current 'supplying' activities (seizing control of the militia, etc.) were thus justified by 'that original frame of this coordinate government of the three Estates in Parliament consented in, and contrived by the people in its first constitution, and since in every reign confirmed both by mutual Oathes between King and people, and constant custom... time out of mind'.[70]

In 1642–43 Parker and the other theorists of resistance believed (or at least hoped) that while expounding the 'ascending' theory of politics they could avoid the untoward eventuality of lower-order initiatives in politics, an eventuality which, as the royalists never ceased to point out, was implicit in that theory. Parker maintained that to distrust Parliament was akin to distrusting God himself, but Henry Ferne wanted to know how, if Parliamentary violence was justified by a princely violation of trust, popular violence could be opposed in the event of a Parliamentary violation of trust: '[T]hen may the multitude by this rule and principle now taught them take the power to themselves... [and] as Cade and Tylar, boast themselves Reformers of the Commonwealth and fill all with rapine and confusion.'[71] At the same time, Bishop Bramhall shrewdly warned the Parliamentarians that those who expected obedience from their servants had better be careful to obey their king.[72]

The second type of attack upon the *status quo* theory can be labelled (for want of a less unsatisfactory word) 'Puritan', and we shall observe that Puritanism also carried with it the possibility of 'untoward eventualities'. Puritanism was plainly a set of beliefs attractive to independent, thrusting people, some of whom unquestionably belonged to the bourgeois class.[73] It had probably always had a subversive potential, but it was the hammer of William Laud (supported by Charles) which aroused the fury and resentment that issued in what used to be called 'the Puritan revolution'. Under Laud's leadership, the 'Arminian' faction within the Church bore down heavily upon its opponents, and to these people Arminianism, with its emphasis on ceremonies and with its anti-predestinarian theology, smacked of Popery. And it is clear that Charles's association with the Laudian faction cost him dear in terms of reputation, especially when it was seen together with his marriage to a Catholic zealot and his failure to make any positive contribution to the Protestant cause in the Thirty Years' War.

The Puritan took himself to be guided by God's word as found in the scriptures, and, as a member of God's elect, he believed himself to have a special responsibility for the condition of earthly life. He was therefore indisposed to acquiesce in what he often regarded in the 1630s as Antichrist's attempt to reverse the Reformation in Britain; and in so far as Charles and his Arminian bishops were held to be involved in this attempt they became his enemies. He thus felt impelled to transcend his (usually) middling position in society in an endeavour to correct (or even to destroy) the 'worldlings' further up the social hierarchy. Consequently, even before hostilities had unloosened the most extreme passions, we find a famous Puritan declaring unequivocally that the performance of Christ's business belonged to the private man: 'if thou beest a soldier of Jesus, whatsoever by place or calling thy rank or degree be, be it higher or lower, yet if he call for thy service, thou art bound, though others stand still, to maintain his power and glory to the utmost of thy power and strength, yea to the shedding the last drop of thy blood . . .'[74] To the royalists this kind of pronouncement indicated 'overmuch sauciness and familiarity with God',[75] even an intention 'to be God's good maisters, not his good servants',[76] and such intentions were bound to alarm men who believed in a traditional hierarchical society.

In a very real sense royalist prognostications found justification in the activities of such groups as the Levellers, Diggers, Fifth Monarchy Men and Ranters, and this 'rebellion within the Revolution' has found a prominent place in Marxist historiography.[77] The conflict in England produced a land 'ablaze with inner lights',[78] wherein virtually all the beliefs of the leading men of 1642 were agonisingly called in question by their social inferiors. To a degree, therefore, Engels' assertion about the bourgeoisie being 'shadowed' by the lower orders finds vindication. It was, for instance, an 'inner light' which sent Gerrard Winstanley and his fellow Diggers to St George's Hill in Surrey to cultivate the common land, and thus to provide a communistic example which (hopefully) would be followed everywhere. In the more specifically constitutional context, the *locus classicus* for the confrontation of what might be called 'the principles of 1642' and the radical theories to some extent derived from them was the Putney debate of October 1647 wherein rank-

and-file representatives (Agitators) of the New Model Army challenged the general officers in a debate about the future of the
commonwealth. For the officers, Henry Ireton argued that the war
had been fought to ensure 'that the will of one man should not
be ... law'; laws should properly be made by Parliament representing those who had 'a permanent fixed interest' in the country. In his
view, substantial property owners had taken up arms against a
would-be tyrant 'because they were immediately concerned and
engaged'; lesser men 'who had no other interest in the kingdom but
this, that they should have the benefit of those laws made by the
Representative, yet fought that they should have the benefit of
this Representative'.[79] To the Agitators these were dismaying views:
influenced by Leveller political theory, they thought in terms of a
much wider (even a natural) right to participate in politics, and felt
themselves 'much deceived'[80] to have seen the war through merely
to secure the dominion of a rich man's Parliament.

What conclusions are suggested by the preceding discussion? Putting aside the Marxist's prejudicing assertion that only a Marxist-
inspired interpretation of this (or any other) period can be correct,[87]
it is clear that (the reservations indicated above notwithstanding)
he has much to offer the student of seventeenth century English
history. He has pointed to the defects of the 1640 regime from the
standpoint of the bourgeoisie as a leading cause of the hostilities
which broke out two years later; he has indicated the degree of
success which the bourgeoisie had in removing these defects and in
clearing the way for further economic expansion; he has enlightened
one's understanding of the 'backsliding' tendency displayed so
copiously throughout the whole period of 1640–60 by members
of that apparently solid front by which Charles was confronted at
the meeting of the Long Parliament; finally, he has suggested a not
implausible framework for the comprehension of some of the leading
ideologies of the period. The intellectual dividends of Marxist 'total
history' are thus seen to be considerable.

At the same time, it seems to me that the 'facts' offer the theory
of 'base' and 'superstructure' (upon which this particular type of
'total history' rests) two serious challenges. First, there is the
apparently impermissible disjunction between 'base' and (political)
'superstructure' in the republic/protectorate period and again in
the Restoration period, especially between 1683 and 1688: the
political events of these two periods, it would appear, call in

question both the Marxian notion of a bourgeois revolution enjoying considerable success, and that of the State as an instrument of the ruling class. From the Marxian point of view, would it not have been much more satisfactory to have found that Charles (or another member of the Stuart family) had been restored as a 'Doge of Venice' in 1648, that Parliament had retained control of the armed forces, that it had not weakened the legislation with respect to the regularity of its meetings, that Filmer had been forgotten, that Charles II and James II had not had an expanding standing army at their disposal, that the Exclusion Bill had succeeded, that James's assault upon the judiciary and the corporations had been more effectively resisted, and that the 'political nation' had taken a more active part in getting rid of him? A consideration of the 'facts', and of a scenario more favourable to the Marxist interpretation, leads, secondly, to the supposition that political activity may have more autonomy than Marxists commonly concede. The 'facts' (as I have shown) are not infrequently recorded in the Marxist's own work, and it seems to me arguable that he thereby provides some implicit acknowledgement of the autonomy of politics which is in question here. In the end, then, it seems that I must confirm Dr Hill in his suspicion that the bourgeois historian's use of Marxism can be no more than eclectic:[82] for it is indeed my conviction that Marx should have same status as Harold Laski's expert, on tap but not on top.

Acknowledgement

For his assistance with this essay I am grateful to Mr Cameron Chisholm, research student in the Department of Politics, Strathclyde University.

Notes

[1] *The Times Literary Supplement*, 24 November 1972.

[2] C. Hill, 'Historians and the rise of British capitalism', *Science and Society*, XIV, 1950, p. 319.

[3] *The Times Literary Supplement, loc. cit.*

[4] Victor Kiernan, *New Left Review*, No. 11, 1961, p. 62. It is surely Hill's overriding determination to make the past more intelligible than the mere narrative historian ('two hundred facts do not make an interpretation' was his comment on C. V. Wedgwood's *The King's War*: see *The Spectator*, 12 December 1958) that has occasionally exposed him to criticism: see especially H. R. Trevor-Roper in *History and Theory*, V,

1966, pp. 61–82; and Charles Wilson in *The Historical Journal*, v, 1962, pp. 80–94. Both writers complain of the distortions involved when a to some extent preconceived theory confronts the evidence.

[5] *Preface to the Critique of Political Economy*, in K. Marx and F. Engels, *Selected Works*, Lawrence & Wishart, London, 1953, i, p. 329.

[6] *Ibid.*, i, pp. 63–4.

[7] *A People's History of England*, Lawrence & Wishart, London, 1965, p. 229; emphasis in original.

[8] *Ibid.*, p. 228.

[9] F. Engels, *Anti-Dühring*, Lawrence & Wishart, London, 1955, p. 146.

[10] 'A review of Guizot's book *Why has the English Revolution been Successful?*', reprinted in K. Marx and F. Engels, *On Britain*, Lawrence & Wishart, London, 1964, p. 347.

[11] *The English Utopia*, Lawrence & Wishart, London, 1969, p. 93.

[12] *Op. cit.*, p. 148.

[13] *The World Turned Upside Down*, Temple Smith, London, 1972, p. 11.

[14] The question of whether a particular historical development is to be termed 'progressive' involves a transcendence of the professional historian's normal sphere of operation. The question presupposes a value judgement that the moral goal of the historical process is 'a socialist society' characterised by 'equality and a communal spirit, combined with a reasonable and rising standard of living' (C. Hill, *The English Revolution, 1640*, third edition, Lawrence & Wishart, London, 1955, p. 5). Also involved is speculation about what might have happened in the absence of what did happen; thus Dr Hill: 'although I am far from absolutely "approving" of any tendency which I label "progressive" ... the suggestion is that of the then possible alternatives it was that tendency (because it developed the national wealth) without which the advance to a better society would have been impossible' (*ibid.*). I take it that the quotation marks round 'approving' in this passage indicate the intellectual obscurities involved, and I shall not take it as my duty to clarify them. Suffice it to say that the notion of 'progressive' rack-renting landlords is one which even sympathetic historians may find less than wholly satisfactory (see Kiernan, *op. cit.*, p. 64).

[15] *Two Tracts on Government*, Cambridge University Press, 1967, pp. 119–20.

[16] Nelson, London, 1961, pp. 32–3.

[17] *A Judge's Judgement: a Speech penned in the beginning of the Parliament against the Judges*, 1641, *Harleian Miscellany*, 1744, v, p. 467.

[18] 'The outbreak of the Civil War', in R. H. Parry (ed.), *The English Civil War and After 1642–58*, Macmillan, London, 1970.

[19] Milton's *Prose Works*, Bohn Library edition, 1848, iii, p. 147.

[20] D. Brunton and D. H. Pennington, *Members of the Long Parliament*, Allen & Unwin, London, 1954, especially, pp. 177 ff. The other major survey of a section of the 'political nation', G. E. Aylmer's *The King's Servants: the Civil Service of Charles I, 1625–42*, Routledge & Kegan Paul, London, 1961, also concluded that 'nothing like a class struggle can

be said to emerge inside the administration' (p. 395); but then, as Professor Aylmer remarks, the bureaucracy is not the likeliest place to find evidence of such a struggle.

[21] *The Century of Revolution*, p. 122.

[22] For a criticism of Hill on these points (*inter alia*, listing 'royalist' ports) see C. H. Wilson, *England's Apprenticeship, 1603–1763*, Longmans, London, 1965, ch. 6.

[23] On the relevance of Scotland to the problems raised by the Marxist interpretation of the period, see S. A. Burrell, 'Calvinism, capitalism, and the middle classes: some afterthoughts on an old problem', *Journal of Modern History*, xxx, 1960.

[24] *A. People's History of England*, pp. 246 ff.

[25] Reprinted in F. Maseres (ed.), *Scarce Tracts on the Civil Wars*, 1815, I, pp. 191, 307.

[26] *A. People's History of England*, p. 249.

[27] Oxford University Press, London, 1971, ch. 8.

[28] There is also the Marxian hypothesis that in a period of class balance a society's political institutions may attain a certain parasitic independence (see John Sanderson, *An Interpretation of the Political Ideas of Marx and Engels*, Longmans, London, 1969, ch. 4). But this hypothesis does not seem to be in question here, although it has been invoked to explain Tudor absolutism (see, for example, D. Petegorsky, *Left-wing Democracy in the English Civil War*, Gollancz, London, 1940, p. 17).

[29] Quoted in Harold Hulme, *The Life of Sir John Eliot*, Allen & Unwin, London, 1957, p. 122.

[30] *The Case of Shipmoney Briefly Discoursed*, 1640, p. 24.

[31] *Memoirs of Colonel Hutchinson*, Bohn Library, 1854, pp. 85–6.

[32] See H. R. Trevor-Roper, 'Oliver Cromwell and his Parliaments', in his collection of essays *Religion, the Reformation and Social Change*, Macmillan, London, 1967, p. 346.

[33] *A Deep Groan Fetched at the Funeral of Charles I*, 1649.

[34] *Op. cit.*, pp. 19–20.

[35] University of Chicago Press, 1971, p. 64.

[36] *The Century of Revolution*, p. 189.

[37] Burt Franklin, New York, 1962, p. 178.

[38] Caroline Robbins, 'Fact and fancy in 1660', in *The Restoration of the Stuarts: Blessing or Disaster?*, Folger Library, Washington, D.C., 1960, p. 37.

[39] J. P. Kenyon (ed.), *The Stuart Constitution*, Cambridge University Press, 1966, p. 382.

[40] Quoted by Caroline Robbins, 'The repeal of the Triennal Act in 1664', *Huntington Library Quarterly*, xii, 1948–49, p. 137.

[41] Kenyon, *op. cit.*, p. 374.

[42] Quoted by J. W. Daly, 'Could Charles I be trusted? The royalist case, 1642–46', *Journal of British Studies*, vi, 1966, p. 27.

[43] Weidenfeld & Nicolson, London, 1970, p. 177.

[44] *A People's History of England*, p. 273.

[45] *Ibid.*, p. 280.

[46] 'The Civil War as interpreted by Marx and Engels', *Science and Society*, XII, 1948, p. 150.

[47] F. C. Turner, *James II*, Eyre & Spottiswoode, London, 1948, p. 236; see also p. 266 for James's conception of the role of Parliament.

[48] Perry Anderson, 'Origins of the present crisis', in P. Anderson and R. Blackburn (eds.), *Towards Socialism*, Fontana, London, 1965, p. 17.

[49] F. Engels, *Socialism, Utopian and Scientific*, in Marx and Engels, *Selected Works*, II, p. 97.

[50] Hill, 'The Civil War as interpreted by Marx and Engels', p. 150.

[51] Victor Kiernan, 'When England was a republic', *Labour Monthly*, XXXI, 1949, p. 89.

[52]. The discussion in this paragraph has been much influenced by J. R. Western, *Monarchy and Revolution*, Blandford, London, 1972, and by J. P. Kenyon, *The Nobility in the Revolution of 1688*, Hull University Publications, 1963.

[53] *Two Treatises of Government*, Mentor, New York, 1965, p. 172.

[54] *The Very Copy of a letter*, reprinted in G. Orwell and R. Reynolds (eds.), *British Pamphleteers*, Allan Wingate, London, 1948, I, p. 162.

[55] Routledge & Kegan Paul, London, 1946, p. 172.

[56] *Prose Works*, II, p. 24.

[57] Hill, *The Century of Revolution*, p. 127.

[58] William Joseph, 'The great English revolution', *Communist Review*, March 1949, p. 456.

[59] See *The Century of Revolution*, p. 144.

[60] Quoted by C. V. Wedgwood, *The King's War*, Fontana, London, 1966, p. 162.

[61] Quoted by Derek Hirst, 'The defection of Sir Edward Dering, 1640–41', *Historical Journal*, XV, 1972, p. 206.

[62] See Kenyon, *The Stuart Constitution*, pp. 21–3, for the *Answer to the Nineteen Propositions*.

[63] *Works*, Library of Anglo-Catholic Theology, 1843–45, III, p. 381.

[64] For 'ascending' and 'descending' theories of politics, see Walter Ullmann, *Principles of Government and Politics in the Middle Ages*, Methuen, London, 1961, pp. 19–29.

[65] Bramhall, *Works*, V, p. 139.

[66] *Cf.* Daly, *op. cit.*

[67] *Cf.* the suggestion of the royalist Henry Ferne that honourable men had in effect changed sides in the period 1640–43. In his pamphlet *Conscience Satisfied: that there is no warrant for the arms now taken up by Subjects* (1643) Ferne expressed his scepticism concerning the prevalence of the evil counsellors by whom the king was said to have been 'enthralled': for every such counsellor there was 'above a thousand of his good subjects, whose nobleness and honesty hath still engaged them honourably, though to the weaker side; before in behalf of the subject groaning under former grievances, now in service to His Majesty opposed by popular fury, subjects that out of conscience of their allegiance cleave unto him' (p. 30).

[68] Peter Heylyn, *A Letter to a Gentleman of Leicestershire*, 1643, p. 58.

[69] Page 2.

[70] *A Fuller Answer to a Treatise written by Dr Ferne*, 1642, p. 6.

[71] *The Resolving of Conscience*, 1642, p. 18.

[72] See *Works*, III, p. 326.

[73] It seems, at the same time, misleading to regard Puritanism simply as a bourgeois ideology. Its frequent condemnation of lending money at interest (more 'reactionary' than Sir Robert Filmer) comes to mind here (see C. H. George, 'English Calvinist opinions on usury, 1600–40', *Journal of the History of Ideas*, XVIII, 1957); and the evidence of Scotland, where Presbyterianism exercised an ideological hegemony in the lowlands in a context of comparative economic backwardness, is also difficult to reconcile with at least some versions of Marxist history (see Burrell, *op. cit.*).

[74] John Lilburne, *A Work of the Beast*, 1638, reprinted in W. Haller (ed.), *Tracts on Liberty*, Columbia University Records of Civilization, New York, 1934, II, p. 25.

[75] Bramhall, *Works*, III, p. 529.

[76] Sir John Spelman, *Certain Considerations Upon the Duties both of Prince and People*, 1643, *Somers Tracts*, 1809, IV, p. 320.

[77] See especially C. Hill, *Puritanism and Revolution*, Secker & Warburg, London, 1958; *The World Turned Upside Down; Antichrist in Seventeenth Century England*, Oxford University Press, London, 1971; A. L. Morton, *The World of the Ranters*, Lawrence & Wishart, London, 1970; Petegorsky, *op. cit.*

[78] Sheldon Wolin, *Politics and Vision*, Allen & Unwin, London, 1961, p. 258.

[79] A. S. P. Woodhouse (ed.), *Puritanism and Liberty*, Dent, London, 1965, pp. 72, 54, 72.

[80] *Ibid.*, p. 69.

[81] It is somewhat surprising to find the current Master of Balliol writing that because R. H. Tawney and Harold Laski were 'associated with the Fabian Society ... [and] reformists in politics', no proper interpretation of the English Civil War could be expected from them (see 'Historians and the rise of British capitalism', p. 311).

[82] *Ibid.*, p. 310.

Stephen White

14

Political science as ideology: the study of
Soviet politics

Political science, Bill Mackenzie pointed out in *Politics and Social
Science*, has 'in its nature been the social discipline that lies closest
to power, and it has never forgotten the misadventures of Plato
at the court of his pupil, the tyrant (or Duke) of Syracuse ... We
are all now part of what we are studying, and we have to allow for
the disturbances that thus arise in ourselves, as well as for the disturbances we set up in our environment. The problem is not unknown to natural science, but it is present in social science in a
more intense way.'
   Following the French *événements* of 1968 he was later to write,
'neo-Marxist doctrines not accorded the *imprimatur* by any communist regime suddenly became fashionable'; and 'sharp differences
of opinion' developed in regard to the social and intellectual role
of the political scientist.[2] The two, indeed, were related, for the
social role of the political scientist (or 'intellectual') and of ideology
generally was precisely a question to which classical and post-
classical Marxism had drawn particular attention. Gramsci, notably,
provided an illuminating formulation of the problem in his *Quaderni
del carcere*. Intellectuals, Gramsci wrote, did not play a direct role
in the world of production. Their role was rather one of mediation:
they were the 'functionaries' of the superstructure, acting as the
'agents of the dominant group for the exercise of the subaltern
function of social hegemony and political government'. They were
required not simply to carry on the business of state in the interest
of the dominant group: their task was also, and more crucially, to
organise ' "spontaneous" consent' on the part of the government.[3]
   Writing in this spirit, Bill Mackenzie observed that much of the
academic work described in politics and social science was 'recog-
nizably ideological ... One is tempted to ask, "Whose social scientist
are you?" when one sees the proof of results clearly favourable to

the orthodoxy of the sponsoring regime'.[4] The central problem, indeed, had been identified some years earlier: it was the link between 'the conceptual framework and the cash basis'. Political research—any social research, in fact—was 'geared into the process which it purports to investigate . . . Surely what we are engaged in is itself a political activity, or at least a form of public adminstration?'[5] The academic study of Soviet politics, it will be suggested, demonstrates both the importance and the potentially embarrassing character of such a question.[6]

Following the second world war and reflecting the increased importance which the Soviet Union had now acquired in international affairs, centres for research on Russian and communist affairs were set up in Britain and the USA with both foundation and government support. A 'wider and deeper knowledge on our part of Russian ideas and motivations', as an authorised history of the Rockefeller Foundation has put it, was now 'basic to fundamental policy and essential to self-interest'.[7] Recognising the fact that no training programme in Russian affairs existed anywhere in the United States, and 'aware of the seriousness of such shortcomings as the Cold War shaped up', the Rockefeller Foundation, together with the Ford and Carnegie Foundations, contributed major sums towards the endowment and expansion of area studies programmes at new institutions founded for the purpose.[8] Centres for the study of Asian affairs were added after the victory of communist forces in China 'created problems for American policy'.[9] In retrospect, rejoiced one scholar, 'never since the Renaissance [had] research been so lavishly financed as it [had] been in the US since the second world war'.[10]

Soviet and East European studies, linked as they were with obvious strategic and practical needs, were the major beneficiaries of this situation. The new centres had an important role to play, for there was now an intense demand on the part of military and civilian intelligence for reliable information concerning a power which was regarded as a serious threat to the domestic and international *status quo*. The new institutions, equally, had an ideological task to perform, for there was a 'widespread and popular feeling', as a committee of American Slavists put it, 'that most educated Americans should know something about the Soviet system and Communism generally'. Soviet area specialists, whose 'primary concern' was 'Communism, its ideology, strategy and tactics', had an obvious part to play in this connection; and most scholars regarded this as an essential part of their duties. It was considered necessary at the same time to 'deal with extremists who have ready-made violent prescriptions to satisfy this thirst.'[11]

The new area studies programmes often derived directly from military-sponsored programmes organised during the war years. The military programmes differed from traditional academic courses in their interdisciplinary character, for 'in order to be prepared for duty on foreign liaison or occupation service, an officer needed to know a great many things about the people with whom he was to deal—their language, their history and culture, the geography and resources of their country, and their political and economic stake in the current conflict'.[12] Chicago, Harvard and Stanford were among the universities which organised training programmes of an appropriate character. Indeed, it was a curious fact of academic history, McGeorge Bundy later remarked, that the first great centre of area studies in the US had been located not in a university but 'in Washington, during the second world war, in the Office of Strategic Services', which carried overall responsibility, among other things, for the area training programmes. Nor did the connection come to an end with the termination of hostilities, for 'in a very large measure', he added, the area studies programmes developed in American universities after the war were 'manned, directed or stimulated by graduates of the OSS—a remarkable institution, half cops-and-robbers and half faculty meeting'. It was 'still true today', he thought, and he hoped it always would be, that there was a 'high degree of interpenetration between universities with area programmes and the information-gathering agencies of the government of the US'.[13]

At Columbia University, where the first Russian centre was established in 1946, a School of International Affairs and a series of associated area institutes developed from a School of Military Government and Administration which had been organised by the university during the war on behalf of the US navy. Four of the first five profesors appointed to the Russian Institute, the first area institute to be established, had had 'substantial periods of government service as specialists in the handling of Russian problems'; and staff members continued, both formally and informally, to act as consultants to government agencies and research institutions, as well as to lend their support to such bodies as the East European Fund Inc.

Without the financial support of the Rockefeller and later of the Carnegie Foundations, however, 'neither the Russian, East Asian nor European Institutes could have been established'. Negotiations between the Russian Institute and the Rockefeller Foundation took place in 1945, and the institute eventually received an initial grant of a quarter of a million dollars. A further substantial grant followed in 1951; and financial support was also received from the Carnegie Foundation and from the Rand Corporation.[14]

The second major American centre for Russian area studies was established at Harvard University in 1948. The initiative in this case appears to have come not from the university but directly from the Carnegie Foundation, which approached Harvard in the spring of 1947. The foundations' enthusiasm, it was noted, reflected their 'belief in the direct or indirect utility of academic training and research on the Soviet Union' and also a 'national sense of the urgency of these studies and of their relevance to questions of national policy', as well as more traditional academic values. The Carnegie Foundation agreed in this instance to provide an initial five-year grant for general purposes, which was subsequently extended for several periods of comparable length.[15]

The new institutes were at pains to emphasise that the foundations were content simply to provide them with material support, and that they did not attempt to bring their influence to bear upon properly academic questions. It should be noted, however, that the major foundations were at this time often directed by former or current OSS or CIA agents or associates (the Carnegie Foundation, for instance, was headed by a former OSS officer);[16] and they appear to have been not unwilling deliberately to lend their support to conceptual approaches within the social sciences which they found congenial.[17] At times, indeed, they appear to have been ready to use their considerable persuasive power more directly: as when the Ford Foundation played a role in the closure of a distinguished but radical-minded Institute of Latin American Studies at Stanford University.[18] Given that the foundations constituted the area centres' most important source of general financial support, however, it seems reasonable to assume that open disagreements of this kind have been notably infrequent.

Foundation support was extended to the study of Soviet affairs through other channels. The Ford Foundation, for instance, established an East European Fund, which in turn subsidised the activities of a publishing house and of a research programme on the USSR, whose director was on the staff and for some years acted as director of the Columbia University Russian Institute. The fund provided financial support for some years for the *American Slavonic and East European Journal*, the premier journal in the field.[19] The Ford Foundation also provided in excess of one million dollars to allow the Rand Corporation, a body established originally by the US Air Force, to construct a headquarters building and to expand its research programme.[20] Rand's research activities were originally concentrated in scientific and technical fields, but increasingly the corporation devoted its attention to social science research, and in particular to Soviet affairs.

The corporation sponsored a meeting of social scientists working in this field in 1947. The recently enunciated doctrine of 'containment' was justified, they thought, only if it was 'correct to assume the existence of internal weaknesses in the USSR which can be exploited for American aims. The task is therefore one of locating actual and potential tensions within the elite, among rival sub-elites, and between elite and mass.' The programme led eventually to the publication of influential studies by Leites, Fainsod, Garthoff, Selznick, Bergson and others.[21] The foundation also extended its support to the Research Program on the History of the CPSU, one of whose products was perhaps the most widely used text on that subject, Schapiro's *Communist Party of the Soviet Union*.[22]

The role of the Central Intelligence Agency in academic life became somewhat clearer in 1967, when it was revealed that the agency had furnished covert support for foreign educational and cultural activities for some fifteen years. The field of Soviet and communist affairs, it appeared, had been a major beneficiary. The CIA had subsidised the Congress for Cultural Freedom, which in turn had subsidised *Survey*, a well known British journal in the field and an obvious counterweight to the then more Soviet-aligned journal *Soviet Studies*. The Congress for Cultural Freedom also organised meetings and conferences for the discussion of Soviet affairs, at least one such conference being sponsored jointly by the congress and by St Antony's College, Oxford.[23] Major sums were provided for the support of radio stations and research institutions in Germany, whose activities were directed against the 'Soviet bloc'; and *Ost-Probleme*, a major German journal of Soviet affairs, 'is or was financed by the US embassy'.[24]

Within the USA itself the CIA appears secretly to have funded studies dealing with the national income and product of the communist countries at Columbia's Russian Institute, and to have made financial provision for teaching and research on Eastern Europe at that university. The CIA also provided funds for the Centre for International Studies at the Massachusetts Institute of Technology, where several influential studies of the operations of communist systems were completed by Walt Rostow, and where a Research Project on Communism, Revisionism and Revolution has more recently been in operation. The centre's director, Max Millikan, had himself served as assistant director of the CIA in Washington.[25] Most important of all, it emerged that a link existing between the CIA and the American Political Science Association itself: its executive director and treasurer were found to have been linked with Operations and Policy Research, a CIA-funded research organisation, and the association was found to have received additional funds from the CIA through conduits such as the Asia Foundation.[26]

Not surprisingly, the new centres found little favour in the Soviet press. *Pravda*, in the flat-footed style of the time, denounced the Russian Institute at Columbia as a 'hotbed of American slanderers, spies and diversionaries', where 'ignorant "professors" deliver lectures in a course of deliberate drivel to young listeners selected on the basis of greatest mental defectiveness and the least moral decency' (24 July 1951). It is easy to dismiss such inept criticism. It may, in fact, be altogether too easy to do so: for the Russian area centres were engaged in research and training programmes which in many ways complemented their often unusual sources of finance.

At Columbia University the School of International Affairs and the area institutes from the beginning 'sought to supply the demands of government agencies and private industry for specialists trained in international affairs and with a particular knowledge of a specific area of the world'.[27] A survey of the careers of the graduates of the US Russian centres ten years later found that most of them had indeed found employment in such fields. Some 25 per cent of the graduates had entered careers in academic or government research, while a further 27 per cent had entered government service related to Soviet affairs.[28] In some cases additional training programmes were organised for those already in government service: Columbia's institute, for instance, sponsored a 'junior specialist training programme' for the US air force. A few found employment in more esoteric organisations such as the US Psychological Warfare Centre or the American Committee for Liberation from Bolshevism.[29]

Others again sought employment with the Central Intelligence Agency. 'In actual numbers,' declared Admiral William Raborn, then the agency's director, 'we could easily staff the faculty of a university with our experts. In a way, we do. Many of those who leave us join the faculties of universities and colleges. Some of our personnel take leave of absence to teach and renew their contacts in the academic world. I suppose this is only fair; our energetic recruiting effort not only looks for the best young graduate students we can find, but also picks up a few professors from time to time.'[30]

The research programmes of the new Russian centres were generally designed for a similar audience. Research in international relations at Columbia's institute, for instance, was intended ultimately to 'equip American policy makers with skills in forecasting and eventually influencing the behaviour of the Soviet Union and of the international Communist movement'; while the institute's research in the field of Soviet politics was 'directed largely towards an evaluation of Soviet strength in terms of the effectiveness of political institutions in the leadership and control of the population'.[31] Harvard's Russian centre similarly devoted a 'substantial part' of its energies for five years to a project on the Soviet social system carried out under contract for the US air force. Some 'fifty major reports' were eventually delivered to the USAF.[32]

Efforts on such a scale could not fail to exert an influence upon the academic study of Soviet affairs. Most of the research and writing in the field in the post-war period, indeed, was carried out in the new area centres under government or foundation patronage, considerable attention being devoted to political science. In fact the 'bulk of research' since the end of the war, John Armstrong noted in 1959, was 'attributable at least in part to these programmes'.[33] The steady and unspectacular process of academic advance, moreover, had now been pre-empted in the Soviet field, as in many other branches of the social sciences, by a new pattern: the provision of generous funds by a public or private 'client' for unprecedentedly large-scale and intensive research towards the achievement of a prescribed objective. The new methods of research came increasingly to dominate the frontiers of research, at the expense of 'cottage industry' techniques; and equally, they required a scale of financial support ordinarily beyond the means of all but government and the wealthier foundations. This in turn made it easier for these institutions to bring influence to bear upon developments within academic social science, and to ensure that they accorded, so far as possible, with the social interests they represented.

The scholars upon whom these major research grants were lavished at the same time acquired enhanced respect and prestige in their field, and were more likely to secure the more senior academic positions and to be invited to join the editorial boards of scholarly journals and series of monographs. The positions of authority which they thus acquired in the profession, strengthened by a high degree of mutual citation among such scholars and a high level of deference on the part of the graduate students they supervised (some of whom, working upon secret projects, might be awarded classified Ph.D.s), tended in turn to confirm and reinforce the academic orthodoxy with which they were associated.

It would, of course, be absurd to attempt to account in this way for the fact that (as Byrnes has put it) 'American scholars generally lack a conceptual framework, except that implied by the cold war.'[34] The majority of scholars, no doubt, had impeccably anti-communist inclinations in any case; while it would be difficult to regard, for instance, Herbert Marcuse, who was employed in the Office of Strategic Services and later carried out research at the Columbia and Harvard Russian centres, as a conscious agent of US business interests. There can equally be no doubt that many, and perhaps even the majority, of the studies carried out with government and foundation support at US Russian institutes have conformed to acceptable and even distinguished standards of scholarship. Indeed, in many cases the studies would not exist had such support not been available: and some may find this sufficient justification in itself.

The real point, however, is a more subtle and a more important one. For no scholar (with rare exceptions) can determine for himself the set of implicit and consensual agreements upon the 'legitimate area of debate' within which his individual study, if it is to be recognised as a 'contribution to the field', must locate itself. Science, as Kuhn and others have shown, proceeds rather in terms of dominant 'paradigms' to which scholars, for the time being, agree to relate their individual research. Social science is hardly less beholden to dominant orthodoxies of this kind, which define the parameters of debate for the individual scholar. Unlike the natural sciences, however, the social sciences deal (or, not less significantly, fail to deal) with the distribution of wealth and the construction of social order, questions to which dominant social groups cannot remain indifferent. In order to examine the ideological character of the academic study of Soviet politics, accordingly, we must attempt to locate a dominant paradigm within the field, and then seek to relate it to its financial and institutional sources of support.

This is not to suggest that faults of a more straightforward character are not to be found in the academic study of Soviet politics, as in other areas of scholarship. Perhaps the most important single study of Soviet politics, for instance, published in a revised edition in 1963, makes little attempt to conceal its preferences. The rebels among the intelligentsia, Fainsod notes, were 'denied an opportunity to acquire experience in the arts of responsible government and were condemned to pursue their dream of justice in loose word-spinning or conspiratorial violence'. Lacking full emancipation and the invigorating challenge of market forces, the bourgeois stratum of society remained 'weakly developed and . . . hampered in its aspiration for independent power' by what Fainsod sternly terms its 'excessive dependence on the State'. Tsarist policy towards labour organisations was similarly a 'tragic story of wasted opportunities'. Reasonable demands were rejected, and no opportunity was allowed for the development of a responsible trade union movement, which, as in Western Europe and the USA, 'might have contributed greatly to stabilise industrial relations and to give Russian workers a stake in the community'. Tsarism's 'most disastrous blunder' was above all that it 'prepared the seedbed out of which Bolshevism grew'.[35]

Open partisanship of this kind has generally been the exception rather than the rule among serious students of Soviet politics. Other faults have been less elementary: the ethnocentrism, for instance, of those scholars who sternly reprove the USSR for its lack of a 'rule of law' on Western lines (Soviet citizens in fact appear to attach no great importance to formal procedures of this sort), and of those who crudely extrapolate Western 'interest group' theory to the very different Soviet setting. By far the most influential approach, however, remains the totalitarian model, which for all its manifest inadequacies has remained the stock-in-trade of the majority of

Western political scientists until very recent years.[36] The totalitarian approach, accordingly, as the 'dominant paradigm' in the field, must receive our crucial attention.

Whatever totalitarianism as a concept may lack, it has not been attempts to define it. It has been equated with 'total terror', the 'politicization of society', even with the 'creeping rape of man' and 'economic planning'. The definition which 'still dominates nearly every discussion of the question', however, is that proposed by Friedrich and Brzezinski.[37] Their list of defining characteristics embraced: 'an official ideology...'; 'a single mass party led typically by one man...'; 'a system of terroristic police control...'; a 'near-monopoly of control...of all means of effective mass communications...'; a 'near-complete monopoly of control...of all means of effective armed combat'; and 'central control and direction of the entire economy...'. This composite definition amplified a five-point list proposed by Friedrich in 1954, and the second edition of their work added two further elements, expansion and administrative control of the courts. Friedrich in 1969 proposed further modifications, suggesting in particular that monopolistic control might 'not necessarily [be] exercised by the party'. It is both authors' six-point definition, however, which continues to hold the field; and it is this definition whose adequacy we shall now consider.

Some of the Friedrich–Brzezinski characteristics, in the first place, are simply descriptions of distinctive institutional features of the communist-ruled countries. An 'official ideology', for instance, is defined so as virtually to be synonymous with Marxism–Leninism: other ideologies—the belief system of *apartheid*, or the uninstitutionalised hegemony of bourgeois political ideas in the advanced capitalist countries—conspicuously fail to qualify. In totalitarian systems, similarly, it is specified that a near-monopoly of the means of effective mass communications shall be exercised by the 'party and its subservient cadres': thus neatly excluding States in which it could be argued that a ruling class exercises precisely such a near-monopoly. In both cases it is difficult to resist the conclusion that the terms of the definitions are—as the phrase has it—'not accidental'. The authors have isolated the distinctive features of the Soviet regime, and have then proceeded to employ them as the defining characteristics of 'totalitarianism'. The Soviet Union accordingly emerges, not altogether remarkably, as a regime 'totalitarian' in character.

A second shortcoming is that many of the defining features of regimes considered 'totalitarian' are by no means unique to such regimes. A 'single mass party led typically by one man', for instance, is a fairly common feature of many newly independent States, where the absence of a competing multi-party system arguably minimises tribalism and the wasteful duplication of political elites. Many of these States (and others) have similarly instituted systems of 'central control and direction of the entire economy'. A 'near-complete monopoly of control ... of all means of effective armed combat', indeed, Friedrich and Brzezinski's fifth point, is characteristic of virtually all modern States.

It may finally be noted that the definition provides a description of the contemporary USSR less adequate than may have been the case at the time of its composition. The 'totalitarian' party, the authors specify, must be selective in character: it can comprise only a 'relatively small percentage of the total population (up to ten per cent)'. The CPSU, however, now includes some 9 per cent of the adult population, a figure which is slowly but inexorably increasing; and in some of the other communist-ruled countries a figure in excess of 10 per cent already exists. Above all, a 'system of terroristic police control, ... characteristically directed not only against demonstrable "enemies" of the regime, but against arbitrarily selected classes of the population' is a characteristic difficult to reconcile with the more limited (although by no means negligible) role played by overt coercion in contemporary Soviet society, whatever may have been the case in the Stalin era.

These criticisms of the concept and of its applicability have little claim to originality. Interestingly, however, and illuminatingly, the force of such arguments has not (until very recently) led to the abandonment of the concept. It has, rather, been redefined so as to continue to accord with the changes, and especially with the easing of coercive controls, within the contemporary USSR. 'Mature totalitarianism' has been offered as an alternative, or 'totalitarianism without teror' (although terror had hitherto been considered the crucial element in the definition): even 'totalitarianism with a human face'. The term itself, however, has stubbornly persisted; and this appears to reflect rather less the scholarly virtues of the concept than its striking ideological merits.

For as surely as 'democratic' serves as a term of approbation, the 'totalitarian' label is sufficient to discredit any regime thus characterised. In particular, it serves to equate Fascist Italy and Nazi Germany, regardless of the differences of principle between them, with the USSR of Stalin and his successors. Although the term originated as early as the late 1920s, notes Spiro, it 'became an anti-communist slogan in the cold war. Its utility for propaganda purposes has tended to obscure whatever utility it may have had for systematic analysis and comparison of political entities.'

Perhaps more important, its use has served to mystify crucial features of bourgeois hegemony in the advanced capitalist countries. The term posits a sharp distinction between the 'State' and an 'individual' who is considered to enjoy an unconstrained freedom except in so far as the State impinges upon his activities. This, however, is a patently ideological statement, for it may with equal justice be argued that social power inheres rather in a capitalist class, whose control over the life chances of individual citizens is in no sense restricted to the acts of government, and whose actions are exposed to no democratic controls of any sort. In directing attention at formal institutional arrangements rather than at the social nature and uses of political power, political scientists are playing the ideological role which Bill Mackenzie ascribed to learned men: they were the custodians of history and precedent, sometimes even adding the role of 'myth-maker and poet'.[38]

Times change, however, and with them the 'myths' required of political scientists). The changes which have altered prevailing paradigms reflect in part the increasing self-awareness of scholars within the social sciences generally. Codes of ethical conduct, for instance, have been elaborated by professional associations to guide the work of political scientists, sociologists and anthropologists, and to attempt to ensure that overseas fieldwork is informed by properly academic purposes.[39] Academics have become more willing to acknowledge their implicit value premises; and the professions, indeed, are now regularly polled for their political preferences (political scientists emerge as marginally less radical than sociologists, but more so than other social scientists).[40] New journals, associations and (often disappointing) 'anti-textbooks' have emerged to challenge the established orthodoxies.

It is to the wider society, however, that we must mainly look to find the origin of recent paradigm changes. The future of Soviet and communist studies, it has long been recognised, would be 'affected favourably or adversely by the course of international affairs and the progress of the cold war';[41] and it has been changes of precisely such a character which have undermined the original rationale of the Soviet area studies centre. That rationale was not a matter for serious debate in the early post-war years, when anti-communism, in Fulbright's expressive phrase, was a 'national ideology'. This, however, is no longer the case, for the present administration, as Fulbright goes on to point out, has made a 'significant departure from the ideological anti-communism which so strongly influenced the foreign policy of American Presidents from Truman to Johnson'.[42] The super-powers, indeed, have moved so far from hostile confrontation that it became almost more appropriate to speak of a community of interest (a development susceptible of several interpretations, as the Chinese have not refrained from pointing out). The era of doctrinaire anti-communism, at least, appears at last to be over.

The development of Soviet–American *détente*, however, has been something of an embarrassment for the Russian area centres, whose foundation and purpose derived from an altogether different situation. Recent years, accordingly, have seen a 'period of straitened circumstances' for the area institutions. Both the government and the foundations (whose support had earlier been 'crucial') appeared likely to reduce the level of their financial assistance; and altogether, warned the director of the Columbia centre, a 'serious reduction in financial support' might be expected. Some area programmes might be compelled to close down and to terminate the employment of their staff, while others would have to reduce the scale of their activity.[43] These gloomy predictions have, on the whole, been borne out: programmes have been curtailed or suspended, support for journals has been terminated, the Institute for the Study of the USSR has been forced to close. Academic research in the Soviet field, in default of institutional sponsors, now depends primarily for such support as it enjoys upon the universities themselves.

In view of what has been suggested above, it would be surprising if such changes in (so to speak) the material 'base' of academic Soviet studies were not reflected in its 'superstructure': that is to say, in the nature of the assumptions informing the work of social scientists in the field. We have no wish to propose a simple one-to-one correspondence (one cannot overlook, in particular, the independent process of change in the USSR itself); but it has, nevertheless, been the case that the totalitarian model, admirably calculated, as it was, to accord with the ideological requirements of government and business during the cold war years, has more recently been succeeded by a variety of other approaches of a less straightforwardly anti-communist character. Indeed, it has been suggested that as its ideological rationale became exhausted, 'totalitarianism' itself might simply disappear as a concept, and might find no place in a future third edition (as it had found no place in the first edition, published in the 1930s) of the *International Encyclopedia of the Social Sciences*. A cue may already have been provided by *Problems of Communism*, a publication of an agency of the US government which, although formally independent, may be expected to reflect its views. In a recent issue the journal has endorsed the need for 'objectivity and high standards of scholarship in our study of Communist affairs', and has invited contributions from scholars in the socialist countries who 'find it possible to respond or to put forward their own perception of the human dilemma and of the Marxist response to it'.[44] Forsaken by its sponsors, the concept of totalitarianism has become politically obsolescent.

In every age, Marx has urged, the ruling ideas will be those of the ruling class. Our analysis of the academic study of Soviet politics tends, on the whole, to confirm this dictum, provided that attention is focused not on the integrity of the individual scholar but rather upon the (admittedly complex) manner in which the working assumptions of scholars are constructed and the 'legitimate areas of debate' delimited: a process which derives, in however mediated a form, from the distribution of political power in a class society. We have examined, in other words, the social construction of knowledge. The story, however, has a moral for the individual scholar: for if its point is taken, he may be able to offer at least a more subtle (if not necessarily a more honest) answer to the question with which Bill Mackenzie has taxed him: 'Whose social scientist are you?'

Acknowledgements

The preparation of this paper was facilitated by the Carnegie Trust, which made possible a visit to the Hoover Institution, California. I should like to express my gratitude also to the Russian Institute, Columbia University, for the provision of documentary materials.

Notes

[1] W. J. M. Mackenzie, *Politics and Social Science*, Penguin Books, Harmondsworth, 1967, pp. 19–20.

[2] W. J. M. Mackenzie, *The Study of Political Science Today*, Macmillan, London, 1971, pp. 10, 24.

[3] A. Gramsci, *Gli intellettuali e l'organizazzione della cultura*, Einaudi, Turin, 1966, p. 9.

[4] Mackenzie, *Politics and Social Science*, pp. 20, 303.

[5] W. J. M. Mackenzie, 'The conceptual framework and the cash basis', *Political Studies*, x, 1962, p. 43. (The title was not in fact chosen by the author.)

[6] Recent exercises in the demystification of academic social science in other fields include L. H. Tribe, 'Policy science: analysis or ideology', *Philosophy and Public Affairs*, ii, 1, autumn 1972, pp. 66–110; S. Wolin, 'The politics of the politics of revolution', *Comparative Politics*, v, 3, April 1973; and T. Pateman (ed.), *Counter Course: a Handbook for Course Criticism*, Penguin Books, Harmondsworth, 1972.

[7] R. B. Fosdick, *The Story of the Rockefeller Foundation*, Harper, New York, 1952, p. 219.

[8] R. Shaplen, *Towards the Wellbeing of Mankind*, Doubleday, New York, 1964, p. 147.

[9] G. M. Lyons, *The Uneasy Partnership: Social Science and Government in the Twentieth Century*, Russell Sage Foundation, New York, 1969, p. 175.

[10] R. F. Byrnes, in W. Laqueur and L. Labedz (eds.), *The State of Soviet Studies*, Cambridge, Mass., and London, 1964, p. 29.

[11] *American Slavic and East European Review*, xviii, 3, October 1959, p. 426; H. H. Fisher, *ibid.*, xvii, 3, October 1958, p. 350; R. F. Byrnes, *Slavic Review*, xxi, 1962, p. 492.

[12] Lyons, *The Uneasy Partnership*, p. 112.

[13] E. A. J. Johnson (ed.), *Dimensions of Diplomacy*, Johns Hopkins University Press, Baltimore, 1964, pp. 2–3. This study is cited by Bill Mackenzie in *The Study of Political Science Today*, where he notes that 'in the USA this close connection with intelligence services is not denied' (p. 93).

[14] L. G. Cowan, *A History of the School of International Affairs and Associated Area Institutes*, Columbia University Press, New York, 1954, pp. 12, 21, 42, 44, 45, 46, 52, 55, 59.

[15] Harvard University, Russian Research Center, *Ten-year Report and Current Projects, 1948–1958*, Cambridge, Mass., 1958, pp. 4, 5, 6.
[16] P. Hoch, *Academic Freedom in Action*, Sheed & Ward, London and Sydney, 1970, p. 97.
[17] Fosdick, *The Story of the Rockefeller Foundation*, p. 217.
[18] N. Chomsky, *Problems of Knowledge and Freedom*, Fontana, London, 1972, p. 58.
[19] C. A. Manning, *A History of Slavic Studies in the United States*, Marquette University Press, Milwaukee, 1957, p. 78.
[20] B. L. R. Smith, *The Rand Corporation*, Harvard University Press, Cambridge, Mass., 1966, p. 84.
[21] Lyons, *The Uneasy Partnership*, p. 171.
[22] L. B. Schapiro, *The Communist Party of the Soviet Union*, Eyre & Spottiswoode, London, 1960, p. xii.
[23] A. Inkeles and K. Geiger (eds.), *Soviet Society*, Constable, London, 1961, p. 36.
[24] Laqueur and Labedz, *The State of Soviet Studies*, p. 36.
[25] D. Horowitz (ed.), *Corporations and the Cold War*, Monthly Review Press, New York and London, 1969, p. 40.
[26] M. Surkin and A. Wolfe (eds.), *An End to Political Science*, Basic Books, New York, 1970, p. 3.
[27] Cowan, *A History of the School of International Affairs*, p. v.
[28] C. E. Black and J. M. Thompson (eds.), *American Teaching About Russia*, Indiana University Press, Bloomington, 1959, pp. 64, 71.
[29] Hoch, *Academic Freedom in Action*, p. 97.
[30] Quoted in T. Roszack (ed.), *The Dissenting Academy*, Chatto & Windus, London, 1969, p. 121.
[31] Cowan, *A History of the School of International Affairs*, pp. 60, 61.
[32] Harvard University, Russian Research Center, *Ten-year Report*, p. 7.
[33] H. H. Fisher (ed.), *American Research on Russia*, Indiana University Press, Bloomington, 1959, p. 51.
[34] *Ibid.*, p. 28.
[35] M. Fainsod, *How Russia is Ruled*, Harvard University Press, Cambridge, Mass., 1963, pp. 8, 25, 28, 30.
[36] It is employed, for instance, in what Bill Mackenzie finds the 'most useful single book' for undergraduate students of comparative politics, S. E. Finer's *Comparative Government*, Allen Lane, London, 1970.
[37] L. Schapiro, *Totalitarianism*, Pall Mall Press, London, 1972, p. 19. The discussion which follows is based in part upon this text and upon C. Friedrich (ed.), *Totalitarianism in Perspective*, Praeger, London and New York, 1969; C. Friedrich and Z. Brzezinski, *Totalitarian Dictatorship and Autocracy*, Praeger, New York, 1956, revised edition, 1966); H. J. Spiro, 'Totalitarianism', *International Encyclopedia of the Social Sciences*, second edition, XVI, Macmillan, New York, 1968; D. Lane, *Politics and Society in the USSR*, Weidenfeld & Nicolson, London, 1970, pp. 188–90; and H. J. Spiro and B. R. Barber, 'Counter-ideological uses of totalitarianism', *Politics and Society*, I, November 1970, pp. 3–22 (I am indebted to Professor Spiro for a copy of this paper).

[38] Mackenzie, *Politics and Social Science*, p. 40. A recent study, 'Bias and blunders in American studies on the USSR', published after this paper had been completed, reaches gratifyingly similar conclusions. Its author, Alexander Dallin, draws attention to a 'tacit and quite unwitting selectivity in the choice of trends and topics to be researched and brought to public attention', and notes the continued existence of a 'film of political preconceptions . . . diffuse premises and unspoken assumptions not related to any particular topic or body of evidence or any one discipline': biases, in other words, which are absorbed 'from our political environment' (*Slavic Review*, XXXII, 3, September 1973, pp. 567, 575, 576).

[39] *Politics and Society*, I, I, winter 1969, pp. 5–15 and 17–21; *Sociology*, IV, 1970, pp. 114–17.

[40] *Politics and Society*, II, 3, summer 1970, pp. 382–86; *ibid.*, IV, spring 1971, pp. 135–44.

[41] J. Ornstein, *Slavic and East European Studies: their Development and Status in the Western Hemisphere*, Department of State, Office of Intelligence Research, external research paper No. 129, Washington, 1959, p. 60. For an exploration of the notion of paradigm and paradigm change in political science, see S. S. Wolin, 'Paradigms and political theories', in P. King and B. C. Parekh (eds.), *Politics and Experience*, Cambridge University Press, 1968, pp. 125–52.

[42] J. W. Fulbright, *The Crippled Giant: American Foreign Policy and its Domestic Consequences*, Random House, New York, 1972, p. 4.

[43] M. Shulman, 'The future of Soviet studies in the United States', *Slavic Review*, XXIX, 1970, pp. 582, 586.

[44] *Problems of Communism*, XXI, 2, March–April 1972, p. 1.

Maurice Wright

15

Looking back at 'looking forward'

The significance of the Plowden report was its demonstration of the need of a more effective system for planning and controlling public expenditure: its achievement was the recognition and acceptance of that need in Whitehall and in Cabinet, and the commitment by both to move the conception of public expenditure control on to a new plane.[1] This was not accomplished quickly nor without a struggle, especially by central departments, who saw in it at first a potential threat to their growing independence of an increasingly moribund system of Treasury control.[2]

Plowden did no more than prescribe the basic principles of a new approach to public expenditure control. From the initial premise that control was determined by the efficacy of the system of decision-making, his committee formulated four principles for reconstructing that system: long-term surveys of expenditure and resources, stability of expenditure policy, improved tools of Treasury and departmental financial control, and collective decision-making by the Cabinet. Their continuing validity is unquestionable and unquestioned, witness their constant invocation by both the Treasury and its critics. But has the Plowden doctrine become current orthodoxy? Has the decision-making system at the very centre of government been reconstructed along the lines laid down? One difficulty in answering such questions arises from the steady evolution of the original doctrine. The concept of planning and controlling public expenditure is now both broader and more complex than it was a decade ago. Moreover, the process of implementation begun in 1961 has been slower and tougher than envisaged originally, and is very far from conclusion.

I have chosen to emphasise difficulties rather than achievements. By now the cult of PESC is sufficiently established to survive any mild corrective which might be administered here. If I have deliberately diverted attention away from the Treasury's success story[3] it is because of an anxiety that until quite recently the continuing debate about the meaning of Plowden and whether and how it could be implemented had been perhaps too private, conducted mainly by a very small group of people within Whitehall. This narrow circle has been widened since 1971 by the arrival of an equally small but enthusiastic and tireless group of Treasury critics, composed of a half-dozen MPs on the Expenditure Committee, their specialist adviser, Mr Wynne Godley, a former deputy director of the Treasury's economic section, and a few academic and professional economists.[4] As a result, private doubts and difficulties have become more public, as the Treasury has been obliged to explain and defend what it was doing. Their dialogues deserve a wider audience. In what follows I deal with only one of four factors whose interdependence has shaped the development of the planning and control system since Plowden, that which Sir Samuel Goldman has called 'the intellectual factor'—advances in the theory of public expenditure, elaboration of relevant concepts, and progress in the techniques of measurement and methods of presentation; about the other three factors—the political, Parliamentary, and circumstantial, I have little to say here.[5] I shall deal with it by drawing attention to some of the conceptual and administrative difficulties which have had to be faced, and many of which remain.

Defining public expenditure

The need to plan public expenditure over a number of years ahead is not nowadays contentious: what remains controversial is whether estimates of planned expenditure can be made with sufficient credibility to enable more rational choices to be made between competing and diverse claims from all parts of the public sector, and whether subsequently these estimates can be used as effective control figures for the containment of expenditure within agreed limits. PESC (Public Expenditure Survey Committee) is the Whitehall and Westminster name for the annual exercise whereby allocations of resources within the public sector are made by individual programmes grouped under broad functional headings, such as Defence, Transport, Social Services, for four to five years ahead. These forward projections of estimated programme costs are revised annually with each PESC review, and note is taken of policy decisions made in the previous twelve months, together with revised estimates of costs of the allocations previously decided upon.[6]

The PESC exercise is based upon the assumption that the public sector can be defined and dealt with as a whole, and that the commitment of resources to it, and their use, can be defined and described. The assumption conceals an inherent difficulty in designing and operating a planning and control system in a liberal democracy where the responsible central authority may be able to influence but not directly control the policies, of a number of disparate public bodies comprising the defined 'public sector'. The Treasury's definition of 'public expenditure' is more comprehensive than that used before 1961, but it is only one among several alternative definitions.[7] As the totals of public expenditure, and their annual growth, have become important political weapons, how 'public expenditure' is defined and used by the Treasury is important. For example, using the Treasury definition it is not possible to use the PESC figures to determine the proportion of GNP consumed or used collectively through public provision, although Treasury administrators as well as politicians persist in making such calculations.[8] If, under the Treasury definition, public expenditure is said to have been reduced, that does not necessarily mean that there has been a reduction in what is provided or used collectively and an increase in what is provided or used privately.[9] In brief, the Treasury definition fails to answer several basic questions about the division of national expenditure between private and collective spending. Nor is it useful for measuring, even crudely, the tax burden resulting from the expenditure of the public authorities. The definition overstates the burden on the citizen by leaving out sources of revenue, e.g. the gross trading surpluses of the nationalised industries, and local authority rents.

In defining and classifying public expenditure into its component parts, and for the purpose of public presentation in the annual surveys, the Treasury broadly follows the practice and conventions of national income accounting. One important difference, however, is the omission of the receipts side of the NI accounts from the Public Expenditure Survey (PES). In consequence some kinds of 'negative expenditure' do not appear in the public expenditure projections. To this extent the Treasury's definition of public expenditure is a restricted and, some have argued, an unreal one. Most critics have argued that a more rational presentation of public expenditure would include both receipts and expenditure.[10] Not so very long ago the Treasury thought so too: 'Public expenditure figures may always be misleading so long as the revenue side is not presented at the same time,' it said in the Green Paper *Public Expenditure: a New Presentation*.[11] 'It is important to show the receipts side of the account along with the gross expenditure' in order that the use of real resources should be more correctly measured by showing the tax offsets and tax flow-backs on some kinds of expenditure.[12] Since then the Treasury has sometimes provided partial information about receipts and sometimes excluded them entirely.

The Treasury's objection to the publication of the projections for receipts (which, however crude, it is itself obliged to make in order to make an annual allocation of prospective resources) is on the grounds that any figures would be highly uncertain, e.g. assumptions about the growth of incomes, the level of profits, trends in world trade, and rates of saving and investment. Most critics take an opposite view: that those outside Whitehall (including MPs) would be helped by the publication simultaneously with the PES of projections of receipts founded on well specified 'conventions' about the growth of the economy and the behaviour of tax rates.

The vexed question of the publication of projected receipts, passionately argued on both sides before a recent Expenditure Committee inquiry, revealed that the assessment made by the Treasury, an integral part of the whole PESC exercise of planning expenditure a number of years ahead, was so uncertain and tentative that the Treasury did not feel confident enough to publish it. Indeed, the Treasury expressed doubt about the usefulness of making any assessment at all.[13]

Planning public expenditure

The government cannot make plans for public expenditure over four to five years ahead unless it forms some judgement about the prospective level of resources likely to be available to it. It is obliged to take a view about the future performance of the economy. While there are short-term economic *forecasts*, the Treasury insists that those for the medium term are merely *assessments*. The medium-term economic assessment (MTA) is prepared annually in parallel with the PESC exercise, but is never made public.[14] This reflects the basic uncertainty and technical difficulty of making an assessment and Treasury reluctance to discuss publicly the assumptions about the movement of the key variables which underly it. In any case, the macro-economic model used is a short-term one 'stretched' five years forward. In practice the level of public expenditure is determined not so much by a view about what resources are likely to be available over a five-year period as by political judgements about priorities and about what needs should be met by the public rather than the private sector. The economic acceptability of the resultant expenditure programmes is then tested in a number of ways, one of which is by reference to the MTA. But 'in no way is it a determining factor or in the sense that it dictates the Government's decisions on public expenditure'.[15]

A more important check is the expected rate of growth of productive potential.[16] During the 1960s and until 1972 the 'prudent rule' was to allow public expenditure to grow at roughly the same rate.[17] Since the 1972 budget, however, the rate of growth of public expenditure is planned (for political and economic reasons) to increase annually by more than the expected rate of growth of productive potential, and the 'rule' governing the relationship between the two is now less invoked than formerly. Its 'prudence' seemed to owe less to any economic causal relationship than to the attractiveness of its political simplicity: Ministers could easily grasp the direct correlation between the two.

Central to the whole exercise of planning expenditure is the process for forecasting the resource costs of the programmes over the plan period. The success of the exercise turns very largely on the skill with which this is done. Persistently inaccurate or erroneous forecasts which have to be revised frequently will eventually destroy the usefulness and validity of the whole system. (Revisions due to genuine changes in policy or new policies are a separate matter, of course.) The exercise is fundamentally one in reducing the level of uncertainty about the future, and like all such exercises is itself inherently uncertain and technically difficult. Two criteria for judging the effectiveness of the forecasting techniques are, first, the extent to which forecasts of programme costs (measured on a constant price basis) are changed year by year as the plan is 'rolled forward'; and, secondly, the extent to which there are found to be differences between the forecast expenditure of a programme and what is actually spent (out-turn).

Until 1970 it was impossible to apply the first criterion. The projections of costs in one PES could not be compared with that for previous or succeeding years because the prices used in each survey were measured in terms of unique survey prices. The 1970 public expenditure White Paper showed for the first time all the main programmes presented in the two previous published PESs revalued to the price basis of the new survey. Even so, the amount of information provided by the Treasury and the way in which it is presented are too limited to enable anything more than comparisons by broad programmes to be made, which may conceal considerable variations in the estimated expenditures for individual programmes. Until urged to do so by the Expenditure Committee, the Treasury had not itself conducted an exercise of this kind to test the variation in the annual estimates of the costs of programmes.[18] It was impossible for the Treasury or the public to judge how accurate its forecasting was year by year. Without special effort, the Treasury had no 'means of knowing quickly how and why new estimates of programmes differ from the old'.[19]

Some departments tend to spend less on their programmes year by year than the expenditure forecast in the PES. In practice there occurs a consistent and predictable tendency for 'shortfall', for which the Treasury makes a block deduction from the total cost of all programmes. The size of shortfall is considerable. In 1969–70 departments underspent by £362 million (1·8 per cent of the total public expenditure). The provisional out-turn for 1972–73 is even higher, £600 million.[20] One major cause of shortfall is that the level of expenditure in some programmes is not directly controlled by the government in its day-to-day management, e.g. agricultural support, the promotion of local employment, payments out of the redundancy fund, local authority housing investment. Another reason is that the timing of expenditure is not always very closely predictable. As the Treasury freely admits:

We have to live, largely, I think, because of the way this country is constituted, without a system which enables the government of the day to lay down with precision exactly what is going to happen in the form of public expenditure at any time in the future . . . shortfall arises as part of the reflection of the absence of a perfect system of commanding £x to be spent everywhere on a certain day.[21]

By attempting to predict what the overall level of shortfall will be for the future on the basis of past experience, and by making substantial provision for it in each of the five years ahead, the Treasury's forecasts of expenditure are given a greater appearance of accuracy than is the case. In fact, by so doing the Treasury is estimating and providing for a level of inaccuracy in its forecasts. But because it does not attempt to make an allowance for shortfall (and for contingency)[22] in each individual spending programme, the estimates for the latter are not the 'very best estimates that can be made of the cost of existing policies', as the Treasury claims.[23] Its 'present method of allowing for shortfall appears to be excessively casual', Professor Prest told the Expenditure Committee in 1971.[24] There was striking confirmation of that judgement two years later, when the accuracy of the Treasury's estimating techniques was directly challenged by the Expenditure Committee following the announcement by the Chancellor of the Exchequer in May 1973 of a reduction in the levels of public expenditure forecast in the White Paper of December 1972 of £100 milion in 1973–74 and £535 million in 1974–75.[25] By May the provisional out-turn figures for 1972–73 pointed towards an estimated shortfall twice that forecast four months earlier in the White Paper. Despite the Treasury's argument that the reduction in the forecast public expenditure of £535 million for 1974–75 was unforeseen, the result of policy changes, it seemed probable that a revision downwards of the estimates for that year would have been necessary even without any policy changes. As the Expenditure Committee pointed out, the Treasury's information system was inadequate to determine what would have occurred without the May cuts, and cited in support of that contention the Treasury's inability to predict the £600 million shortfall in the 1972–73 programme. Mr P. R. Baldwin, Treasury deputy secretary, was forced to admit that

The people in control of these expenditures tell us until very late in the year that they expect to spend the money, and this has been true consistently, even within central government, for decades; and the actual owning up, so to speak, to the prospect that they are not going to spend all the money comes very late in the financial year. What we do to correct that is to write in the expectation of shortfall before they tell us. But we cannot say to each of them, 'You are going to spend less' because we are not entitled to, we do not know.[26]

The Expenditure Committee claimed that the Chancellor's May cuts for 1974–75 would have the effect more of reducing a greater anticipated shortfall than that originally predicted in the PES than of making an actual cut in expenditure. More seriously, the committee contended that the provision for shortfall in the annual PESs enabled the Treasury subsequently to rescue hard-pressed Chancellors looking for cuts; that what happened in such circumstances was often not a real cut in forecast expenditure but a reduction of what they called the 'up-the-sleeve' element. This contention was strongly denied by the Treasury, but its evidence failed to remove doubts expressed about the effectiveness of its estimating techniques and the use made of the provision of shortfall.

Provision for shortfall represents estimates of anticipated inaccuracy in expenditure forecasts: the contingency reserve provides for those expenditures which it is impossible to predict or unnecessary to determine at the time the forecasts are made. The need to provide a contingency reserve in each PES arises from inadequate knowledge about the factors which determine expenditure beyond year 3. In itself this is sufficient testimony to the continuing technical difficulty of forecasting resource costs throughout the plan period.[27]

Stability of expenditure policies

The contingency reserve provides also for the development of a policy which could not be anticipated when the policy was originally costed, and ensures that the system is flexible enough to accommodate changes which a government may want to make from time to time in its policies without having to review the whole range of priorities as set out originally. Nevertheless, as Plowden emphasised, stability of decision-making is an essential ingredient of a planning system. The size and composition of public sector spending and its susceptibility to more direct governmental influence make it inevitable that governments will use it as a tool of short-term economic management. Some kinds of public expenditure can be altered at short notice, up or down, and their use as tools for the short-term management of demand is accepted by the Treasury and its critics; their effectiveness is, of course, hotly argued.[28]

Undoubtedly the introduction of forward planning has introduced greater stability into the commitment of real resources. There is a good deal of evidence that most expenditure decisions for years 1–3 in the PES are not merely 'firm', in the PESC language, but difficult to revise (certainly downwards) even with the advent of a new government. When the Conservative government came to power in June 1970 it was committed to the reduction of the size of the public sector and the proportion of total resources pre-empted by it. The early months in office were spent searching for ways to cut back public expenditure. It found that, short of making decisions which would be economically and socially wasteful and disruptive, what could be achieved in the short term or even within three to four years was circumscribed by the scale of existing commitments. The so-called public expenditure cuts announced in the White Paper of October 1970, *New Policies for Public Spending*, were not real cuts in the sense of a reduction of public sector claims on total resources, but reflected changes in charges and cash transfer payments *within* the public sector.[29] In the White Paper of January 1971, *Public Expenditure, 1968–69 to 1974–75*, the government claimed further that public expenditure would rise more slowly over the next five years than had been planned for the same period by the previous Labour government. In fact the claims on real resources envisaged by the Conservative government in its programmes were very similar to those implied in the previous government's programmes.[30]

By November 1971 unemployment was rising so quickly, against a background of stagnant private investment, that the government was forced to take corrective action. It turned, as its predecessors had turned, to the public sector. In its second annual White Paper it restored in aggregate virtually the whole of the 'cuts' announced since it took office, adding over £1000 million to public expenditure in the current and the following years.[31] By May 1973 unemployment had been brought down to an acceptable level, and the government took steps to reduce the level of demand in the economy by cutting back future commitments in the public sector—the 'May cuts'. The result of all this activity stands out in sharp relief if we look at the expenditure plans for the year 1974–75. In the space of three years these have been revised on three separate occasions. In October 1971 forecasts for that year were revised downwards to reflect policy changes by £911 million. Subsequently, as part of a larger package of measures to correct rising unemployment, spending plans for 1974–75, were revised upwards by an additional £1,524 million. In the 'May cuts' of 1973 planned expenditure of 1974–75 was reduced by £535 million. Looking at this succession of policy changes between 1971 and 1973, the Expenditure Committee commented in a bitingly critical report that they

[depart] drastically from what we have understood to be a central principle of public sector planning: that since the lead time between the taking of decisions and the generation of expenditure is so long, the scale of the

main programmes should be related to long-term trends in the economy, not to short-term fluctuations in it ... It therefore seems likely that the changes will have caused much expensive and, since taken as a whole they virtually cancel out, *needless* disruption.[32]

Such exercises, conducted hastily, partly for political and 'public' reasons as well as for economic and social ones, tend to diminish the rationality of the previous decision-making. In an attempt to respond quickly to an unfavourable economic situation the spending on some programmes is boosted or cut back without a searching review and careful consideration of commitments across the whole range of public sector activity, the principal criterion being what can be done most easily and most quickly to increase or reduce the level of demand. In such situations governments have to do what they can, even if the effects of what they do are rather longer delayed than is often claimed by them publicly. But the frequency and the extent of these exercises make each successive PES less credible: forecasts of prospective commitments of resources within the public sector remain stable to the extent that governments do not disturb them for short-term management purposes.[33] One consequence may be that both participants and the public become cynical about the survey procedures. While the greater part of the PESC arguments each year are not about the bulk of public expenditure, which is fairly stable and its annual growth inescapable, but about making changes upwards or downwards at the margin, then the rationality of that allocative process is diminished if subsequent changes are made, involving perhaps a much greater proportion of GNP, without a similar analysis and review of different options between and within programmes.

Against this view, the Treasury argues that some expenditure programmes may prove to be more flexible in the short term than was once supposed, and that changes for short-term conjunctural reasons may not be as damaging. However, experience so far has been limited to expanding rather than contracting programmes, and it has yet to be shown that short-term constraints on public expenditure are other than wasteful and disruptive.[34]

Collective decision-making

Plowden emphasised the need of a planning system in which decisions about commitments of resources for the future were made collectively by the Cabinet, rather than separately by the Chancellor and each departmental Minister. The desirability of doing so is obvious enough: to enable a more rational discussion of expenditure priorities in the context of the government's overall strategy. But more than this, it was hoped to enlist the aid of all Ministers in the forward planning of expenditure by getting them to appreciate the consequences on all other decisions of any particular decision to commit a greater or lesser amount of total resources—'to force Ministers to face up to the situation that they can have this or that but not both', in the words of a former Chief Secretary to the Treasury.[35]

In one of the unpublished papers written by the Plowden committee a proposal was made for the establishment of a committee composed of senior Ministers to scrutinise, under the chairmanship of the Chancellor of the Exchequer, all departmental programmes. The Macmillan government preferred a weaker solution, and appointed a Chief Secretary to the Treasury whose function was to look after the public sector programmes and to whom Ministers were supposed to refer, with the Chancellor and, ultimately, the Cabinet sitting in final judgement.[36] In practice senior Ministers have tended to ignore the Chief Secretary when a controversy arises over an important item of spending between their department and the Treasury, and to appeal over his head to the Chancellor personally. For a short while after taking office in 1964 the Labour government had a group of senior Ministers, none of whom had large departmental responsibilities for any particular block of expenditure, who met under the chairmanship of the Chancellor to consider the public sector programmes.[37] The arrangement lapsed, and by 1967 there had been a return to a system of bilateral haggling between the Chancellor and each departmental Minister, with final decisions reserved for full Cabinet. There are advantages and disadvantages for both sides in conducting the annual review in this way, but none of them contributes to greater rationality in deciding upon spending priorities.

Very little is known about the process by which Ministers arrive at the final set of decisions reflecting their judgement about the priorities of different expenditure programmes. By definition this is as much, maybe more, a political exercise as an economic or financial one. The final choice, or set of choices, is political, reflecting the values and judgement of those Ministers concerned; it can never be otherwise. There is as yet no management tool for measuring the allocative efficiency of committing extra resources to a road rather than a hospital programme; and even if there were, it would still be necessary and right for Ministers to exercise a political judgement (in the widest sense), which might give a greater priority to using resources in a way apparently contrary to some test of economic efficiency. From the outside it is almost impossible to know anything of the process whereby Ministers, after the conclusion of the PESC exercise, faced with the 'factual presentation' of the surveys 'showing where present policies are likely to lead in terms of public expenditure at constant prices if they remain unchanged over the ensuing five years', decide what the balance shall be between different programmes.[38]

No government has been prepared to publish that 'factual report' and risk revealing discrepancies between it and the final approved estimates published in the annual White Paper. Any variation between the two would have to be explained and defended by the government. If the decisions had been made on the basis of comparing different 'costed options', then the Chancellor or the government would be obliged to explain what those options were and to defend the choice of one rather than another. While some critics of the Treasury have pressed for the publication of such options,[39] Ministers, ex-Ministers and civil servants have consistently argued against it, one ground being that 'if there is a public presentation of the horse-trading that goes on between departments and Ministers over the final agreement, the effect might be that Ministers would be much less willing to make concessions than if it was kept behind closed doors'.[40] In other words, *how* the government makes up its mind on the allocation of public money is its own business. In any case, there are now no 'costed options' for Ministers to discuss before finally settling the survey estimates, as the Treasury was forced to admit to correct the impression given by its own second secretary, Sir Samuel Goldman, and other Treasury witnesses, before the Expenditure Committee. 'The question of choices between alternative courses ... arises in practice continually ... [and] policy and its resulting cost as part of the general body of "existing policies" has to be determined at a far earlier stage than Ministers' consideration of the total costings of existing policies expressed in the annual Surveys.'[41]

Controlling expenditure

Traditionally the Treasury's task has been to try to ensure that what was spent by departments matched as nearly as possible what had been estimated by them and appropriated by Parliament. Even on an annual cycle this was never an easy task, and it was apparent by the end of the 1950s that the tools of traditional Treasury control had lost their cutting edge. With the lengthening of the time horizon during which commitments were entered into, it became still more difficult to ensure on an annual basis that what was committed by a department annually corresponded to the estimated and approved expenditure for that year. Moreover, with a more comprehensive definition of public expenditure the process of physical control became that much more difficult, partly because of the diversity of the spending authorities—local authorities and nationalised industries, as well as central government departments—and partly because of the nature of the expenditure itself in some cases. The Treasury has no precise control over the level of local authorities' expenditure 'even in any one year, let alone in the trend running five years ahead'.[42] Nor can it be sure that the nationalised industries in their dealings with suppliers will spend £x rather than £y in any one year. In addition, some of the central government's commitments are open-ended—social security payments or regional development grants, for example, where the precise take-up year by year is difficult to estimate, and even more difficult to ensure that expenditure matches it.

Merely to measure and compare estimates of expenditure with out-turns presents a difficult technical problem. Following the implication of the Plowden report, the annual PES expresses the commitments in physical or 'real resource' terms, rather than in money terms. But in order to compare estimates with out-turns, and successive estimates of expenditure for a given year with each other, a methodology and an information system relating to price changes are required. In brief, a satisfactory method of measuring expenditure at constant prices. Further, the system for measuring public expenditure has to be consistent in terms of its information and its accounting conventions with that in terms of which the economy is controlled. Unless the public expenditure estimates can be fitted into the National Income system, it is impossible to measure the opportunity cost of increasing one type of expenditure in terms of reducing another, or of increasing taxation. The difficulties of devising such a system have proved formidable.[43] For example, central departments have devised statistical systems to provide them with information about cash appropriations to local authorities which help them with the accountability to Parliament for these grants. But public expenditure may differ considerably from those appropriations. Local authorities may receive the grant at one time and incur expenditure at another, while the total expenditure generated by the grant will normally be greater than the grant itself when the central government provides a fixed percentage (e.g. police). Thus the process of reconciling cash appropriation by the central government with total expenditure by local authorities requires new types of information.

To approach the Plowden objective of more effective control requires very much more hard work by the Treasury and the departments to generate more information and to develop an appropriate methodological system for using it. The limitations of the present system of controlling public expenditure are not denied by the Treasury, who 'envisage that several years of substantial effort would be required at the present level of improvement work before most of the problems . . . could be resolved'.[44] Despite the prompting of the Expenditure Committee, and in particular its specialist adviser, Mr Wynne Godley, it is by no means certain that the Treasury and the departments are convinced that the results of such slow and laborious work would be worth the use of very expensive manpower.

Much has been achieved in planning and controlling public expenditure since Plowden reported, but as much or more remains to be done. While there is much to admire in the way the system has been developed and operated by the Treasury and the departments —in particular, the increasing sophistication of the resource allocation, the growing firmness of departmental control since 1968, the development by the Treasury of concepts and methodology for measuring and verifying expenditure—the limitations of the present techniques for estimating resource costs over a five-year period have become even more apparent in recent years; there is still no realistic and credible medium-term economic forecast; projections of receipts remain tentative and uncertain for all but the short term; and the reconciliation of the PES with the national income accounts has still to be achieved, although the prospects are encouraging.

Even if all the conceptual, methodological and administrative problems could be handled satisfactorily in the next few years, and it became possible to forecast with much greater accuracy the costs of programmes over a five-year period and to ensure that in each year out-turn was consistent with planned expenditure, there would remain the problem of deciding whether the original resource allocations had resulted in the achievement of the objectives of the different programmes. The search for a system to 'complement and reinforce' PESC, which would provide an analysis of expenditure according to policy objectives began in the late 1960s. Just ten years after Plowden reported, it was decided to introduce programme analysis and review (PAR) throughout central government. Already PAR is firmly linked conceptually with PESC, but there is a long way to go before PAR becomes an integral part of the whole system of planning and controlling public expenditure.[45] Little progress has yet been made in defining 'needs' in the different expenditure programmes, and measuring what is obtained in return for the money spent.[46] As with the further development of control procedures, the attitude of the Treasury and the departments will influence what is done and how quickly it is done. There is a similar reluctance to commit time and energy to the development of a comprehensive information system which would be the basis for evaluating planned expenditure and monitoring performance. While the idea of a set of statistics of outputs over the whole range of public expenditure is an ambitious one, the Expenditure Committee has set its sights that high and will expect the Treasury and the departments to adjust accordingly. Now that we have

one of the most sophisticated analyses of inputs in the world ... we think that the possibilities inherent in the present system will not be fully realised until the analysis of inputs is matched by an analysis of outputs. We are not suggesting that such a system will ever obviate the need for subjective judgments on how resources are to be allocated; no analysis of outputs will ever tell us whether we prefer, say, an old people's home to a nursery school. But when a subjective judgment is made we need to know how many old people's homes and how many schools would be involved and how far aims are near achievement.[47]

Notes

[1] Recognition and acceptance of that need by Parliament came very much later. It was very little involved before the publication and debate of the 1969 White Paper on Public Expenditure, and the setting up of the Select Committee on Expenditure in 1971. Both developments have their immediate origins in a report by the Select Committee on Procedure: *Scrutiny of Public Expenditure and Administration*, 1968–69, H. C. 410.

[2] How departments learned to stop worrying and learned to live with, if not love, PESC is one theme explored in chapter 5 of H. Heclo and A. Wildavsky, *The Private Government of Public Money*, Macmillan, London, 1974. On the origins of Plowden see Henry Roseveare, *The Treasury*, Allen Lane, London, 1969, ch. 9. Professor F. J. M. Mackenzie's classic 'The Plowden report: a translation', which appeared first in the *Guardian*, is reprinted in R. Rose (ed.), *Policy-making in Britain*, Macmillan, London, 1969. On the evolution of the system, 1961–72, see Sir Samuel Goldman, *The Developing System of Public Expenditure Management and Control*, Civil Service College Studies, No. 2, HMSO, London, 1973, pp. 1–14.

[3] The most recent account is by Sir Samuel Goldman, a former Second Secretary at the Treasury and head of the Public Sector Group: *The Developing System of Public Expenditure Management and Control, op. cit.*

[4] In particular, I have in mind the Expenditure Committee's Public Expenditure (General) Sub-committee. Mr Godley is, of course, gamekeeper turned poacher. In the Treasury he was responsible for economic forecasting and the analysis and presentation of the public expenditure figures. He is at present Director of the Department of Applied Economics at Cambridge.

[5] Goldman, *op. cit.*, p. viii.

[6] For a detailed but formal account of PESC see 'Public expenditure survey system', memo by Treasury to the Public Expenditure (General) Sub-committee, in the third report of the Expenditure Committee, 1970–1971, H. C. 549. Heclo and Wildavsky, *op. cit.*, provide a necessary corrective to the Treasury's gloss.

[7] For some others see S. Brittan, *Steering the Economy*, Penguin Books, Harmondsworth, 1971, p. 92.

[8] See, for example, Sir Samuel Goldman, then Second Permanent Secretary, Public Sector, H.M. Treasury, in evidence to the Public Expenditure (General) Sub-committee, 'Command papers on public expenditure', 1970–71, q. 256.

[9] Third report, Expenditure Committee, 1970–71, *op. cit.*, qq. 466–7.

[10] See memoranda by Professor A. R. Prest, pp. 117–20, and by Peter Jay, p. 96, and evidence of Jay and Samuel Brittan, qq. 453–76, third report, Expenditure Committee, 1970–71, *op. cit.*

[11] Cmnd. 4017, April 1969, para. 30.

[12] *Ibid.*, paras. 20–2.

[13] Third report, Expenditure Committee, 1970–71, qq. 8 and 45.

¹⁴ The Labour government's 'roll-forward' of the National Plan, *The Task Ahead*, was a public version of the current MTA, HMSO, 1969. In 1972 the government agreed after considerable pressure from the Expenditure Committee to publish as an experiment the main elements of the MTA.

¹⁵ Mr. Patrick Jenkin, Chief Secretary to the Treasury, q. 346, seventh report, Expenditure Committee, 'Public expenditure and economic management', 1971–72, H.C. 450.

¹⁶ See appendix 1, pp. 113–19, seventh report, Expenditure Committee, 1971–72, *op. cit.*, for the Treasury's definition and use of this concept.

¹⁷ Seventh report, Expenditure Committee, 1971–72, *op. cit.*, q. 169.

¹⁸ See Treasury memo, 'Public expenditure: comparisons with previous estimates', pp. 76–9, third report, Expenditure Committee, 1970–71, *op. cit.* The Treasury is now producing a historical series of programme expenditures on a common basis over time. Some results were published in the Public Expenditure White Paper, December 1971, Cmnd. 4829.

¹⁹ Goldman, *op. cit.*, p. 40.

²⁰ As announced by the Chancellor of the Exchequer on 21 May 1973.

²¹ Mr P. R. Baldwin, then Under-Secretary, General Expenditure Division, H.M. Treasury, in evidence before the Expenditure Committee, third report, 1970–71, *op. cit.*, qq. 380–1.

²² See below.

²³ Baldwin, *op. cit.*, q. 382. As the Treasury admit, 'very best' does not mean that they are always very good.

²⁴ Third report, Expenditure Committee, 1970–71, *op. cit.*, q. 478.

²⁵ *Public Expenditure, 1976–77*, Cmnd. 5178, 1972.

²⁶ Eleventh report, Expenditure Committee, 1972–73, Public Expenditure (General) Sub-committee, *The May 21 Expenditure Cuts*, q. 18.

²⁷ Shortfall and the contingency reserve are discussed at length in the oral evidence taken by the Public Expenditure (General) Sub-committee, third report, Expenditure Committee, 1970–71, *op. cit.* See also *Public Expenditure White Papers: Handbook on Methodology*, HMSO, London, 1972.

²⁸ See seventh report, Expenditure Committee, Public Expenditure (General) Sub-committee, 1971–72, 'Public expenditure and economic management', H.C. 450.

²⁹ Wynne Godley, 'The Barber "package" under the microscope', *Financial Times*, 3 November 1970; S. Brittan, 'Package in Perspective', *Financial Times*, 28 October 1970.

³⁰ Wynne Godley and Christopher Taylor, 'Public sector's rising claim on resources', *The Times*, 17 February 1971; Godley and Taylor, 'Heavier tax burden and reduced consumption', *The Times*, 22 February 1971.

³¹ *Public Expenditure to 1975–76*, Cmnd. 4829.

³² Eleventh report, Expenditure Committee, 1972–73, *op. cit.*, para. 10.

³³ The criteria for the use of public expenditure for short-term demand management, and the limitations, were explained by the Treasury in evidence to the Expenditure Committee, seventh report, 1971–72, *op. cit.*, specially qq. 1–80.

[34] On this see Goldman, *op. cit.*, p. 54, seventh report, Expenditure Committee, 1971–72, and eleventh report, Expenditure Committee, 1972–1973.

[35] Mr John Boyd-Carpenter, third report, Expenditure Committee, 1970–71, *op. cit.*, q. 166.

[36] See Heclo and Wildavsky, *op. cit.*, chapter 4.

[37] *Ibid.*

[38] But see Heclo and Wildavsky, *op. cit.*, chs. 4 and 5.

[39] See third report, Expenditure Committee, 1970–71, *op. cit.*, paras. 43–54. On the wider question of the relationship of expenditure to 'needs' see eighth report, Expenditure Committee, Public Expenditure (General) Sub-committee, *Relationship of Expenditure to Needs*, 1971–72, H.C. 515.

[40] Third report, Expenditure Committee, 1970–71, *op. cit.*, q. 440.

[41] Appendix 8, 'Costed options', note by the Treasury, third report, Expenditure Committee, 1970–71, *op. cit.*

[42] Third report, Expenditure Committee, 1970–71, *op. cit.*, q. 378.

[43] See the Treasury memo 'Public expenditure: measurement and verification', Mr Wynne Godley's memo, 'Measurement, forecasting and control of public expenditure', and the Treasury's note on Godley's memo, third report, Expenditure Committee, 1970–71, *op. cit.*, pp. 134–46.

[44] Treasury's note on Godley's memo, para. 15.

[45] An account of the PAR 'launch' is given by the former Special Adviser to the Chief Secretary to the Treasury, R. J. East, in 'Improving government expenditure decisions through programme analysis and review', *Long Range Planning*, VI, 1, March 1973. See also Sir Richard Clarke, *New Trends in Government*, HMSO, London, 1971, ch. 2, and Sir Samuel Goldman, *The Developing System of Public Expenditure Management and Control*, pp. 45–51.

[46] See eighth report, Expenditure Committee, 1971–72, *op. cit.*

[47] *Ibid.*, report, para. 19.

Sheila Hamilton and John Money

Bibliography

Napoleon both travelled and read a lot; and, being a busy man, he did much of his reading on long journeys. It is said that whenever he finished a book he casually tossed it out of his carriage window, where it was retrieved by the local inhabitants and made the basis of a new public library. Professor Mackenzie's published work shows that his peregrinations over the last thirty years have in their own way been equally fruitful, his passage being marked by work on elections in Africa, the politics of resistance in Norway, regionalism in Italy, and administration in America, to name but a very few of the subjects on which he has written; and translations of his work have been made into a variety of languages, including Spanish, French, German and Japanese.

All academics hope to influence thinking in their subject fields by their own spoken and written words. Many hope to extend this influence by participation in the counsels of the official and unofficial bodies which influence the practical affairs of the world. In Professor Mackenzie's case the latter as well as the former hope has long since become a reality. To some extent his publications reflect this practical interest in government and administration, but a mere listing of what he has written is not a true reflection of his work and influence in these fields. We feel it is right, therefore, that the bibliography should also include reference to some of his more important activities in this sphere. Though not publications in the conventional sense, documents and evidence submitted, e.g. to the Fulton Committee on the Civil Service, have been of equal if not greater importance in giving actuality to his constitutional, political and administrative ideas than material presented in the more familiar academic dress of published articles and books. And how can one possibly estimate the influence flowing from his unpublicised but profound contributions to the constitutional structure of newly emerging African States? All else apart, his academic colleagues all over the world are indebted to him not only for the stimulus of his ideas but also for the personal guidance and help of which he has been such a prolific and generous donor.

Professor Mackenzie refers modestly to having found himself by accident on that index in the heart of the British system of government wherein are listed 'the good and the great' who are regarded as suitable for service on official committees. We know that the entry was no accident, for we feel that at the present time our profession contains few so good and none so great as Bill Mackenzie.

1. *Books*

British Government since 1918 (jointly), Allen & Unwin, 1950.
Central Administration in Great Britain, with J. W. Grove, Longmans, 1957.
Free Elections, Allen & Unwin, 1958.
Five Elections in Africa (ed. with K. Robinson), Oxford University Press, 1960.
Politics and Social Science, Penguin Books, 1967.
The Study of Political Science Today, Macmillan, 1972.
Power, Violence, Decision, Penguin Books, 1974.
Explorations in Government: Collected Papers, 1951–68, Macmillan, 1974.
Public Policy and Private Interests: the Institutions of Compromise (ed. with D. C. Hague and A. Barker), Macmillan, 1974/5.

2. *Contributions to books and works of reference*

Preface to *English Regional Government: a Study of the North West*, J. W. Grove, Royal Institute of Public Administration, 1950.
(Ed., as chairman of group) *The Scope of Enterprise in Local Government*, NALGO, 1951.
'Constitution making', in *Man in his Relationships*, ed. E. Westmann, Routledge & Kegan Paul, 1955.
(Ed., as chairman of group) *The Manchester Mental Nursing Survey*, Manchester University Press, 1955.
Foreword to *The Spirit of British Administration*, Charles Sisson, Faber, 1958.
Preface to *European Volunteer Workers in Britain*, J. A. Tannahill, Manchester University Press, 1958.
'Local administration of the social services', in *The Future of the Welfare State*, CPC, No. 178, 1958.
Blurb for *Provincial Metropolis*, L. P. Green, Allen & Unwin, 1959.
'The civil service, the State and the Establishment', in *Essays on Reform, 1967*, ed. Bernard Crick, Oxford University Press, 1967.
'Models of collective decision-making', in *The Social Sciences—Problems and Orientations*, Mouton, The Hague, for UNESCO, 1968.
'The functions of elections', in *International Encyclopedia of the Social Sciences*, Macmillan Co. and Free Press, New York, 1968, vol. 5.
(Ed., as chairman of group) *Social Work in Scotland: a report on the Social Work (Scotland) Act, 1968*, University of Edinburgh, 1969— Joseph Rowntree Memorial Trust grant to the Department of Social Administration, Edinburgh University.
'Political science', in *Main Trends of Research in the Social and Human Sciences*, part 1: Social sciences, chapter II, Mouton, The Hague, for UNESCO, Paris, 1970.

3. Translations of articles and books

'Le autonomie locali nell'ordinamento amministrativo britannico', in *Problemi della pubblica amministrazione*, vol. III, 1960, Ciclo di conferenze promosso dalla scuola nell'anno accademico 1958–59, Università di Bologna, Scuola di Perfezionamento in Scienze Amministrative.

Elecciones libres, trans. F. Condomines Perena, editorial Tecnos, Madrid, 1962.

'Die Struktur der zentralen Verwaltung', in *Strukturwandel der modernen Regierung*, ed. Theo Stammen, Wissenschaftliche Buchgesselschaft, Darmstadt, 1967.

'Civil service, Staat und Establishment', in *Die Verwaltung*, Duncker & Humblot, Berlin, 1968.

La politica e le scienze sociali, trans. Ada Cavazzani and Giordano Sivini, Laterza, Bari, 1969.

'La science politique', *Tendances principales de la recherche dans les sciences sociales et humaines*, part 1: Sciences sociales, chapter II, Mouton, The Hague, for UNESCO, 1970.

Politica y ciencia social, trans. Jose Cazorla Perez, Aguilar, Madrid, 1972.

Politics and Social Science (in Japanese), trans. Hideo Uchiyama, Mirai Sha, 1972.

4. Articles and published evidence

'The House of Lords: who does its business?' (with Margery Jackson), *Manchester Guardian*, 17 May 1950.

'Federalism and regionalism', *Modern Law Review*, vol. 14, 1951 ('A note on the Italian constitution of 1948', with B. Chapman).

'The study of public administration in the USA', *Public Administration*, vol. XXIX, 1951, pp. 131–43.

'The conventions of local government', *Public Administration*, vol. XXIX, 1951, pp. 345–56.

'The government of great cities' (Percival lecture, Manchester University), *Memoirs and Proceedings of the Manchester Literary and Philosophical Society*, vol. 93, session 1951–52, pp. 1–13.

'Science in the study of administration' (lecture at the London School of Economics, 5 November 1951), reprinted in *The Manchester School*, vol. XX, 1952, pp. 1–24.

'The professor as administrator: a comment', *Universities Quarterly*, vol. X, 1953, pp. 333–41.

'Committees in administration', *Public Administration*, vol. XXXI, 1953, pp. 235–44.

'Co-operative politics in a Lancashire constituency' (with Cynthia Arditti), *Political Studies*, vol. II, 1954, pp. 112–27.

'Representation in plural societies', *Political Studies*, vol. II, 1954, pp. 54–69.

'Changes in local government in Tanganyika', *Journal of African Administration*, vol. VI, 1954, pp. 123–9.

'The co-ordination of public passenger transport in south-east Lancashire' (with G. M. Higgins), *Manchester School*, vol. xxii, 1954, pp. 276–311.

'Local government in Parliament—a note', *Public Administration*, vol. xxxii, 1954, pp. 409–23.

'The protection of civil liberties: Britain and the USA', *Bulletin* of Committee on Science and Freedom, 1955.

'Political theory and political education', *Universities Quarterly*, vol. ix, 1955, pp. 351–63.

'Pressure groups in British government', *British Journal of Sociology*, vol. vi, 1955, pp. 133–48.

'Partis politiques et classes sociales en Angleterre' (with A. H. Birch and P. Campbell), *Revue française de science politique*, vol. v, 1955, pp. 772–98.

'Pressure groups in Gran Bretagna', *Occidente*, vol. xii, 1956, pp. 128–47.

'Local government elections in towns', *Journal of African Administration*, vol. viii, 1956, pp. 61–8.

'The Royal Commission on the Civil Service', *Political Quarterly*, vol. xxvii, 1956, pp. 129–40.

'The south-east Lancashire conurbation', *Manchester Guardian*, May 1957.

'Theories about elections', *Central African Examiner*, 6 June 1957.

'Electoral studies and the politics of emergent States', *APSA News*, vol. 2, 1957.

'The export of electoral systems' (the Sidney Ball lecture, Oxford University), *Political Studies*, vol. v, 1957, pp. 240–57.

'Political science courses in Manchester', *Political Studies*, vol. vi, 1958.

'Mr T. D. Weldon: an appreciation' (obituary), *Manchester Guardian*, 16 May 1958.

'Idiom in political studies', review of *Models of Man, Social and Rational*, H. A. Simon, *Political Studies*, vol. viii, 1960.

'Theories of local government' (public lecture at LSE, 25 May 1961), *Greater London Papers*, No. 2, London School of Economics and Political Science.

'Oxbridge myths—and others', contribution to a symposium, 'The popularity of Oxford and Cambridge', *Universities Quarterly*, autumn 1961.

'The conceptual framework and the cash basis', *Political Studies*, vol. x, 1962.

'Town and gown—the role of the university in relation to local government', Society of Town Clerks' annual conference, Brighton, 31 May 1962.

'The export of elections', *New Society*, October 1962.

'Does our administration need reform?', *Listener*, 21 February 1963.

'Problems of administrative reform', *Listener*, 28 February 1963.

'The Plowden report: a translation', *Guardian*, 25 May 1963, and *Public Administration* (Australia), June 1963.

'Regionalism and local government structure', annual conference of the Institute of Municipal Treasurers and Accountants, Torquay, 12 June 1963.

'How to train administrators', *New Society*, 27 February 1964.

'Administrative aspects of "Buchanan" and "Crowther"', golden jubilee conference of the Town Planning Institute, 24–26 June 1964.

'Attention to graduates' (contribution to the fourth Gulbenkian Educational Discussion, 1963), *Universities Quarterly*, vol. XVIII, 1964.

'Administrative reform', Fabian Society lecture, November 1964.

'Les institutions politiques en Angleterre', *Futuribles*, No. 937, supplement No. 2, 10 December 1965.

'Government and management', *Bulletin* of the Association of Teachers of Management, May 1965, and in Association of Teachers of Management occasional papers, No. 4, *The Academic Training of Management*, ed. D. Pugh, Blackwell, 1966.

'Higher education for the professions' (contribution to the sixth Gulbenkian educational discussion, 24–31 October 1966), *Universities Quarterly*, March 1966.

'Our island library', *SSRC Newsletter*, November 1967.

'The political science of political science', *Government and Opposition*, vol. 6, No. 3, summer 1971, p. 277.

'Recruitment to the civil service', evidence to the Estimates Committee, in *The Sixth Report from the Estimates Committee* (H.C. 308, 1964–1965). Extracts also published in *Taxes*, journal of the Inland Revenue Staff Federation, October 1965.

'Scrutiny of public expenditure and administration', evidence to the Select Committee on Procedure, in *The First Report of the Select Committee on Procedure* (H.C. 410, 23 July 1969).

5. *Book reviews*

Public Administration, autumn 1949. *An Introduction to Public Administration*, by E. N. Gladden.

Public Administration, June 1951. *Planning in Practice: Essays in Aircraft Planning in War-time*, by Ely Devons.

Manchester Guardian, February 1951. *William Goodwin: a Study in Liberalism*, by David Fleisher.

Public Administration, 1950, *The Study of Public Administration in the USA*, by H. A. Simon, D. W. Smithburg and V. A. Thompson.

Manchester Guardian, October 1951. *Modern Constitutions*, by K. C. Wheare.

Manchester Guardian, November 1951. *Principles of Social and Political Theory*, by Sir Ernest Barker.

Journal of African Administration, vol. IV, No. 4, October 1952. *The Local Government Service*, by J. H. Warren.

Political Studies, 1953. *Parliament: a Survey*, ed. J. J. Craik Henderson; *Problems of Nationalised Industry*, ed. W. A. Robson.

Public Administration, 1953. *Ideas and Issues in Public Administration*, ed. Dwight Waldo; *Public Administration*, by John M. Pfiffner and R. V. Presthus.

History Today, October 1954. *Political Parties: their Organisation and Activity in the Modern State*, by Maurice Duverger.

Political Science Quarterly, December 1955. *Great Cities of the World: their Government, Politics and Planning.*

Political Studies, 1955. *British Political Parties*, by R. T. McKenzie.

Local Government Finance, November 1955. *Report on Local Government in British Guiana*, by A. H. Marshall.

Journal of Education, vol, 88, No. 1042, May 1956. *Man on his Past: the Study of the History of Historical Scholarship*, by H. Butterfield.

Political Studies, vol. v, No. 1, 1956. *The Constitutional and Administrative Law of the Commonwealth*, first issue of *Public Law.*

Africa, 1957. *Government and Politics in Tribal Societies*, by I. Schapera.

Socialist Commentary, May 1958. *British Pressure Groups: their role in Relation to the House of Commons*, by J. D. Stewart; *The British Political System*, by André Mathiot (Hogarth Press).

Public Administration, summer 1958. *Leadership in Administration: a Sociological Interpretation*, by Philip Selznick.

Public Administration, summer 1959. *Education for Administrative Careers in Government Service*, ed. Stephen B. Sweeney.

Political Studies, December 1959. *Decision-making: an Annotated Bibliography*, by Paul Wasserman, with Fred S. Silander; *Measurement and Evaluation of Organizational Performance*, by Paul Wasserman; *Models of Man, Social and Rational*, by H. A. Simon; *Organizations*, by James G. March and Herbert A. Simon, with Harold Guetzkow.

Archiv für Rechts- und Sozialphilosophie, vol. XLVI, No. 1, winter 1959–1960. *Political Theory: the Foundations of Twentieth-century Political Thought*, by Arnold Brecht.

Political Studies, vol. VIII, No. 1, February 1960. *Models of Man, Social and Rational*, by Herbert A. Simon.

Political Studies, vol. IX, No. 1, 1961. Review of seven books on Africa (in one general review) by E. Clegg, D. A. Low and R. C. Pratt, Colin Leys and C. Pratt, P. Mason, C. Seinger, Susan Wood, and R. E. Wraith.

Journal of Commonwealth Political Studies, vol. I, No. 3, May 1962. *The Kenyatta Election*, by George Bennett and Carl Rosberg.

Political Studies, October 1962. *Aucuparius: Recollections of a Recruiting Officer: the Empire as Squirearchy*, by Major Sir Ralph Furse.

Universities Quarterly, December 1962. *Rationalism in Politics and other Essays*, by M. Oakeshott.

Public Administration, autumn 1963. *The World Role of Universities*, by Edward Weidner.

Journal of Local Administration Overseas, October 1963. *Central Authority and Regional Autonomy in Indonesia*, by C. R. Legge.

New Society, 17 October 1963. *The History of English Local Government*, by Beatrice and Sydney Webb.

Public Administration, winter 1963. *Papers in Comparative Public Administration*, ed. Ferrel Heady and Sybil L. Stokes (Institute of Public Administration, University of Michigan).

Yorkshire Post, 2 January 1964. *Education for a Developing Region*, by Guy Hunter.

Political Studies, vol. XII, No. 1, February 1964. *Government and the Atom: the integration of Powers* and *Science and Politics*, by H. P. Green, Alan Rosenthal and the Rt. Hon. Viscount Hailsham, Q.C.; *The Theory of Political Coalitions*, by W. H. Riker.

Urban Studies, vol. 1, No. 1, May 1964. *Victorian Cities*, by Asa Briggs.

Journal of Commonwealth Political Studies, May 1964. *The Nigerian Federal Election of 1959*, by Ken Post.

Public Administration, summer 1964. *Bureacracy and Political Development*, ed. Joseph La Palombara.

Political Studies, vol. XII, No. 2, June 1965. *The Peaceful Atom and Foreign Policy*, by A. Kramish; *Operational Research in the RAF: Administering the Atom for Peace*, by J. E. Hodgetts; *Scientists and National Policy-making*, ed. R. Gilpin and C. Wright.

Journal of the Town Planning Institute, vol. 50, 1964. *The Administrators: the Reform of the Civil Service*, a Fabian Group tract No. 355.

Town Planning Review, January 1965. *Southern California Metropolis*, by W. Crouch and W. Dinerman.

Race, October 1965. *Colour and the British Electorate, 1964*, ed. N. Deakin.

Municipal Review, December 1965. *Regionalism in England, 2: its Nature and Purpose*, by Brian C. Smith.

Journal of Commonwealth Political Studies, July 1966. *Technical Cooperation*, by F. J. Tickner.

Journal of Commonwealth Political Studies, December 1966. *The British and their Successors*, by Richard Symonds.

Political Quarterly, January 1967. *Central Departments and Local Authorities*, by J. A. G. Griffith.

Journal of Commonwealth Political Studies, December 1967. *Politicians and Politics: an Essay on Politics in Acholi, Uganda, 1962–65*, by Colin Leys.

Journal of Administration Overseas, January 1968. *New Federations: Experiments in the Commonwealth*, by R. L. Watts.

Tidsskrift for Samfunnsforskning, No. 4, 1968. Review of *Scandinavian Political Studies*, vol. 2, 1967.

SSRC Newsletter, January 1969. *Communications Systems and Resources in the Behavioral Sciences*, by the National Academy of Sciences.

Sociology, June–July 1969. *The Electoral System of Finland*, by Klaus Törnudd.

Journal of Administration Overseas, vol. VIII, No. 3, July 1969. *Ombudsmen*, by Geoffrey Sawer.

New Society, March 1969. *The Making of British Foreign Policy*, by David Vital.

Public Administration, vol. 47, autumn 1969. *The Novelist on Organisation and Administration: an Inquiry into the Relationship between Two Worlds*, by Dwight Waldo.

Sociological Review, 1970. *The Ten Thousand: a Study in Social Organization and Action in Xenophon's 'Anabasis'*, by G. S. Nussbaum.

Urban Studies, 1970. Volumes 1, 2 and 3 in the series *International Urban*

Studies of the Institute of Public Administration, New York: vol. 1, *Urban Government for the Paris Region,* by Annmarie Hauck Walsh; vol. 2, *Urban Government for Metropolitan Lagos,* by Babatunde A. Williams and Annmarie Hauck Walsh; vol. 3, *Urban Government for Zagreb, Yugoslavia,* by Eugen Pusić and Annmarie Hauck Walsh.

SSRC Newsletter, March 1970. Review of the National Libraries Committee report (the Dainton report), Cmnd. 4028.

Journal of Administration Overseas, July 1972. *A Gust of Plumes: a Biography of Lord Twining of Godalming and Tanganyika,* by Sir Darrell Bates.

Political Quarterly, vol. 44, No. 3, July–September 1973. *Administrative Theories and Politics: an Inquiry into the Structure and Processes of Modern Government,* by Peter Self.

Inlogov, October 1972. *Style in Administration: Readings in British Public Administration,* ed. R. A. Chapman and A. Dunsire.

Political Studies, vol. xxi, No. 3, September 1973. *An Introduction to Metapolitics: a Brief Inquiry into the Conceptual Language of Political Science,* by A. James Gregor.

Journal of Administration Overseas, vol. xii, No. 4, October 1973. *Aid and Liberation: a Socialist Study of Aid Politics,* by Judith Hart.

Political Studies, vol. xxi, No. 4, December 1973. *Foundations of Political Sociology,* by Irving Louis Horowitz.

The Economist, April 1974. *Size and Democracy,* by Robert A. Dahl and Edward R. Tufte.

Index